DOWNFALL

DOWNFALL
HOW RANGERS FC SELF-DESTRUCTED

PHIL MAC GIOLLA BHÁIN

Foreword by ALEX THOMSON C4 *News*

FRONTLINE
NOIR

Phil Mac Giolla Bhain is an author, blogger, journalist and writer. He is an active member of the National Union of Journalists, a member of the Irish Executive Council and the Irish representative on the NUJ's New Media Industrial Council. Phil has contributed to publications as diverse as the Guardian, the Irish Independent, Magill magazine and the Irish Post. He has also built up a considerable online readership through his blog - www.philmacgiollabhain.ie. His use of the online platform to break stories, particularly on the extent of the financial dealings at Rangers, has brought him acclaim from media commentators and colleagues.

The book is to be dedicated to:
Mick Derrig

This edition published 2012
by Frontline Noir, an imprint of Books Noir

Copyright © 2012 Phil Mac Giolla Bháin

ISBN 978-1-904684-26-8

A CIP record for this book is available from the British Library

Typeset in Garamond by Park Productions

Cover design by James Hutcheson

Printed and bound in the EU

CONTENTS

FOREWORD

By Alex Thomson, Channel 4 News

It is, I'd have to agree, a pretty reasonable question, and that's probably why I've been asked it so many times. But the answer as to why someone with years of experience as a news correspondent in Somalia, Afghanistan, Iraq, the Balkans and Middle East should suddenly get all tangled up with the Incredible Ibrox Implosion, is, frankly, by accident.

Lying in bed in a hotel in the West End of Glasgow, I'd been looking into a story from the previous day about big banking and the Royal Bank of Scotland in Edinburgh. I was on the point of heading to the airport and back to London when I made a cursory check-call to the news desk to make sure there was no reason to stay. The Channel 4 News programme editor for that day said, almost as an afterthought, "You know, this Rangers thing's pretty weird, isn't it? Maybe nothing in it but there's this tax hearing or something in London today. Why don't you stick around and maybe make a few calls – see if there's anything to it?"

Within a few hours it was clear there most certainly was "something to it". And coming from investigating Big Banking, suddenly it was plain this was Big Football – but this was no football story. The parallels are striking, and that is why charting what happened, as this book does, matters so much.

For where there was (Sir) Fred Goodwin there is Sir David Murray with knighthood still appended and intact at the time of writing. Where there was RBS and big banking, there was RFC and big football. Big ideas, big dreams and all let loose in the era of the credit frenzy where anything seemed possible and "living the dream" was reality amid wild promises to outspend Celtic to win – literally – at all costs.

Fred thought big, played big, won big – for a while. Dave thought, played and won in equal style and again – for a while. It was all possible in the free-market, light-touch "regulation" of big banks and big sport. Just as the FSA didn't ask enough questions in the City so, four hundred miles north at Hampden Park, the SFA were busy not asking the right questions about the voodoo economics down in Govan as Dave outspent not just Celtic but his own resources at Ibrox.

The Scottish Football Association and the Financial Services Authority: in parallel worlds both charged with governing, both about to witness major catastrophes on their respective watches, both institutionally incapable of preventing the meltdown.

There is a famous story of the Queen, concluding a trip around the City of London, clutching her handbag and surrounded by besuited Masters of the Universe; they expected more polite enquiries of the "So-what-do-you-do?" style. Instead, addressing the financial meltdown partly caused by credit over-extension, Mrs Windsor turned to the assembled bankers and said, "Why didn't anybody see this coming?" Cue awkward silence, nervous coughing and mutual gaze-avoidance syndrome.

So, too, around Ibrox. Except as you'll see here the question is, "How come they didn't see it coming *twice*?"

For what's set out here in gripping style is the extraordinary ability of the Scottish Football authorities and much of the Glasgow football media to fail to ask the reasonable questions – not just of Sir David Murray as his dreams collapsed into debt-ridden chaos, but of Craig Whyte too.

Here, the parallel universe with the City unfolds all over again as Craig – like the Queen – paid no tax. The small difference being the Queen's allowed – but hell! why worry? There was "off the radar" wealth for Craigy Boy to call on, wasn't there?

Well, no.

But nobody asked. What unfolds across these pages is a story where even the culture of media deference to Sir David Murray among Glasgow football journos became so engrained it had its own name.

Outside Glasgow succulent lamb's a pleasing culinary experience. Inside the city it's a bitter and ironic symbol of how a city's desire to sell newspapers and promote the Ibrox myth teetered close to sycophancy and often went right over the precipice into it. Ask no tricky questions of big Sir D. and he'll see you right with a string of harmless exclusives.

To this day there is a deep, unthinking desire among some in Glasgow's mainstream media to promote the latest saviour, this week's phoenix, today's new salvation for Ibrox.

Across recent months the same old unquestioning nonsense has been pumped out. How an aged US businessman was coming to make everything alright at Ibrox . . . How the cumbersome Company Voluntary Arrangement was going to stop a bankrupt FC going bankrupt . . . How a Yorkshire businessman was going to lead the Bears back into Premier League glory . . .

In the newspapers hardly anyone questioned any of this nonsense. It was as if Sir David Murray had never left the Big Hoose. It did not help Rangers. It did not help the club's legions of beleaguered, confused, sold-out fans. And it was wrong.

Yet, yet, all the while there was an alternative voice. Alternative coverage. Not always right, of course, and often motivated – let's be frank – by a loathing of Ibrox and all it stands for. The authors of this narrative blogged away online. They were often anonymous. They were shadowy. But they were very often right and very often first.

They – not the Glasgow MSM – were the ones who examined Sir David Murray's "wealth" and his banking and credit arrangements. They were the ones to point out that Wee Craigy Boy's oceans of wonga might actually be rather smaller puddles in reality with a vulnerability to evaporation.

Time and again they were either ignored or their truths and exclusives were reluctantly taken up by the mainstreamers in Glasgow when even they could no longer deny that Rangers might soon no longer exist.

This book emerges from one such blogger who has taken his obvious skills and contacts as a mainstream newspaper journalist into the Rangers blogosphere to brilliant effect.

It is a thankless task in some respects. Football fans do not take kindly to having the painful, embarrassing truth of what they hold dear laid dispassionately before them. The bigger the club, the prouder the history, the harder some take it. Rangers were bigger than most, prouder than most.

That is why another such blogger, Rangers Tax Case, has wisely decided to preserve his anonymity even while winning the Orwell Award for Online Journalism. And he is far from alone in doing so. In the intense world of Glasgow football some close to the old Rangers were not above threatening reporters; others have attacked and intimidated people more violently, of course.

Astonishingly, the author – like myself – received overt physical threats from a former Glasgow-based sports journalist for having the temerity to investigate the mess at Ibrox. It remains a dispiriting fact, both to myself and the author that Strathclyde Police, armed with a dossier of evidence to prosecute, chose to do nothing.

Welcome then to the bizarre world of Glasgow football and the spectacular death of the old Rangers – how the Old Firm became the Firm when it had nothing to do with scoring goals. The world of Minty, Duff and Duffer, of Jabba, Britney and Craigy Boy – of OldCo, NewCo, Sevco and the CVA. A world where the local cancer of Rangers, toxic and potentially lethal, was allowed to spread and potentially engulf clubs from Elgin to Annan.

Ibrox will never be the same and the face of Scottish football is changed forever, with more changes coming. It was Robert Burns who famously wrote: "O wad some Power the giftie gie us, To see oursels as ithers see us!"

What unfolds now is the story of how the renegade "internet bampots" took on the mainstream "laptop loyal" and beat them on their home ground, without needing extra time, let alone penalties. In so doing they let the light in and laid bare the facts. Finally, even the Glasgow media, the Scottish football authorities and, yes, many a Rangers fan, finally saw themselves, their club, their sport in Scotland, as so many others had seen them for years.

Here, from the inside, is the extraordinary story of just how that happened.

Alex Thomson
Chief Correspondent, *Channel 4 News*
August 2012

ACKNOWLEDGEMENTS

There are many people to whom I owe a huge debt of gratitude for this book. Some of them, for reasons of their personal situation and the nature of the assistance they afforded me, do not wish to be publicly acknowledged.

A journalist wouldn't get anywhere without good sources. Over the years that I have written about the Rangers saga many people approached me to help. Sometimes it was a one-off snippet of information that proved very useful. However, with others it would be the start of a long-term collaboration.

Many people took risks to get me the information. They received no payment and their motivations were to get the news out there. A lack of trust in the mainstream media seemed to be a common theme with many of them. They all have my heartfelt thanks for their help.

Thanks must also go to Bob Smith of Books Noir for spotting that today's "underground" writing is often the mainstream of tomorrow. My gratitude also goes to his talented team for the high standards and the meticulous eye for detail that they brought to the project.

Special thanks are due to Angela Haggerty. She is a fine young journalist and her abilities as a sub editor on the manuscript, working to a very tight deadline, were an invaluable asset to this project. She has a great future in front of her in Scottish journalism, of that I am sure.

To Seamus Dooley and Paul Holleran of the NUJ whose support and guidance through many challenging times was always appreciated. *Mile Buíochas* to NUJ President Donnacha DeLong for his unstinting support for my online reporting on this story and for seeing the value of new media to the craft of journalism before just about anyone else in the union.

Brian McNally of the *Sunday Mirror* was also a great friend throughout and always provided me with sound advice.

Throughout this journey I have always been able to call on Professor Roy Greenslade of the City University, London. A prolific blogger himself for the *Guardian* on media matters he took a keen interest in what I was doing on the Rangers story and he was a constant source of help and good counsel.

I am sorry that the late Paul McBride QC will not hold a copy of this book, because we discussed the subject matter often enough. On more than one occasion he gave me the benefit of his brilliant legal mind; him on the steps of the High Court and me in my kitchen in Donegal. He understood fully what I was trying to achieve by writing so persistently about this scandal.

As this story picked up others came on board and were valued added and great assistance to me in my work, most notably the RTC blogger, a worthy winner of the Orwell prize, and Paul McConville and his Scots law blog. They both analysed and assessed a developing story with a diligence and precision that was totally lacking in the mainstream. Their generous help to me at different junctures in this journey cannot be overstated.

I know he is far too young to be called the grand old man of the fitba internet, but Paul Brennan of Celtic Quick News has been at this caper for a very long time. His daily online output is elegantly written and he manages to be witty and often prescient in very few words. He was a constant source of support and good humour throughout the time that I was working on this story. If he ever stops being a computer wizard then he would make a damn fine journalist.

I also owe a debt of gratitude to Archie Macpherson for allowing me access to the vast archive of Scottish football memories that he calls his head.

This is a book about online content and I could not have maintained this level of output without my tech team. They both ticked the box marked "no publicity", but they know who they are and they have my thanks.

A very special thank you must go to Alex Thomson of *Channel 4 News* for coming over the hill at just the vital moment and tipping the balance against the official narrative about Rangers. I am deeply honoured that he agreed to write the foreword for this book. His contribution to the dénouement of this saga is difficult to overstate.

As ever the greatest source of support was from my own clan. To my big guy at Trinity College Dublin and the man he is becoming in front of my eyes. Many late-night snacks were consumed as we discussed what I had achieved that day on this story. Now he pops up on Skype to get an update. His *súil eile* will always be precious to me. His two amazing sisters scuttle around this kitchen in Donegal wonderfully disinterested in what their old befuddled dad is writing about, but proffering tea at vital moments. They have an excellent role model in their mother who, through all of this stuff, knows what is truly important for all of us.

Although many people have kindly assisted me in the preparation of this book any errors contained within here are, of course, my own.

Phil Mac Giolla Bháin
Ireland
August 2012

Introduction

This book is the product of several years of journalism investigating the scandal emanating from Rangers which rocked Scottish football to its foundations and changed the national game forever.

For me, it has been an unplanned and fascinating journey. Originally, my work had been focused on tackling racism in Scottish football, specifically the anti-Irish racism coming from a section of Rangers fans and, in particular, their singing of the illegal "Famine Song".

Once I had become established as a writer interested in the Ibrox club, I started to acquire sources who were keen to let me know of the internal financial problems at Edmiston Drive. People very close to the action were willing to share highly sensitive information with me, either directly or through third parties. As I continued to publish, more sources approached me. I was hooked.

The book is organised into four sections and within those the work is published chronologically. The sections represent the key themes in this drama. Each one has an introductory chapter which provides context to the story, as well as some new material.

Many reputations were consumed as this rumbling saga exploded into a full-blown fiasco and none more so than that of the mainstream media in Glasgow. The greatest sporting scandal in British history was on the doorstep of Scottish journalists and they largely looked the other way. Too long in the pocket of Rangers owner, Sir David Murray, and fearful of any adverse reaction from Rangers supporters, they regurgitated PR fluff about billionaires, casinos and star players.

This book will be of interest to anyone who has been enmeshed in the Glasgow football feud, because this is how the vendetta was finally ended. It will also engage anyone who has studied the chaos that has been created by the neo-liberal economics of "light touch regulation". The "big bang" in banking deregulation in the UK and the repeal of the Glass-Steagall Act in the USA in 1999 created the era of casino capitalism. Banks became gambling houses, betting with the money of their customers. These self-proclaimed masters of the universe claimed that they could create wealth out of nothing, when in reality what was being experienced was just a re-run of the

South Sea Bubble. It was an illusion of easily acquired wealth which fooled and, subsequently, ruined the lives of millions of people. Plus ça change . . .

The downfall of Rangers is a small, if high-profile, part of that boom and bust. David Murray's ownership of the Ibrox club spanned that era. He took over at Edmiston Drive the year after UK banks had been let off the leash and he was a dream customer for any bank. He had an insatiable appetite for borrowing and, to a bonus-incentivised high flyer, he was the kind of customer you could build your career around. Add to this the cultural cachet and establishment clout of Rangers in Scotland and it appeared to be an impregnable trinity. The banks, Murray and Rangers seemed rock solid. Nothing could go wrong and the mainstream media in Glasgow told the world that everything was fine.

I entered this journalistic journey into Rangers in the same week that Lehman Brothers collapsed and the securitised dominoes started to fall across the financial industry. Rangers were part of that global story. David Murray was every inch the spawn of the fictional Gordon Gekko in Hollywood's 1987 movie, *Wall Street*.

Rangers fans partied in the 1990s like people here in Ireland who suddenly thought of themselves as shrewd property speculators, when in reality they were becoming increasingly indebted due to hallucinatory consumer dreams. The people of Ireland, impoverished for generations and the butt of racist jokes, suddenly became cubs of the Celtic Tiger. Rangers fans, so long starved of a prolonged period of success, caught silverware fever and wanted more and more. However, more was never enough and they thought it would last forever.

When people are in a bubble they can never see an end to it. When the new millennium dawned, the Ibrox klan realised that their city rivals had rebuilt. Celtic had a bigger stadium and a winning team on the park. David Murray borrowed extravagantly and scammed Her Majesty's revenue in order to buy more glory for the Queen's Eleven. It was the road to ruin, but no one listened to Rangers director Hugh Adam when he shouted "Stop!"

A decade after his warning, the club he had served well was liquidated. The NewCo is now in the Third Division of the Scottish Football League. There has never been a humiliation so public for any group of football supporters.

This book also addresses the changing nature of Scottish society and how a hatred that had been part of the culture for generations suddenly started to appear out of step with the post-devolution zeitgeist.

Although a football club is at the centre of this story, it should not deflect readers from the wider import of the real drama within. This is not a story about who scored the goal or who was offside. This is a modern tale about what happens when light touch regulation becomes an abdication of responsibility and creates a complete collapse of corporate governance across many organisations and institutions. The banks, the financial regulators, the people in charge of Rangers and those entrusted to safeguard Scotland's national game all failed in their own specific ways.

It is also a tale of the failure of my own trade. The mainstream media and the fans of the Ibrox club were locked into a parasitic relationship that ultimately failed both of them.

And there was a human cost; people at Ibrox lost their jobs and that must not be forgotten in the stramash of headlines. However, the biggest existential price was paid by the Rangers fans. For many of them, the club was the centre of their very self-identity and now it is gone. They believed that their club stood for the things they aspired to. For them, being a "Rangers man" was about upholding positive values, such as upstanding behaviour at all times, dignity and fortitude. Instead, the tale that was revealed to them was one of tax evasion, cheating and chiselling. The club they loved had become FC Lehman Brothers, surfing along on a tidal wave of cheap credit that would lead Rangers to the grave.

Under Sir David Murray, Rangers was meant to establish itself at the top table of European club football and, in the process, strive to break and belittle its East End rivals for a generation, perhaps forever. This book is the story of how that hubristic dream turned out to be a chimera.

Instead of becoming the Real Madrid of the north, David Murray sold the club for a pound to a man who didn't have much more than that in his pocket. A year later the club was liquidated. Subsequently, Celtic are now the biggest, richest club in Scotland – a position that they will only be dislodged from by their own folly, should they choose to behave like their deceased rivals.

The Rangers fans were sold a dream by a snake oil salesman. They believed in his vision because it was so seductive. However, the reality of the Rangers story is an ugly and cautionary one. Scotland's establishment club was a permanent fixture of the national game, yet it was destroyed. A new club with Rangers' assets, bought for a mere £1.5m in a liquidation sale, was ordered to begin in the SFL Division Three as a result of a rebellion by fans of other clubs.

Rangers Football Club (established 1872) is no more. The club expired in its 140th year and this book will tell you how the impossible happened.

Phil Mac Giolla Bháin
August 2012

Part I: Finance

Introduction

Finance and, ultimately, the lack of it sits at the heart of this story. Readers will note that the blog posts in this section tend to be shorter and sharper by 2011, a reflection of how fast-moving events had become. These were communiqués from the frontline as opposed to what we call in the newspaper trade "colour pieces". It tended to be "tight and newsy" and as soon as I was able to verify the information I was receiving, it was being posted on my site.

However, the saga of Rangers downfall could not be told without understanding the historical period that it happened in. Moreover, it would be incomprehensible without looking at the man at the centre of the Shakespearean fate that befell Scotland's establishment club. What follows now is an attempt to sketch in some of the historical and sociological "colour" of the period.

The story of Rangers' downfall is the tale of one man's hubris and how his vanity fed the collective dreams of thousands. When David Murray bought Rangers from Lawrence Marlborough for £6m in 1988, Britain had been under Margaret Thatcher's leadership for almost a decade. The British prime minister saw the world very differently from her post-war predecessors. Mrs Thatcher told Douglas Keay, in an interview for *Woman's Own* on 31 October 1987, that: "They're casting their problem on society. And, you know, there is no such thing as society. There are individual men and women, and there are families."

David Murray, who had not been knighted at that point, was very much a child of the Thatcherite revolution. The "Iron Lady" had a worldview that Britain had declined on the global stage partly because nationalised industries at home were inefficient. It had spread a culture of failure and had smothered the natural entrepreneurship of the country.

Like Calvin Coolidge across the pond fifty years earlier, Mrs Thatcher thought the business of Britain should be business. In the same way that a wise manager would not shackle a naturally gifted footballer to a specific position on the field, the "wealth creators" should be allowed to get on with it. The job of government was to be minimal; look after the currency and let market forces do the rest. Many would fail, but those who succeeded would drive the economy forward. For her, men like the new owner of Rangers were the future of Britain. Self-made self-starters like David Murray would be the entrepreneurial shock troops of her reborn Britain.

Yet, despite a lot of fluffy PR about his amazing business acumen, Murray had prospered by simply buying and selling on as the markets rose inexorably. In an economy that was booming, it was difficult to fail. The trick was in knowing what genuine economic growth was and what was just an inflated bubble. If it was the latter, fortunes could be made if you knew when to get out. If you got the timing wrong, you could be ruined. Murray got his timing badly wrong.

The man in Charlotte Square liked to sail close to the wind. Perhaps it was in his blood. His father, David Ian Murray, was a coal merchant in Ayr. His company was called Murray Forrest. The company had interests in large tracts of land that could be used for open cast mining. They lived on Racecourse Road, Ayr. Following his bankruptcy, he was sentenced to eighteen months in prison for "fraudulent conversation". This was a rather genteel term for tax evasion. No succulent lamb journalist has ever had the temerity to ask Murray how he was affected by that childhood event.

Murray's father had failed to declare all of his assets, especially his interest in Tudor Treasure, the winner of the 1961 St James's Palace Stakes and the Victoria Cup in 1963. He also had an interest in Water Skier, the winner of Kempton Jubilee in 1962 and 1963. Another horse he owned won the prestigious Royal Hunt Cup. Tudor Treasure was one of the wonder horses of that period, with incredible stud value. It is thought the horse could make around £70,000 per year at stud, an incredible figure in the sixties. He had other horses, usually named after his mines and local areas, like Pennyvenie and Morelands.

A man of excess, Murray senior was known for his boorishness and arrogance. During one incident at the Open Championship at Royal Troon, the famous golfer Peter Thomson found himself in the bunker at the infamous postage stamp, the third hole. Murray shouted across the bunker to his "runner" Alex Wylie, "I bet you he doesn't get down in two from there." Without looking up, Peter Thomson said, "I'll have twenty pounds on that!" Having got out of the bunker and putted for par he walked across the green and demanded £20 from Murray.

I am not a betting man, but as I found out more about the perilous state of Rangers' finances in 2010 I became convinced of two certainties about the Ibrox club: death by taxes. We are told that "all is fair in love and war"; David Murray took that to heart. I don't know if the knight of the realm reads the classics, but he seems to have grasped Cicero's observation that "the sinews of war are infinite money".

In the 1990s, the Rangers owner boasted to veteran sports journalist Archie Macpherson: "I'll buy the league!" Murray spent like a Lottery winner at Rangers and there seemed no end to it. In this digital age, where any footie fan can manage his favourite team, this was like playing *Championship Manager* with the cheat codes on. If your club had a bigger budget than its rivals by many multiples then the game was pretty easy. Reduced to a simple monetary calculation, the club with most money would win the league. That's how it was throughout the 1990s.

Funded by Murray's largesse, the light blue legions had never known such success. With their brash new Thatcherite owner, the Ibrox outfit could simply outspend everyone else in Scotland by some distance. The league trophies were won with ease. It was no longer a championship campaign, more of a seasonal coronation.

Rangers, with very few hiccups, jogged to the title year on year for nine consecutive seasons. Even when Graham Souness left in 1991 it didn't alter the trajectory of the championship. In the heyday of Bill Struth, the Ibrox martinet, the best that Rangers could manage was five league championships in a row in the 1930s.

Murray's aim was to give the Rangers supporters what they craved domestically more than anything else. Having won a record nine league titles on the bounce during the Jock Stein era, it was the fans of Celtic Football Club who had held the domestic bragging rights. When Rangers equalled that feat in the 1990s, anything seemed possible for Murray and Rangers. "Ten-in-a-row" became the Holy Grail for the Ibrox faithful and Murray came within an inch of delivering it.

By failing to better Celtic's record, a one-time chance to get the bragging rights over the green and white tribe had been lost, probably forever. The only thing that remained for Murray was to reach the heights that Stein's Celtic team had in their day: European glory at the highest level. No matter how browbeaten Celtic fans were throughout the 1990s, they could still warm themselves with the glow of that iconic picture of Billy McNeil lifting the European Cup on 25 May 1967. That day, Celtic became champions of Europe.

Rangers fans could never say that their team had been on that pinnacle of sporting achievement and their city rivals took a great deal of time reminding them.

For Murray, Rangers was a vanity project. He hadn't grown up supporting the club as a boy. As a young man his sporting interests lay with the oval ball. He had made overtures to the owners of Ayr United before turning his attention to Rangers. When he bought the club in 1988, the Ibrox side had only won the league title four times in the previous twenty years. It was an astonishing statistic.

Murray got his timing perfect when he bought Rangers. Celtic, under the old board, was slipping inexorably into bankruptcy. The "new firm" of Aberdeen and Dundee United had passed its zenith and was entering a period of decline. The Edinburgh clubs were perennial under-performers, especially when they travelled to Glasgow on league business. However, in the first half of the 1980s, things had been different. Three clubs – Aberdeen, Celtic and Dundee United – won the league and Hearts came within a whisker of the double in 1986. Aberdeen won the Cup Winners Cup in 1983 and Dundee United contested the UEFA Cup final in 1987.

Most of the players in the league were Scottish. However, entering the 1990s, Murray's Rangers would be stuffed with highly paid imports. No club would be able to keep up. Scottish football, under David Murray's reign, was entering a period of unipolarity. The Rangers fans, already equipped with a Herrenvolk mind-set suddenly had some evidence to back up their feelings of cultural superiority. Rampant Rangers on the field of play nurtured the worst aspects of their belief system.

When I first wrote of Rangers' financial problems in January 2009, I knew that it was the tale of one man. It was always going to be about David Murray and his rise and inevitable fall. I suggested his life would make a great biopic. When I learned more about his background and where he had come from, I was even more convinced that one day someone would be playing David Murray in a movie. It would, however, take a Cecil B. DeMille-type panoramic view to capture Murray's ego on celluloid.

Murray loved the adulation of the crowd. Buying Rangers in 1988 had made him a rock star in Scottish society. He was immediately transformed from being a well-got entrepreneur to an "A-list" celebrity. The cachet of owning Scotland's establishment club opened doors for him in the circles where big deals were done in Edinburgh's high finance village.

Rangers' fans craved ten-in-a-row and Murray dreamt of glory, but it was cruelly snatched from them by Celtic. After the vanity project was derailed by Wim Jansen and Harald Brattbakk in 1998, the only option open to Murray was to hit back at the city rivals – but it wouldn't be easy. Celtic was no longer financially crippled and was in the process of building a stadium that would have a bigger capacity than Ibrox by 10,000. If the men around the Parkhead boardroom could encourage enough people into the new Celtic Park, they would have a genuine financial advantage over Rangers. Michael Kelly, from the deposed Celtic board in 1994, had scoffed that the stadium was too big and it would never be finished, never mind filled with paying customers. He was utterly wrong and Fergus McCann's vision was vindicated.

Celtic Park was full in the early years of the millennium and there was a waiting list for season tickets. The Parkhead club started to pull away from their city rivals in the battle of the balance sheets.

Murray, as always, had the media on his side and the handpicked hacks gushed about Murray's big plans. Ever the gambler, he went double or quits at the poker table and waited to see if Celtic would fold. He boasted that he would simply outspend the Parkhead club. As has been covered extensively in the media section of this book, this was the era of salivating journalism; the succulent lamb was served and handpicked hacks were VIPed to five-star junkets.

Murray also brought in fresh investment. While he was still chasing nine-in-a-row, he brought in Joe Lewis of English National Investment Company (ENIC). In 1996, ENIC Group invested £40m in Rangers. Although the cash was welcome, the input was not. Murray wasn't a team player and board meetings were rare. It was a case of irreconcilable difference. Disagreements with Murray over the extent of Rangers manager Dick Advocaat's spending madness led to ENIC's Howard Stanton resigning from the club's board of directors in May 1999. In the same year, Bob Brannan only lasted six months as chief executive on the Rangers board. He warned that the company was trading while insolvent and that the level of debt would eventually kill the club.

Murray, as always, wanted other people's money but he didn't put much value on their opinions. Dave King, a Rangers supporter from Glasgow who had made his fortune in South Africa, came onto the board in 2000 and invested £20m. Dick Advocaat, the Rangers manager, was allowed to spend lavishly and the objective was clear: reassert domestic dominance and, most important of all, achieve Champions League glory.

As Celtic, under manager Martin O'Neill, assembled a capable team, Murray famously boasted in 2000: "For every five pounds Celtic spend, we will spend ten." What this meant, in effect, was that Murray was willing to pay twice what a player was worth. He authorised the purchase of Norwegian Tore Andre Flo in 2000 for £12m from Chelsea. Celtic paid the same club £6m for the accomplished Chris Sutton. The big Englishman's first goal for the Parkhead club was in a 6–2 thrashing of Rangers. Sutton spoke of "putting Rangers in their place" as a key part of his job description. It wasn't an idle boast. Celtic won the treble in season 2000/2001 and Advocaat was sacked in the same year.

The Dutchman, dubbed "the little general", had reasserted Rangers as the pre-eminent power in Scotland following their stumble at ten-in-a-row. However, he had failed to progress in the Champions League. Basically, he did what Walter Smith had done throughout the 1990s; he won in Scotland but failed in Europe. This just wasn't good enough given the resources he had been given.

By 2001, Rangers' European dream was in tatters and they were instead in a street fight with Martin O'Neill's skilful scrappers. Ironically, it would be Advocaat's successor, Alex McLeish, who would steer Rangers to the last 16 of the Champions League. However, by that time the financial damage had been done. The ex-Aberdeen stalwart had to work under circumstances of extreme austerity compared to those Advocaat had enjoyed.

Off field there were plenty of portents of the troubles that were to come. When Hugh Adam resigned from the Rangers board in January 2002, he could not have been clearer in his warnings about where Murray was taking the club. His words, published in the *Scotsman*, were chillingly prescient and worth quoting at length here: "That's the logical conclusion to a strategy that incurs serious loss year-on-year. In the past five years – and it's all there in the last annual report – Rangers have lost £80m. Now, the banks are well known for being a bit more tolerant of companies whose core business is a popular pursuit like football. But there is a limit to how far backwards they can bend to accommodate you. David Murray has always had an amazing persuasiveness when it comes to getting people to put money into his businesses, but the signs are that those sources have dried up. The £40m worth of shares that ENIC bought a few years ago are now worth about £15m, with no evidence to suggest that they will recover. The money itself, that which was actually invested, was lost some time ago. Now the latest investor, Dave King from South Africa, will know that his £20m shareholding is worth around half, or even less, of what it was when he bought. No proper businessman will want to buy into that kind of loss."

On 5 July 2002, Murray relinquished the chairmanship of Rangers. This took him out of the firing line to some extent. Given his cosy relationship with the media, he wasn't very eagerly pursued by intrepid hacks from Glasgow. On 1 September 2004, Murray was back, and with a conjurer's flourish he announced a rights issue to raise funds which would reduce the club's debt, which by that stage was over £80m. Murray knew he had to act. The share issue was a total flop, and it fell short of its £57.2m target, but he had underwritten the issue to the tune of £50m.

As it turned out, it was a mere paper shuffling exercise and the debt went into Murray International Holdings' main debt burden. Although the Rangers accounts looked better, it was a complete flop, raising little over £1m in new money. A £50m dent was moved from Rangers' balance sheet onto Murray International Holdings'. Moreover, he had used the bank's money to achieve this accounting three-card trick. It bought him some time, but not much.

This was the first time that anyone inside the Murray media tent had publicly questioned what he was doing with the club financially. Graham Spiers pointed out the "financial vandalism" that Murray was inflicting on Rangers. He was frozen out of the magic circle of hand-picked hacks for his efforts. That aside, all that it really achieved was for Murray to see his shareholding in the club increase to around 90% of the total stock. It was these shares that he would sell for one pound to Craig Whyte in May 2011.

David Murray stated in July 2006 that he had his own "fit and proper person test" for anyone wishing to own the club. Claiming that the Ibrox outfit was worth £66m, he told the *Daily Record*: "It's not about money. It's about who would run the club in the correct way and that's not happened. There's no point in selling Rangers to people who can't invest money."

The year after he put the club up for sale, Murray was knighted for "services to business in Scotland" at a ceremony in Holyrood Palace.

When the club was eventually sold, it was Lloyds Banking Group's guy on the board, Donald Muir, who had the final say.

The Whyte takeover of Rangers is now the subject of a criminal investigation by Strathclyde police's fraud squad. They enlisted the specialised services of a handwriting expert from Scotland Yard to examine documents. A police insider told me that the common law offence of "fraud and uttering" was central to the investigation. Essentially, this is a probe into whether or not documents were forged as part of a fraud during the period of Whyte's takeover of the club in early 2011. It is believed that a preliminary report has been prepared for the Crown Office. At time of writing, no charges have been preferred and no arrests have been made.

Murray broke cover and, in a typically fluffy series of interviews, he said he had been "duped" by Craig Whyte. His hold over the mainstream media in Glasgow appeared intact. When Murray first put Rangers up for sale he regaled the hacks with tales of having almost sold the club but, after looking into the eyes of the prospective buyer, he refused to sign the papers. It was ripping yarns stuff and the poodles in his press pack loved it.

Alastair Johnston, who had been club chairman under Murray, said of the knight of the realm in May 2012: "He got too immersed in the fans' perception of himself – as well as his own ego and invincibility, probably. In the last few years he lost his business discipline, and then panicked when he saw Armageddon coming."

Johnston was less than delighted when the bank pushed through the sale of Rangers to Whyte in May 2011. The ex-chairman told Mark Daly of the BBC in his 2011 documentary about Craig Whyte that the bank had threatened to turn the credit line off unless the sale went through.

By then Murray was out of the picture. Of course, there was a time when the knight of the realm had a much more convivial relationship with those who provided his banking services. When I was researching this story in early 2010, I was put in touch with someone who worked for the Bank of Scotland in the 1990s. He related two occasions where he was present at several meetings between bank officials and David Murray. He told me: "It was more like a royal visit. Murray could do no wrong. This was the man with the Midas touch. The bigwigs were desperate for his business."

When the banking world changed after 2008 it was important that any new owner of Rangers had the cash to fund the club over and above what it earned. In November 2008, Murray gave an interview to the *News of the World*, where he referred to the Ibrox outfit requiring the "benefactor element" and saying that without it, there would have to be downsizing of up to 25%. As ever with Murray, the representation was often at odds with reality. He bought Rangers in 1988 with borrowed money. The cash he put into the club over the years was also accessed through corporate borrowing. The idea that Murray was a "sugar daddy" for Rangers did not stand up to serious scrutiny. With Murray it was always "OPM" (Other People's Money), whether it be the bank's or new investors'.

When he did make a killing on selling Murray International Metals in 2005, Rangers didn't see a penny of it. What wasn't known in 2005 was that he was the largest beneficiary from the Murray Group Remuneration Trust. Basically, Murray used the MIH employee benefit trust (EBT) as a way to access tax-free cash. The man with the billionaire lifestyle had expensive tastes, which is where some of the £6.3m he acquired through the EBT scheme went.

If you are reading the words "employee benefit trust" for the first time in relation to matters fitba then you have obviously been away on a very long cruise. David Murray was one of 72 Ibrox staff – including 55 players and five former managers – who benefited from the scheme. Although a gushing media mentioned his great wealth, it was largely notional, in much the same way that people find out that they are "millionaires" during a property boom.

The month before that interview with the *News of the World*, it was starting to become evident within Scottish football that all was not well financially at Rangers. In October 2008, Hamilton Accies visited Ibrox to play in a League Cup tie. This match deserves a little footnote in Scottish football history, not for the quality of the fare on the pitch, but because the club put a warning up on the electronic screens before the match started. It informed the Rangers fans that if they sang the "Famine Song" they were liable to be arrested. The week before, their travelling support had subjected Republic of Ireland under-19 starlet, James McCarthy, to appalling abuse at Accies' home ground, New Douglas Park. The youngster, born and reared in the west of Scotland, qualified to play for Ireland under the grandparent rule.

The Accies were due £38,000 from the match at Ibrox. When it didn't arrive after an appropriate length of time the club officials at Hamilton chased it up, but with no luck. Eventually, Rangers agreed to pay the Accies half of the amount due. The men from Hamilton told them £19,000 wasn't good enough and they wanted the £38,000 that was rightfully theirs. At the time it made no sense to the guys at New Douglas Park. However, it was clear evidence that Rangers were in financial trouble in late 2008. The dispute went through a tortuous process of tribunals and appeals which lasted 22 months. Finally, the SFA ruled in favour of the Accies. Within a week of that ruling, Rangers paid out the £38,000.

When I spoke to the Hamilton official who dealt with the incident, he hadn't taken it personally, he realised it was only business.

What the general public was not aware of at the time was the extent of the cash crisis that was enveloping the club as the bank turned the screw. Some of the roots of that crisis could be traced back to the interference of Celtic's Dermot Desmond in imposing Martin O'Neill on the Parkhead club instead of the favourite for the manager post, Guus Hiddink, in the year 2000. O'Neill, a success at lowly Leicester, brought out the best in Henrik Larsson. No one was really sure how, but Celtic had themselves a world-class striker for the first time in at least a generation. O'Neill was allowed to bring in a solid core of competent English premiership performers at considerable cost to the club. Celtic was also borrowing at a level that was unsustainable. Even when the club reached the UEFA Cup final in Seville in 2003, it made a loss.

This was the arms race that Murray had forced upon anyone who wanted to catch Rangers. However, a resurgent Celtic – with many more season ticket-holders than Rangers – was not part of Murray's plan after he had failed to deliver ten-in-a-row. Martin O'Neill's first Glasgow derby ended in a 6–2 thrashing of the city rivals. The wheels had started to come off the Advocaat express. The little Dutchman appeared to be able to get anything he asked for from Murray. This included a state-of-the-art training complex. Resources, even for Murray, were scarce and he halted work on a hotel at Ibrox in order to build Murray Park. Dick Advocaat told Murray bluntly that if he didn't get a training facility worthy of his coaching talents, he would walk. Murray blinked.

Archie Macpherson told me of the day that John Greig was sent out of Ibrox to the guys building a hotel adjacent to the stadium: "They were told to stop immediately. That was the day that Murray decided that the training ground, and not the hotel, would be built." This facility was meant to rear star players so that there would be less need to go into the transfer market. It never really materialised and the Rangers first team continued to be built around senior pros bought into the club.

The reality is that Dick Advocaat was effectively allowed to bankrupt Rangers between 1998 and 2001. Murray tried everything at his disposal to give him the resources to get the job done in Europe. With the opportunity to win ten-in-a-row gone, the Rangers owner upped the ante and looked for ways of affording better standards of player. Of course, these stars would be on significantly higher salaries.

This was the period when Murray decided to pay the players through employee benefit trusts. Over a ten-year period £48m was paid into these trusts. Over the last twenty years, thousands of companies in the UK utilised this tax efficiency strategy. Monies would be placed in a trust for an employee and then they would draw down loans. Those loans would have to be paid out of the person's estate when they died. However, this could be written off against inheritance tax if there was money in the deceased person's estate to pay back the loan. What the EBT could not be used for was paying normal contractual obligations to an employee – like wages and bonuses.

This is what HMRC allege that Rangers used the Murray Group Remuneration Trust for over a ten-year period. Pretending that players were getting loans from the trust when in fact it was money due to them as part of their salary was, in the opinion of HMRC, a "sham transaction" and, therefore, tax evasion. The Murray Group's lawyers – Rangers was defended by MIH in the tribunal – argued that the Dextra Case of 2005 was the test case and that they had not evaded tax. HMRC demurred.

What was not in dispute was that the use of EBTs allowed the Ibrox club massive financial advantage over its city rivals in terms of what it could pay players. For this tax evasion scheme to work, players had to be paid a substantial amount of their salary "off contract". This meant that they were not properly registered and were, under FIFA rules, ineligible to play. The dénouement of this saga that became known as the "big tax case" has yet to be delivered.

However, the decision by David Murray to pay players via this method rather than the normal PAYE system "saved" the club some £24m over a decade. The flamboyant tax lawyer Paul Baxendale-Walker sold Murray on the ingenious use of this tax efficiency strategy. EBTs were perfectly legal as long as they weren't used to pay "contractual obligations", like wages.

Celtic had also looked at EBTs as a way of paying players. The club did have an EBT for the Brazilian, Juninho, in 2004. However, the Celtic chairman, Brian Quinn, immediately saw the danger of this method of remunerating employees. As the former number two at the Bank of England, his point of view carried extra weight. The EBT for Juninho was the first and last at Celtic. The money that would have been ordinarily paid to HMRC if the Brazilian had been put through the PAYE system was sent to the taxman. Celtic has much to thank Brian Quinn for in this regard.

What HMRC investigators found, thanks to the material given to them by City of London police in 2007, was evidence of a policy of "wilful connivance" within Ibrox to evade tax. The main functionary for this scheme at Murray International Holdings was Ian MacMillan. He was the man who understood the complexity and the consequences of what was being operated. His job description indicated that he managed the group's tax compliance. It was an Orwellian title for Murray's bookkeeper.

MacMillan was the guy that Elliot Ness would have gone after, but it wouldn't have been personal. When Rangers' tax polices came to be discussed in the first-tier tax tribunal in Edinburgh, his scheduled half day in the witness box turned into three days. He was "spit roasted", according to one insider. Another MIH employee, a female, broke down under questioning; she suddenly got her memory back and was escorted to her hotel room to get some paperwork.

The main defence, put forward by Andrew Thornhill QC, was that Rangers thought what they were doing was illegal when they were doing it, but it turned out not to be. Former player and now broadcaster, Neil McCann, was brought in for the defence of his former employers. However, his honest testimony did much to augment HMRC's case.

Rangers could have challenged the evidence gleaned from the "Boumsong raid" at Ibrox in July 2007 on the grounds of admissibility. The information that was so crucial to HMRC on this case had been delivered to them by the City of London police. After this raid, the club was in serious trouble with HMRC. The tax man now knew that senior people inside Ibrox had been consistently telling lies about their tax affairs. City of London police delivered an entire armoury of smoking guns.

It was made clear to Rangers officials that if they did challenge the evidence gathered from the Boumsong raid on the basis of admissibility – which was their right – and they were successful, HMRC could forgo the tribunal route and go for a straight criminal prosecution of several well-known names up the marble staircase. The admissibility play was not utilised by Rangers, and HMRC were able to put before the three judges all that had been discovered by City of London police. It was damning stuff.

The Boumsong raid revealed a paper trail of deception, including

Martin Bain's now infamous email where he asked to be paid via an EBT and asked for the paper trail to be shredded. Despite the clear financial advantages of paying players through EBTs, the money problems at Rangers throughout those years did not go away. Alex McLeish took over from Advocaat in 2001 and he was the first manager at Ibrox under Murray's reign not to have huge amounts of money to spend. Indeed, he was the first to experience austerity. The days of crazy spending were over at Ibrox, something that must have stung Murray.

Martin O'Neill left Celtic to care for his wife. In an age where mangers are summarily dismissed or "moved upstairs", it was an end to a managerial reign with a difference. He was replaced by Gordon Strachan in June 2005. Rangers were SPL champions and it was his job to get the title back. He took the job on the proviso that he also cut an eye-watering £24m from the budget. Celtic's chairman, Brian Quinn, realised that the Parkhead club's borrowing had to cease. In trying to keep up with Murray's Rangers they had dug themselves into their own hole. Strachan would be an extraordinarily successful manager in modern times. He delivered three SPL titles on the bounce and got the club to where even Martin O'Neill with Larsson couldn't get.

Celtic navigated through to the last sixteen of the Champions League twice. It was a magnificent achievement while making those massive savings on the playing squad. This success by the city rivals may have had a bearing on how Rangers reacted to the bad news from the taxman in 2008. With the assessment in from HMRC, they knew they had to find £24m in unpaid taxes. There was interest and penalties on top of that.

Murray could have come clean with the fans, treated them as adults and told the whole truth about the EBT scheme and the huge tax bill they were facing. A player sale, brutish but necessary, could have brought in the core amount. With a cheque for £24m to HMRC and an apology, "Hector" would probably not have been hard to deal with after that.

It is a mantra of the HMRC chaps that "we are not a bank" when asked for easy terms to pay. However, with the core amount lodged with them, the interest (4% compound) could have been paid over two years. The penalties were, at that stage, perhaps negotiable if the correct, contrite attitude had been displayed. Instead, the Ibrox club played hardball with Hector and went on a spending spree, buying players to stop Celtic doing four-in-a-row.

Had the people in leadership positions at Rangers brought in that austerity programme in the summer of 2008, the city rivals would have been odds-on to win the next two titles. Five-in-a-row would have been a bitter pill to swallow and with each succeeding title the Rangers fans would get more and more fraught. Moreover, the home crowds may have dwindled.

When Walter Smith went on this spending spree it infuriated the bank. This was the last major strategic decision that was taken within the Ibrox boardroom apropos spending until Craig Whyte took over in May 2011.

When Gordon Strachan took over at Celtic in 2005 he should have been in charge just when Rangers were going bust. The Ibrox club should have become insolvent in 2005. All of the signs were there. Rangers were bent double under a huge debt and they were hamstrung by a continued inability to access the riches of the later stages of the Champions League.

However, Murray wasn't finished gambling and a fortuitous revaluation of heritable assets took place – basically Ibrox Stadium and Murray Park. At the start of 2005 the value of those assets was on the books at £48m. Given the level of the club's debt that year, insolvency was a given.

The company DM Hall was brought in to revalue those assets. £48m became £119m overnight. The breakdown between Ibrox and Murray Park was never revealed. In 2005, Murray Park had only been open for four years and had cost £14m to build. The training ground that bore Murray's name was revalued to between £20–25m. Therefore, the majority of the "uplift" was in the value of Ibrox stadium.

It was the paper exercise that prevented Rangers from going insolvent in 2005. This revaluation of assets allowed Murray to revert to type. He borrowed. The following year he had the final throw of the dice when he entered into the JJB deal and received a one-off payment from the clothing giant of £18m and a guaranteed payment of £3m per year for a decade. As part of this deal, Rangers closed their own chain of shops and people were made redundant.

This injection of £18m allowed Murray to bankroll new manager Paul Le Guen's team in 2006. Convincing the Breton to come to Glasgow and replace Alex McLeish was a genuine coup for Murray, probably his last at the helm of Rangers. The ex-Paris Saint-Germain player had a sparkling CV as the coach of Lyon, winning three league championships in a row and getting to the Champions League quarter-final. Le Guen was hot property in 2006 and, like Advocaat, he was meant to deliver European success. However, he did not have the vast budget that had been afforded to Advocaat seven years earlier. Le Guen and Rangers was a bad match. He was gone by 4 January 2007; it was the shortest reign of a Rangers manager on record.

One of the reasons for Le Guen's early exit was that Celtic, guided by the pragmatic and abrasive Gordon Strachan, was cruising to the title. Walter Smith was brought in to steady the ship after the Le Guen debacle. It was during Smith's reign that the club made its last ever important independent decision. Walter Smith needed players in the summer transfer window of 2008. The bad news from the taxman was already known. It was decision time for Murray.

The fans were in an ugly mood after star player Carlos Cuéllar, who had joined the club in July 2007, decided to leave Ibrox and could do so because of a release clause in his contract. The move infuriated Walter Smith. Moving to the English Midlands in a deal worth £7.8m on a four-year contract netted Rangers a substantial profit. He had joined Rangers from Osasuna for £2.37m the year before.

This money could have gone to pay outstanding taxes, but instead, as promised in an interview with Chick Young, Murray spent "every penny". That interview proved, if any proof was needed, that the Rangers owner still had a compliant press at his disposal.

Throughout the middle of the decade, Rangers supporters were regularly updated with breathy reportage about the "super casino for Ibrox". It was highly appropriate that someone like Murray would see financial salvation in a gambling establishment. However, the irony was lost on the domesticated hack pack in Glasgow. This dubious prize of being the city to host the mega casino was eventually awarded to Manchester, before the entire scheme was scrapped completely.

While the destination of this Las Vegas-style social problem was in doubt, the graphics artists in the Glasgow tabloids had great fun with imaging what it would look like next to Ibrox. The Ibrox circus could keep on going for as long as the world would lend high roller David Murray more and more of other people's money. When the Rangers' roulette wheel stopped, it did so abruptly.

When the banking crash came in September 2008, it was the beginning of the end for the football club in Scotland that had been fashioned in the image of Lehman Brothers. By the time the sub-prime carousel had stopped, Rangers was also dealing with a new banking situation at home.

The cosy days of the 1990s, when the Bank of Scotland loved Murray, were long gone. In February 1999, with Rangers' debts mounting, the Bank of Scotland took a 7% stake in the club and secured a charge over the club's income and assets should it default on its repayments. In 2001, the bank merged with the Halifax to form HBOS. As a result of the banking crash, the British government moved in and ordered the merger of HBOS with Lloyds TSB Group. This created Lloyds Banking Group in January 2009, the bank that would effectively take control of the club later that year.

The days of Sir David Murray having a cosy non-questioning relationship with his bankers were very much a distant memory. Rangers were like the doomed investment bank in New York, leveraged beyond any sane level and it could only be kept alive by regular infusions of liquidity. When the credit tap was turned off in Wall Street, the wells ran dry all around the world.

Rangers Football Club, culturally huge in Scotland and Northern Ireland, was but a tiny speck in that global story that would create towns full of swimming pools in the San Fernando Valley turned green by algae, a very visible sign that the good times were over now that the pool guy was unaffordable. Closer to home the same financial madness created ghost estates of empty houses across southern Ireland.

The global financial system was rocked to its foundations and it meant that, for Murray, the easy times were over. The term that everyone had to learn was "credit crunch" and, for Murray, it meant a business future where he was no longer in control of his own destiny. By January 2009, Rangers' bankers, under new ownership, wanted the club to reduce the debt and wanted a fire sale of players in the transfer window. When Rangers entered the January transfer window, Walter Smith knew that all of his players were up for sale. The signal from Rangers was clear: they were willing to sell anyone, even key players from their squad.

The club accepted the first offer that came in for their top scorer, Kris Boyd, but the player could not agree personal terms with Birmingham City, managed by ex-Rangers boss Alex McLeish. With no sales in the January window, the club then felt a firmer hand from the bank. First, a project team was sent in to start going through every transaction, every invoice, and every expense. This was happening across Murray International Holdings and Rangers was no different.

MIH owed the bank almost £1bn by 2009 and it looked a racing certainty that Murray's company would default on two loans. In April 2010, the bank increased its stake in Murray International Holdings to

24%, arranging a debt-for-equity swap. Lloyds Banking Group, realising that Murray couldn't pay, was taking a chunk of his business in the hope that the bank would benefit from an upturn in MIH's fortunes down the road and get its money back. When Donald Muir was put onto the board it merely formalised what had been going on for months – the bank was running Rangers.

In 2009 I met with a contact in Glasgow. In a quiet bar in Royal Exchange Square, he opened his laptop and showed me a screen grab image of an email from Donald Muir to Martin Bain, the Rangers chief executive. It was clear evidence that the bank had an austerity plan for the Ibrox club and that it was Muir's job to push that through.

My source allowed me to take down the details of the email, which was referring to an attached word document. Infuriatingly, I could only glean some of the import from the covering memo. Basically, the club would not pay any new player more that £15,000 per week. All of the higher earners, i.e. anyone above that level, would have to be shifted out of the door at the next available transfer window. No player should be allowed to drift in contract to where he left on a Bosman. The objective was to have a first team squad based on 14–16 professional players on a maximum of £15,000 per week. This core would be augmented by kids promoted from the youth ranks. This represented a massive cut in the football budget at Ibrox.

Muir's objective was simple: drive down the debt by cutting costs and maximising revenues. Walter Smith delivered on that end handsomely. However, it was his expensively assembled squad that had provoked the bank to act in the first place. The guys at Lloyds had "understood" that the cash that was spent on players in 2008 was going to come to them instead.

Still, the uneasy partnership of Muir and Smith produced excellent trading figures. The debt, once at £30m, was brought down over two years to £18m. However, the big tax case hovered over Rangers like impending doom. In fact, it wasn't "like" impending doom, that's exactly what it was. If the big tax case became the big tax bill, it was game over at Edmiston Drive.

Alastair Johnston, who had succeeded David Murray as chairman of Rangers Football Club on 26 August 2009, had deep reservations about the big tax case and said so at a press conference at Ibrox on 1 April 2011. Despite the date, he wasn't in any mood to joke. He was asked a question apropos the big tax case: "Could Rangers go bust?" In response, he nodded his head. Asked to clarify what the nod of the head meant, he added: "There's a 10,000lb gorilla in the room and you don't know what its appetite is . . . even accessing all the resources we have access to, we couldn't pay the bill."

The big tax case, of which the details were made public in May 2010, made the club unsellable to any serious buyer. Only an insolvency entrepreneur like Craig Whyte could have had an interest in the dying club. Everyone at Ibrox knew the import of the big tax case and the only strategy was to kick it into touch, play for time and hope for a saviour.

When Mr Whyte turned up on the scene, despite the risible reportage about him having "wealth off the radar", one person who wasn't convinced was Alastair Johnston. Johnston had clear concerns that the man advertised as a "billionaire" by the Scottish press didn't have the money to pay the regular bills. However, the bank was insistent that the sale had to go through and it wouldn't back down, so the club was sold to Whyte the following month.

Craig Whyte bought Rangers for a pound in May 2011. With money advanced to him from Ticketus, he was able to pay off the bank, which was in effective control of the club. This well-established company buys futures in season ticket sales. It is a way for football clubs to raise money in the short term. Most clubs go into negative cash flow in the couple of months just before season tickets are renewed. Rangers were no different and had used the company in the past.

What Whyte did was of a different order. He securitised a substantial chunk – 60% – of the next three years of the club's season tickets. When he couldn't make the first repayment, he went for a fourth season. He had used money that the fans would undoubtedly pay in the years to come to buy the club. Moreover, it emerged that the paperwork had been created by "clip art" on a computer and had not gone through the normal Ibrox invoicing system.

When I wrote about this a month after he had taken over the club, his PR people went into fire-fighting mode, writing to journalists and hinting that legal action against me was in the pipeline. For the record, I never even received so much as a lawyer's letter never mind a writ. It was all bluster designed to frighten off journalistic inquiry and to quietly rubbish my work in the eyes of other journalists.

Despite the fact that the club would have a huge hole in its finances for four years, the bank got its £18m and left the premises very happy. Like the bank, Whyte was happy, as he wasn't planning on staying around for much longer.

I was told, very early on in the life of the new regime, that there was a problem with working capital. There wasn't any. Rangers would need to operate on their own resources. They could not do that and satisfy the tens of thousands of season ticket-holders who expected a certain standard of player on the field. Their club had just won three SPL titles in a row. They wanted four and more.

European income was the key to Whyte's plans. Rangers played a Champions League qualifier against the un-fancied Malmo, from Sweden. If the Ibrox side triumphed, they would gain entry to the lucrative group stages. The Swedes won the first game in Glasgow 1–0. The Scottish champions had it all to do in Sweden.

Because of UEFA sanctions on the club for "discriminatory chanting" by their fans the previous March during a game against PSV Eindhoven, Rangers were not allowed to take a travelling support to the away leg. Perhaps this was the deciding factor in the tie, but Rangers were knocked out of the Champions League. Craig Whyte had some severe budget readjustments to make.

The summer spending spree had brought such soccer luminaries into the club as Alejandro Bedoya, Juan Manuel Ortiz and Matt McKay. There was no disguising that this was bargain basement stuff. After exiting the Europa League to lowly Maribor of Slovenia on 25 August, which meant that the club had no European income at all, Rangers purchased no more players in the summer transfer window. Even the bargain basement was off limits.

The Glasgow hack pack was in a tizzy. After all, the new owner had been trumpeted as a "billionaire". My sources inside the club painted a picture of an impending cash flow crisis. Whyte's own PR people were fire-fighting furiously. Rangers' own media people were also trying to quell any notion that all might not be as it had been painted with Mr Whyte and the club's finances. The photographs of sheriff officers entering Ibrox with arrestment orders for the "wee tax case" was publicity that Mr Whyte and his associates didn't need. Whyte had agreed to pay this £2.8m bill as part of the purchase of the club.

The "wee tax bill" arose from an historic dispute between Rangers and HMRC regarding the company's use of a discounted options scheme. This was another tax avoidance scheme, for two former players – Tore Andre Flo and Ronald De Boer – between 2000 and 2003. In Planet *Fitba* it became known as the "wee tax case".

HMRC issued Rangers with a bill totalling £4m in early 2011 for outstanding amounts owed from the discounted options tax scheme.

The club accepted the assessment and it did not go into the tribunal system. However, the bill had still not been paid by August 2011, forcing HMRC to send in sheriff officers.

The "wee tax case" also raised the issue of whether or not the SFA should have awarded Rangers a licence to play in Europe for season 2011/2012. The UEFA rules state that a club, to be eligible to play in one of their competitions, must not be "owing to a taxation authority".

After Craig Whyte failed to meet his obligation to pay the bill, monies were frozen in the club bank account. It wouldn't be the last time that Rangers banks accounts were so impeded by legal instrument – Martin Bain was suing for compensation after being sacked by Whyte. When the draft of his legal papers were leaked via the Rangers Tax Case website, the fitba internet went a bit crazy. Here was the former Rangers chief executive spelling out the dire situation that the club was in. He wanted the monies frozen because he didn't think Rangers would be in business for much longer. He was right.

The core of the story was that Rangers had been bought by someone who didn't have the money to bankroll the club. Moreover, he had used season ticket futures to pay off the bank. It was only a matter of time before the club was formally in an insolvency event.

My sources told me that all the ducks were in a row at the end of October 2011. When that didn't happen, the mainstream media crowed, but in the end it was only about timing. At the eleventh hour, cash had been realised from Whyte's parent company, Rangers Football Club Group Limited – formerly known as Wavetower – in the British Virgin Islands.

The British Virgin Islands are a small remnant of the British Empire. They make a living in the world by being a tourist destination, but mainly they are a destination for the offshore financial industry. Rich people like going there for the Caribbean sun, but most of all they like sending their money there. Registering a company offshore in the British Virgin Islands isn't cheap. However, if you wish to avoid scrutiny of your business affairs it is a wise move. The deal is that it is expensive to register a company in the British Virgin Islands, but it is safe from the prying eyes of foreign governments and pesky journalists.

Whyte's company, Wavetower, which was renamed "Rangers Football Club Group Limited", became the club's parent company in May 2011. The man dubbed a "billionaire" never intended to stick around for long. Whyte was expecting the first-tier tribunal to deliver the bad news and he would file for administrators to be appointed. However, due to Andrew Thornhill QC following his brief to delay, more time was needed to conclude the tribunal and the case, instead of concluding in October 2011, had to resume in January 2012.

If the big tax case had found against Rangers in late 2011, Whyte could have filed and would have been relatively blameless. By simply running out of cash, he would be the villain of the piece.

I had been informed by sources outside and within Rangers that normal remittances were not being paid. Whyte was, effectively, using due tax monies as cash flow. It was this behaviour that forced HMRC to act in February 2012 and place the club in administration. At that point, the name "Duff and Phelps" meant nothing to the inhabitants of Planet *Fitba*. However, the court-appointed administrators would assume a reputation of mythic proportions for bungling incompetence.

I was in regular contact throughout this period with someone who had been close to the action when Motherwell Football Club went into administration a decade ago. I asked what was likely to happen in the Rangers administration, given his experience of the same process at Fir Park. He made certain confident predictions and they all sounded very sensible and evidenced based. Interestingly, they were all wrong.

This was a football administration in Scotland like no other. This was confirmed to me by someone who had first-hand knowledge of the trauma that Dundee Football Club had endured, having experienced administration in 2003 and again in 2010.

No one, in fairness, expected that the first move of the administrators at Ibrox would be to sign a new player! From the botched attempt to hire Daniel Cousin, a former Rangers player, the Duff and Phelps reign of error continued. They would run up a bill of over £5m for their services.

There were several suitors for the dying club. There was the "Blue Knights" consortium, headed by ex-Rangers director, Paul Murray. Then Brian Kennedy entered the drama, a man of serious net worth who owns the Sale Sharks rugby club. They would later join forces and Kennedy, clearly an alpha male, would give a riveting press conference about the size of his "quantum". The hacks swooned. This, we were told, was the forceful type of chap that should be at the helm at Ibrox.

Then Tennessee truck tycoon Bill Miller turned up, had a look at the books and left. He stuck around long enough for the Ibrox crowd to demonstrate that their xenophobia was flexible and it wasn't just Irish Catholics who weren't welcome in Govan. Miller's due diligence flagged up that the club would need £30m over three years just to stay still.

The Scottish hack pack, still all giddy from Brian Kennedy and his quantum, was now introduced to the concept of the "incubator" company. The hilarious metaphors just kept coming out of the Rangers fiasco. The reality was grubbier. The club was going to die.

Duff and Phelps published the list of creditors owed money by Rangers, all 276 of them. Creditors ranged from HMRC, which was owed monies that could total £93m dependent on the outcome of the big tax case, to the corner shop near Ibrox, owed £567.45 for newspapers, and even a face-painting service, which was owed £40. Rangers' administrators revealed the club owed at least £55m to the 276 creditors. However, the total bad news could reach £140m.

Duff and Phelps wanted the creditors to accept a Company Voluntary Arrangement (CVA). This is where creditors are offered a "pence in the pound" deal, which means they don't get all that they are owed but they can get a percentage. This allows the company to come out of administration and continue in business. Under UK law, if creditors owed 75% of total liabilities agree to the CVA then it goes ahead. If a creditor, or creditors, owed 26% of the monies do not agree then they can block the CVA. HMRC, even without the big tax case, was owed more than 26% of the liabilities and held it in its power to stop any such deal. The idea that HMRC, as a major creditor, would accept a CVA was a chimera.

Rangers had offered to settle the big tax case for £10m in January 2010. The offer had been dismissed out-of-hand. The only "out-of-court settlement" that HMRC wanted from Rangers was all of the money. The idea that they would accept a CVA in a case where there had been evidence of evasion was nonsensical, yet the mainstream media still kept up with the pretence that everything was going to be OK. At each stage it was wrong.

Even the usually grounded Roddy Forsyth of the *Telegraph* wrote on 22 April 2012 that "highly placed sources within HMRC have indicated that they will not oppose a CVA for Rangers".

Duff and Phelps had to find a buyer and they thought they had finally lucked out when Bill Miller from Tennessee turned up. A self-made man of considerable wealth, he had made his fortune in tow trucks. I found it hugely ironic that the man who was going to save Rangers was in the car wreck business. Miller had his people look at the books over a lazy weekend in May and quickly established that he would have to bankroll the Ibrox outfit to the tune of £30m over three years. With that realisation, he was out, although not before the

Rangers supporters had appeared at a match with a banner telling the American to "Truck Off!"

Meanwhile, Rangers players had agreed to take a wage cut of 25–75% earlier in the administration. With that agreement about to run out, Duff and Phelps said that they did not have any cash left to run the club. When that happens to a company in administration, liquidation automatically follows from that.

Then, with Miller gone, Charles Green and his rather shadowy consortium appeared in the drama as if by magic. Originally, he stated that he was the frontman for twenty investors. However, that number was soon whittled down. His CVA offer was £8.5m. It was a tiny offer and, despite what the mainstream press was saying, HMRC would not go along with this because of the evidence of evasion by the company. The policy is stated on HMRC's own website: "Rejecting a voluntary arrangement. We are also likely to reject a voluntary arrangement where there is evidence of evasion of statutory liabilities or past association with contrived insolvency."

Indeed, an allegation of "evasion" was why Rangers were in the big tax case tribunal in the first place. When the CVA was rejected by HMRC on 12 June 2012, the club established in 1872 went onto the corporate equivalent of death row.

Charles Green bought the assets of the club for £5.5m. That figure would later be broken down when Duff and Phelps had to present papers to Lord Hodge in the Court of Session. The Duff and Phelps report, dated 10 July, stated that the allocation was:

Goodwill £1
SPL Share £1
SFA Membership £1
Leasehold Interests £1
Player contracts and Registrations £2,749,990
Stock £1
Subsidiary Companies Share Capital £5
Heritable Properties £1,500,000
Plant and Machinery £1,250,000

It all neatly added up to £5.5 million. Amazingly, the Albion car park, Ibrox stadium and Murray Park had been sold to Green's Sevco Scotland Limited for only £1.5m. Moreover, Green had parted with £2.75m for player registrations. However, because the club was to be liquidated, these players were free agents and could walk out of their contracts. That is what most of them chose to do, including goalkeeper

Alan McGregor and club captain Steve Davis. For Mr Green, who had been the top guy at Sheffield United, it was an appalling misjudgement.

The adventures of FC Sevco – the liquidators have, at time of writing, yet to approve their use of the name "The Rangers" – are still to play out. However, their purchase of the assets of Rangers marked the end of 140 years of history of a club that David Murray once thought he could turn into a family heirloom. To use the lexicon of Her Majesty's armed forces, so beloved of the Ibrox crowd, this story charts a series of self-inflicted wounds that ultimately proved fatal. No one made David Murray go down the route of employee benefit trusts. There was no outside agency pressurising Rangers to spend in 2008 when they knew that a substantial tax bill was likely to come their way. In the same fashion, it was entirely an internal Ibrox decision in 2011 to use overdue tax monies as working capital.

Their city rivals in the East End were mere onlookers to all of this. However, Celtic played an unwitting role and a long time before any of the current incumbents, like Peter Lawwell, were around the boardroom table. When they meet in the boardroom at Celtic Park, in the trophy cabinet shines a symbol of Rangers' torment: a replica of the cup Celtic won in Lisbon in 1967.

It was trying to emulate that feat that plunged Rangers into a spiral of craziness and self-destruction. With the benefit of hindsight, Jock Stein and his men not only gave Celtic their finest hour, but they inflicted a psychic wound, the extent of which can only now be gauged.

Trying to win the big cup killed Rangers. It was suicide brought on by jealousy. Stein said that football without fans was nothing. As this crisis became a fiasco, the stance of the Rangers supporters seemed utterly out of place. Their swaggering Herrenvolk hubris now seems pitiable. Stein's men reached the pinnacle of European club football on a shoestring budget. His players were all local lads. I would wager that one of the Internazionale movie stars earned more than all of Stein's Lions.

The Inter Milan manager, Argentinian Helenio Herrera, magnanimously conceded that Celtic's victory on 25 May 1967 was "a victory for sport". Had Murray been successful with Rangers, it would have been a victory for Gordon Gekko. Rangers, so long tainted by discrimination and shameful scenes of crowd trouble, completely lost their moral compass under Murray.

The less self-aware among the Rangers fan base cannot perceive how the outside world viewed them. Ironically, Murray was a creation of an ideology that destroyed the local business class that had always nurtured the Ibrox club in the twentieth century. As the crisis unfolded, the fans waited and waited in anticipation of a rich man with an emotional connection to Rangers. That person never materialised.

Much of the native business class on Clydeside that had been so prominent at Ibrox in the interwar years had been destroyed by Thatcherism. A new type of entrepreneur, speaking estuary English and utterly oblivious to the ways of fair Caledonia started to inhabit the Scottish business ecosystem.

It will be recorded that Rangers' 140th year was its last. The cause of death was debt brought on by David Murray's hubris, with the rampant jealousy of the Rangers klan over Lisbon as a complicating factor.

References

http://www.scotsman.com/sport/alan-pattullo-rangers-chief-is-fully-aware-he-has-made-errors-but-he-defends-his-running-of-club-1-754246

http://www.rangers.co.uk/staticFiles/fe/a8/0,,5~174334,00.pdf (Appendix 3 is the list of creditors.)

http://www.scotzine.com/2012/07/will-rangers-actually-bounce-back-quickly-as-many-predict/

http://news.bbc.co.uk/sport2/hi/football/teams/r/rangers/4788114.stm

http://www.scotsman.com/sport/football/top-football-stories/adam-shakes-ibrox-pillars-with-warning-of-bankruptcy-1-595808

http://www.dailymail.co.uk/sport/football/article-2114674/Former-Rangers-owner-Sir-David-Murray-apologises-mess-says-duped.html

http://www.dailyrecord.co.uk/football/spl/rangers/2012/02/14/rangers-in-crisis-timeline-of-ibrox-club-s-spiral-towards-administration-86908-23748464/

http://www.dailyrecord.co.uk/football/spl/2012/05/23/rangers-in-crisis-the-downfall-of-sir-david-murray-by-former-chairman-and-ally-alastair-johnston-86908-23870056/

http://www.scotsman.com/sport/football/top-football-stories/murray-makes-163-112-million-but-not-a-penny-will-be-put-into-rangers-1-1111714

http://www.heraldscotland.com/mobile/news/home-news/claims-murray-pocketed-6m-through-tax-scheme.1340293352

http://www.dailymail.co.uk/sport/football/article-468810/Police-raid-clubs-corruption-investigation.html

http://news.bbc.co.uk/2/hi/uk_news/scotland/glasgow_and_west/8654171.stm

http://www.telegraph.co.uk/sport/football/teams/rangers/8422821/Rangers-
    chairman-admits-the-club-could-go-bust-if-no-white-knight-is-found.html
http://www.hmrc.gov.uk/helpsheets/vas-factsheet.pdf
http://i48.tinypic.com/123s8i8.jpg
http://www.murray-international.co.uk/pdfs/MurrayNewsWinter2007.pdf
http://www.independent.co.uk/sport/football-brannan-steps-down-from-
    rangers-post-1045974.html
http://m.accountingweb.co.uk/article/
    hmrc-calls-administrators-rangers/524397
http://news.bbc.co.uk/1/hi/scotland/4264114.stm
http://www.heraldscotland.com/sport/spl/aberdeen/council-takes-a-gamble-
    on-gbp200m-ibrox-super-casino-rangers-given-first-such-permission-
    in-uk-1.42503
http://www.dailyrecord.co.uk/news/2006/04/05/
    fight-on-cards-for-first-super-casino-86908-16904656/
http://www.rangers.co.uk/staticFiles/a2/b6/0,,5-177826,00.pdf
http://www.bbc.co.uk/news/uk-scotland-glasgow-west-18169502

The fall of the house of Murray

11.01.09

So far, no one has made a movie of the life of Sir David Murray. I can't
think why as there is certainly enough dramatic material. The story arch
is all there and the character bio is engaging. The young businessman
who triumphed despite the appalling personal tragedy of the loss of
both legs following a serious car crash after a rugby match, in 1976. The
loss of his wife, Louise, in 1992 due to cancer.

In this movie there are also strong supporting roles for good character actors, with broody tough guy Souness and the genial white-haired
Walter Smith all good strong dramatic roles. There is even a cast of thousands. The extras should never be the story in a movie, it should be about
the central characters. *Braveheart* was never about the FCA lads at the
Curragh dressed up for the day as Highlanders, it was about the Wallace.

However, in Murray's story it is the extras that are the real story. It
isn't like that in the real movies. Steven Spielberg would have none of
that. How would you shoot the battle scenes from *Saving Private Ryan*
if the US Rangers started to behave like Glasgow Rangers? Heading for
Omaha beach, they suddenly start a drunken barney among themselves

in the landing craft. What would Cecil B. DeMille do if the Israelites, instead of fleeing out of Egypt on cue, decided to use the pyramids as a public urinal while singing the "Billy Boys"?

It is the extras in the David Murray biopic that have been the cause of his greatest misfortune. In the movie of his life, Sir David Murray has wanted to write the script and direct the action. In that, he is no different to any businessman who has made it to the top. Like most powerful men in the western world in the last fifty years, he has known the need for control over the media. He lives a rock star lifestyle, but instead of being known for number one hits, he is known for being the owner of Rangers Football Club.

He made an alliance with Rangers supporters. He will now know the extent to which he is riding a tiger. As Rangers chased a record-equalling ninth championship in a row, Murray attracted investment from ENIC when they bought a 25% stake in the club for £40m in 1997. Then, having lost out on a record-breaking ten-in-a-row, Murray decided that domestic dominance wasn't enough. He would make Rangers a force in Europe and the ENIC money would be part of bankrolling that assault on the Champions League. The man to lead Rangers into Europe would be Dick Advocaat. Murray believed in "the little general" and indulged him.

It looked, initially, like Murray and his Dutch coach would usher in a generation of domestic hegemony and build serious European credibility. Like the economic miracle that Murray had been part of since the 1980s, there was no secret formula. It was actually a global overdraft. The Rangers portion of that credit line was used up by the Dutchman's buying binge. Advocaat was, essentially, allowed to bankrupt Rangers in his treble-winning first season of 1998–99. The Dutchman cost Murray a £32m gross spend on players. For a single season it was a British record.

This was also the period of fawning journalism. Many recall James Traynor's hilarious dinner date piece where Murray held court as the captivated *Daily Record* journalist informed his readers about what was on the menu as he dined with the Rangers owner. Apart from Traynor's complete lack of journalistic objectivity was Murray's hubris following Celtic's title win, stopping the tenth consecutive league win for Rangers. "Neither am I willing to stand aside and allow another club to overtake Rangers. The failure of last season hurt me a lot and that pain was something I didn't need nor want," Murray told the *Daily Record*. "It is also a pain which I never want to suffer again, but by God that sort of thing just makes me even more determined to succeed. I am still as driven, still as enthusiastic and I will welcome the challenge of anyone out there."

This drooling journalism has, inevitably, spawned its own dedicated website. As Rangers spiral towards administration, no doubt a www. humblepie.com would be more appropriate. With a venal media in competition to conjure up the next best compliment to Murray and his business acumen, the Rangers support was also on message. The traditional party tunes of Ulster Loyalism were still allowed within Ibrox. At every home game and in the streets around Ibrox stadium, the words of the "Billy Boys" were clearly audible. The media, with very few exceptions, didn't question Murray's business model for Rangers or the behaviour of the fans. All was well in the world.

The new millennium should have belonged to Murray and Rangers. That was in the script and the funding for the next epic production was in place. Like an out-of-control movie director, the little Dutchman continued to spend like, well, like it wasn't his money. Tore Andre Flo for £12m was the zenith of the lunacy. Advocaat spent like a shopaholic with a no-limits credit card. The problem was that he wasn't spending Murray's money. The Scottish entrepreneur was merely a middleman between the Dutchman and the bank. Murray loved Dick and the bank loved David. It had to end in tears.

Rangers' debts spiralled and the club has never fully recovered. There were warnings from within, but Murray didn't seem to listen. His business model for Rangers, and so it seems Murray International Holdings (MIH), was to borrow, speculate and gamble that the only direction for economy was up.

In 2002, Hugh Adam, who had resigned from Rangers in 2000, went public with his concerns for the club he had served for decades. Adam knew, commercially speaking, where the bodies were buried. He wrote a piece for the *Scotsman*, which was published on 14 July 2002. The sub-editor didn't have to think too hard for an appropriate title. "Murray in over head" was damning and, more to the point, unanswerable.

"I have read the eulogies to David Murray over this past week with amusement and bemusement, for they owe little to the facts. Far from being the master in the market, as he has been portrayed, in purely business terms Rangers fared badly during David's fourteen years as chairman of the club," Adam wrote. "Exactly how else can losses of £80m over the past five years – despite almost £60m of outside investment in that time – be explained? If you are one of the media sources grateful to David for always being available on the phone and giving quotable 'lines', it would seem these can be dismissed as an unfortunate by-product of a necessary outlay to achieve unparalleled success; or the nine-in-a-row years, if you prefer. I beg to differ."[1]

Adam stated upfront that he had parted from Rangers on bad terms with Murray and that, obviously, coloured his judgement of the Rangers owner. However, it didn't mean that his analysis of Murray the businessman and Rangers' financial future didn't have some veracity. "We endured strained relations throughout our time working together because I never depended on him for my income and so could be an independent voice in what was otherwise a one-party state. David tends to only appoint toadies and didn't like the fact I was not prepared to be one," Adam said in the piece. "This is one of his weaknesses as an executive. Another is the fact that he is simply not an astute business-man. Rather, he is an impresario, a showman, what might be termed a buyer and seller, this extending even as far as the manner in which he has sold himself and his club through a willing media. No football club chairman in the history of the Scottish game has found his name in the papers above more sympathetic articles than David. Even when the tales being told amount to bad news stories.

"Perhaps because he was afforded such impunity he too often had lit-tle interest in balance sheets, preferring to splash out recklessly because this appealed to his sense of showmanship. Long-term effects were not considered and the upshot of this is that the new chairman will have to find a way of reducing expenditure to below income in order that debts can be serviced. In his resignation statement last week David practi-cally confessed he did not possess the guile to do this, claiming that the penny-pinching now required was not his style," Adam added.

None of this needs any spin or embellishments. Adam worked closely with Murray, as closely as anyone at Rangers, on the business side. Quite simply, the man described by Adam was no businessman, more of a riverboat gambler.

By 2004 the club's debt stood at £82m. Only Graham Spiers, chief sports writer of the *Herald*, now of *The Times*, broke ranks in Scotland and wrote about the impending financial disaster that Murray was tak-ing Rangers into. Spiers also wrote about the "bigotry issue" which, he claimed, was much worse at Rangers than it was at Celtic. In hap-pier times, Spiers spent time in Murray's holiday home in the Channel

---

1   http://www.scotsman.com/sport/football/top-football-stories/
    murray-in-over-head-1-1375205

Islands, where the entrepreneur told him in an interview that was published in the *Herald*: "I'd love it to become a kind of dynasty thing.
I'd love one of my boys to take over from me at some stage and drive
the club on. I think that would be really satisfying, to have that family
association with Rangers."

That was in 1998, as he marked his decade in control of Rangers.
Now, of course, Rangers are in control of him. Murray, stung by criticism from some brave souls in the media, like Spiers, about the debt
problem at Rangers, moved more flags on maps in his bunkers. Another
share issue raised £51.5m, of which £50m came from Murray's own
businesses. In reality, Murray merely moved the Rangers debt into
MIH's accounts proper. Unlike Fergus McCann's share issue, which
financed the building of a new stadium, the £1.5m of new money generated for Rangers was a humiliating failure for Murray.

Failure is something that Sir David Murray isn't used to. From 2005
onwards, the emotional contract that Murray had with the Ibrox faithful
came under increasing strain. He had promised explicitly to deliver on-
field success. He had also, implicitly, pandered to the darker emotions of
the club's support. The orange away strip, the world was told, was in rec-
ognition of the Dutch manager and the large contingent of Dutch stars
in the team. No one was fooled. Another away top looked suspiciously
like an England top. All the while the traditional songs of settler supremacy in Ireland and empire Loyalism were belted out with impunity.

The first time I saw a different Murray was when he squirmed as he
was, for a change, asked tough questions by a journalist. Screened in
February 2005, Murray was interrogated on *Panorama* about the singing of the "Billy Boys". He didn't know it then, but Murray had UEFA
censure, the Manchester riots and the PR disaster of the "Famine Song"
all in front of him. All delivered by the unruly extras on his epic, a
production that was so over budget there was no longer a budget. Since
2006, the extras have been looking on as the stars in the production
have failed to provide on-field success and their repertoires of songs, old
and new, could end them in court on criminal charges.

Not surprisingly, and never a pretty bunch to start with, the hard-
line Rangers fans are now revolting. Their racist outpourings on message boards and on the streets of Manchester make Rangers even less
attractive to any potential buyer. Like a bad-tempered movie mogul
on his favourite project – the movie that will be his legacy – Murray is
going through managers like so many underperforming scriptwriters.

As I write this, there has been a new development in the Scottish media. The first green shoots of a widespread criticism of Murray. The once timid hack pack, perhaps sensing that Murray's power may be on the wane, feel somewhat safer to tell Murray's customers what everyone in the Scottish media has known for some time. The emperor has no money. He promised the Rangers supporters that he would deliver on-field success.

The reality is that Murray's Rangers last won the Scottish Premier League in 2005. His team currently trail rivals Celtic by five points and the Rangers first team squad is being auctioned off to meet bank payments that are due before the summer.

I will soon post an article, exclusive to this site, by a financial expert in the USA who has been examining the accounts of Murray International Holdings (MIH) at my request. Ray McKinney is President of Chemera Consulting LLC (Philadelphia, PA). He holds a B.Eng (Hons) in mechanical engineering from the University of Strathclyde, and an MBA from Columbia Business School in New York. An experienced turnaround manager, his expertise is in corporate restructuring. In short, he is an excellent person to analyse the current commercial and financial health of any company.

Ray is quite unequivocal that, technically speaking, MIH (and Rangers) is insolvent. Murray's companies owe more than they are worth. The Rangers owner has borrowed massively against assets, including Ibrox stadium, that have been grossly overvalued. Ironically, it is the esteem with which Murray has been held in Scotland for being the owner of Rangers and the man with the Midas touch that has allowed him to construct the scenario which has led his empire to the brink of ruin.

Until recently, most scriptwriters would have tacked the Murray story as a feel-good, uplifting triumph of the human spirit. The only way a producer would give the Murray story the time of day now would be as the story of a man with too much pride who fell in with a bad crowd.

Taxing times for Rangers

07.06.10

EXCLUSIVE
A few weeks ago I spoke with Rangers' chief executive Martin Bain. He kindly took my call on a Saturday morning just after his lad's football match. I told him that I was a freelance journalist commissioned

to do a story for the *News of the World*. After exchanging some jokes about the perils of being, as I termed it, "a maddie at your boy's fitba match", I had to tell Martin Bain some bad news. I informed him that this journalist already knew that Rangers had received a bill from the taxman for £24m and that interest of £12m had been nailed on to that amount.

Over the previous two weeks, the *News of the World* had firstly broken the story that all SPL clubs were being investigated by Her Majesty's Revenue and Customs (HMRC) as part of an ongoing tax probe. The real story, however, was revealed the following Sunday, and it was that the old firm, conjoined twins in so many areas, had very different tax policies.

For the last decade, Rangers had been making a systematic use of Employee Benefit Trusts (EBTs). Celtic looked at this method of being "tax efficient" in 2006, but Celtic chairman, formerly of the Bank of England, Brian Quinn, thought better of it. Initially, Martin Bain said to me that, effectively, the tax issue belonged to the parent company of Rangers – Murray International Holdings (MIH). He told me that there was no tax bill at Rangers.

After going round the houses with Martin Bain on the phone, we nailed down that there had been "an assessment" delivered by HMRC to Rangers FC. Most people would call that a bill. The "assessment" formally becomes a bill when the tribunal system is exhausted. The amount on the "assessment" then "crystallises". That is when the money is due to be paid.

The tax authorities have sent a bit of paper to Rangers and that piece of paper has a number on it. That amount is £24m plus £12m interest. That £36m is greater than the club's well-publicised bank debt.

After my interview with Bain the story was out there and, perhaps because of this, the club chairman Alastair Johnston went public and clarified the position on the tax probe. The Ohio-based businessman confirmed that the assessment from HMRC was indeed "a Rangers issue, but it is being masterminded by the Murray Group's financial and legal advisors," said Johnston. The only question to be answered was what tax penalty would be imposed on Rangers by HMRC should they lose the case.

What has not been previously revealed is that Rangers Football Club has already been served with a tax penalty of £15m by HMRC for their sustained use of "Employee Benefit Trusts" (EBT) for players and other senior employees. This brings the total confirmed amount that HMRC are seeking from Rangers to £51m. This £51m bill has yet to "crystal-lise" – the tax tribunal due process has yet to reach its conclusion.

Rangers can drag out this process by using all the appeals available to them. However, this will incur huge legal bills should they decide to do this. The figure of £15m for the penalty is an indication of the serious-ness with which HMRC view this case and their determination to see it through to a successful conclusion.

The recent press interest and investigation has clearly rattled the Scottish Premier League champions, with the club's chief executive refusing to answer whether or not Rangers had ignored expert tax advice to abandon their tax strategy.

I also put the following question to Martin Bain: "Did Sir David Murray, or other Rangers executives, benefit from this scheme?" Bain confirmed that "employees of the trust" were paid through the EBT. I asked him if that included people at the club other than players. He confirmed that it was not just players. I then asked him if he had been paid through the EBT. "That's a matter for the tax office and my own personal contract so I'd rather not go into that." Of course, a simple denial would have killed that particular part of the story.

When I put it to Bain that his answer was, in fact, a "no comment", he didn't disagree with my characterisation of his answer. Here is what has been confirmed at this time:

– Rangers FC has confirmed that there is a tax probe

– Rangers FC has used EBTs. This will have helped millionaire play-ers pay lower tax rates than most Rangers fans.

– Chief executive Martin Bain has confirmed to this journalist that the bill for core amount has been received.

Initially, Bain told this journalist that the EBT was a matter for par-ent company, Murray International Holdings (MIH). However, after the article was published, chairman Alastair Johnston confirmed that the HMRC issue was, indeed, a matter for Rangers. "It is a Rangers issue, but it is being masterminded by the Murray Group's financial and legal advisors," revealed Johnston.

When I interviewed Martin Bain he suggested that I speak to MIH financial director, Mike McGill. I called McGill on the Monday after I had spoken to Bain. I spoke briefly with McGill. He told me that he had read the *News of the World* story and, subsequently, refused to speak to me.

The day after I spoke to the MIH financial director, I received further news that shocked me. What moves this story on is the following information. I did not know at the time of my interview with Martin Bain that Rangers had already been served with the tax penalty. The amount of that penalty is £15m. Therefore the full amount that Rangers will be due, should they lose this case against HMRC, will be £51m.

It is clear that those in charge of Rangers did not wish this story to break. Since I started writing on Rangers taxing problems, the club's public comments have confirmed my journalism to be accurate. The initial stories were met with disbelief from both sides in Glasgow's football feud, thinking that this news was either too awful or too wonderful to be true. It is true and it will not go away.

The Scottish champions' problems with HMRC will be the dominant story out of Ibrox in the next twelve months. The club's bank debt is serviceable. The tax bill is not. It's a game changer.

Martin Bain, as much as one can ascertain over a fifteen-minute phone call on a Saturday morning, came across as a really, really decent bloke in a difficult position. I'm sure he cringed when he heard the "Famine Song" or saw Manchester policemen kicked to the ground by feral louts in Rangers shirts. The Rangers chief executive told me that wee Bain's team had lost 4–1. I told Martin to tell his lad to keep his chin up, because you usually find out more about yourself when you lose than when you win. His dad agreed with me.

Watch this space.

Rangers offer to settle with HMRC

23.01.11

My sources have informed me that Andrew Thornhill QC, who is representing Rangers in the current tax case with HMRC, recently approached the lawyers of the other side and offered to settle the case. The figure offered to HMRC was £10m. HMRC rejected this offer out-of-hand without any consideration.

The fact that Rangers authorised their legal team to make such an offer does not indicate that the people that currently run the Ibrox club are confident of winning this case in the slightest. On the basis of the first "round" of this case last year, when Rangers got to present their evidence and the HMRC legal team cross-examined, that would be a safe assumption in my opinion.

Of course, any reasonable person might ask: "If Rangers believe that that they have no case to answer and are confident of ultimate victory then why should they offer to pay anything?"

Quite.

Rangers board desperate to settle tax case!

23.01.11

EXCLUSIVE

Rangers' legal battle with HMRC took a serious turn for the worst in recent weeks. The case, which concerns the club's use of an Employee Benefit Trust (EBT) to pay players without paying PAYE or National Insurance contributions, puts Rangers FC's future on the line. In a startling gambit, Rangers' lawyer, Andrew Thornhill QC, has had his second approach to settle the case out of court rebuffed. In this most recent offer, it is understood that the Ibrox club offered an amount just under £10m.

But this was not Rangers' first effort at making this problem disappear. Upon taking the case in the spring of 2010, Thornhill approached HMRC asking what it would take to settle. When that did not elicit a response from the British government's representatives, he threw out an offer of £3–5m. This was summarily rejected. However, at the time, this was not seen as significant; simply a lawyer doing his job to evaluate all options and test the depth of resolve of the opposition.

However, this most recent approach comes with the background of the initial phase of the first-tier tax tribunal, which was held in late October 2010. Several of the witnesses called by Rangers were forced into damaging admissions and retractions under cross-examination. The entire case was scheduled to last for two weeks, but Rangers were not even able to complete their rebuttal of the charges – that they had knowingly operated an illegal tax scheme. HMRC's lawyer is widely considered to have "roasted" several senior representatives of the famous Glasgow club.

With the tribunal scheduled to restart in May 2011, the flat rejection of this offer is sure to send a wave of panic up to the top of the marble staircase and beyond. It is understood that it would take an offer to pay HMRC 100% of the original underpayment and accrued interest – a total of £36m – to get HMRC to engage in negotiations over the amount of penalty which would be added. The final amount of the penalty, which has already been billed to Rangers at approximately £15m, is scheduled to be determined in a separate tribunal if Rangers' guilt in operating a tax evasion scheme is established in the current process.

HMRC's enthusiasm for going to court can be explained by a desire to establish case law and eliminate any doubt over the use of EBTs to pay contractual obligations such as salaries and appearance money (contrary to erroneous speculation in the print media, image rights form no part in the current case against Rangers).

One can only speculate whether Alastair Johnston and the Rangers board still retain their jaunty confidence in the "expert advice" they claim to have followed. Their flat dismissals of the risks surrounding this matter and their willingness to write a cheque for £10m today seem to be in conflict. One financial analyst familiar with the case said, "It looks like the seriousness of their position is dawning on the Rangers board. This looks like they have figured out the maximum amount of money they are able to pay and have decided to offer it now rather than risk almost certain insolvency should they be forced to pay even close to £60m."

What tax experts are saying about Rangers

03.02.11

"Scuttlebutt" is a wonderfully graphic nautical term that has migrated from the days of sailing ships into the world of work to mean "office gossip". Where once it meant the device where sailors congregated to have a drink, it now means workplace bush telegraph. A term originally meaning a cask on shipboard to contain fresh water for a day's use now means an underground communications network where people find out what is really going on, probably because this was the one time in the day the ship's crew could congregate and chat about what was happening on their part of the ship.

All professional groups have scuttlebutt. In the world of tax consultants, the Rangers case is now, as they said in the Glasgow of my childhood, "the talk of the steamie". It is now received wisdom among people that earn their living by advising others on how to be tax-efficient in the UK that Rangers FC is a dead company walking. It is no

secret among these tax professionals that HMRC have, in their possession, documentary evidence that spells "game, set and administration!"

My most recent source on this case, a highly regarded tax consultant,
related the following to me: "Only last week, I was at a presentation
given by a chartered accountant who specialises on tax mitigation strategies. His advice to anyone with shares in Rangers was that it might be
a good idea to sell them quickly."

There is more, much more to reveal about this case. However, I do
not want to prejudice the tribunal. When the time is correct, the entire
case can be revealed here.

The real value of Rangers' fixed assets may soon be known

09.02.11

Something to keep an eye out for is the possibility of a "write-down"
of the book value of Rangers' fixed assets in the coming months. These
are made up almost exclusively of Ibrox Stadium and Murray Park, and
were listed as having a value of £121m in Rangers' last annual report.

With Lloyds Banking Group vigorously implementing a plan to sell
off its distressed loan assets, the bank has been taking steps to clean up
the balance sheet of Murray International Holdings (MIH) – Rangers'
parent company. Recent action to eliminate the £60m in "phantom"
assets – related to the complex web of companies created by Sir David
Murray to manage 30% of Rangers' shares – is a sign that the day of
transparency for Rangers' accounts may be drawing closer.

Multiple revaluations of Rangers' property values during the mid-
noughties was widely seen as simply holding a tissue over Rangers'
technical insolvency to hide HBOS' embarrassment while the bank
continued to extend credit to an absurd degree. In these more prudent
times, Lloyds is paying a hefty price for inheriting HBOS' madness. To
prepare businesses and assets for sale – and to even manage their massive toxic debt portfolio efficiently – accuracy and realism are critical.
Therefore, phantom and overvalued assets are being marked down to
realistic levels at companies across the land. Writing down the value of
Rangers' assets may also simplify matters should Rangers file for administration following resolution of their on-going tax troubles.

The bank likely has a security interest in these assets, but unsecured creditors may claim that receiving assets "worth" £121m should discharge the bank's claims. The bank suddenly claiming that this property has become worth as little as £10–15m overnight would certainly create complications in dividing up the proceeds of the sale of assets in administration. It would all be much simpler if Rangers' property assets were marked down to their resale value before an administration filing is made.

A write-down of Rangers' assets will also cascade through to MIH's balance sheet, so bringing the cleansing light of reality to Rangers' accounts will help clean up MIH's balance sheet. For both of these reasons – protecting the bank's interests in administration and bringing greater clarity to the MIH predicament – Lloyds can be expected to look at a massive write-down.

It is unlikely that a revaluation would be completed (or disclosed) for the mid-year report, but it will be interesting to see the full season's results, which are usually published each September.

Even journalists that are very well disposed towards Sir David Murray in Scotland will then struggle to continue to help him deflect responsibility and blame for Rangers' current financial malaise away from himself.

With a ruling from the first-tier tribunal on the legality of Rangers' tax activities expected at around the same time, autumn 2011 could be the time when the great wall of silence and feigned ignorance surrounding Rangers' efforts to match Celtic since 2001 is finally torn down.

Worth watching.

Will Sir David Murray pay the tax bill for Rangers?

11.02.11

I recently had a useful chat with a senior Scottish sports journalist in the media centre at the AVIVA stadium. We were both there for the Carling Cup. We were discussing the Rangers tax case when he told me of the dominant view of this problem within the upper echelons of the Ibrox club: "I've spoken to various people at Rangers and they say that they are confident that they'll win the case, but if they lose the case then Murray will have to pay the bill."

I asked him why he thought Sir David Murray would pay the bill. "He would have to. I mean, morally he would have no choice. If he didn't, his reputation as the owner of Rangers would be in tatters." When I asked him if he thought that Sir David would have a spare £55m, my journalist buddy merely shrugged.

Much of Sir David's Murray's wealth at the height of his powers was tied up with Murray International Holdings (MIH). Just as people in Dublin discovered that they were millionaires simply because they had a home in a certain area of Dublin, much of MIH's value was notional. Now that the debt for equity swap puts MIH, like Rangers, in the effective control of the bank, it is difficult to see where the cash for the HMRC case would come from. His wine company is doing well and it isn't part of the MIH group, which means that it isn't under de facto effective bank control. Industry sources I contacted disregarded the possibility that Sir David Murray's wine company would have a spare £55m or so in petty cash.

If my colleague is being well briefed from within Rangers then there is a level of wishful thinking at Ibrox apropos the tax case that surprises me.

Another tax case

14.02.11

Dave King, the man who wants to own Rangers FC, hasn't been having it all his own way recently. In October last year, the judgement of North Gauteng High Court in Pretoria stated that King was a "glib and shameless liar". Last week, the company "Ben Nevis" dropped its appeal against the contention by the South African Revenue Service (SARS) that the company and Dave King were, effectively, one and the same. With this appeal dropped, SARS then made an application to go after Ben Nevis for the millions they claim that King owes in unpaid taxes and penalties. SARS is chasing Ben Nevis for around two-thirds of the tax debt, and King personally for the rest. The total amount is thought to be around £250m.

This latest ruling is one in a series over the past few years designed to straighten out who owns and owes what. The appellant in the latest case is Ben Nevis. Technically, Ben Nevis is run by trustees who do not include King, and, as of last month, he was insisting that he was not involved.[1] However, last year's judgment ruled that Ben Nevis and King were, in fact, the same entity.[2] "The question is whether in law X [King] was acting as the appellant [Ben Nevis] when he made default in making the returns. Although he was not an officer of the appellant and he held no other formal position which would normally entitle him to act on its behalf he clearly controlled the appellant as if he was its managing director and was acting with all the powers of the board." So, by dropping its appeal against that judgment, Ben Nevis is accepting that it can't win that case.

An appeal against the majority of the tax debt was dismissed last October. In its devastating judgment, the court said King "has no respect for the truth and does not hesitate to lie . . . if he thinks it will be to his advantage. He is a mendacious witness whose evidence should not be accepted on any issue unless it is supported by documents or other objective evidence. In our assessment he is a glib and shameless liar."

Last Friday, a hearing in Pretoria was told that a further legal challenge by Ben Nevis had now been dropped, allowing the taxman to raise an application to collect the cash. Dave King strenuously denies that the Ben Nevis company, registered in the British Virgin Islands, has anything to do with him.

The SARS case partly relied on emails uncovered at the Bank of Bermuda in 2001. One stated: "Apparently DK [Dave King] wishes to 'dismantle' current structure and transfer the assets of Ben Nevis into a new company, as the 'tax authorities are chasing him'." Another stated: "We are restructuring Ben Nevis to stop the South African taxman in his tracks."

Pesky emails . . .

Rangers mid-term accounts delayed. Why?

06.03.11

It has been brought to my notice that the release of Rangers' mid-term accounts has been delayed. When a company delays their accounts it is almost always a sign that all is not well. Murray International Holdings (MIH) delayed their accounts in 2009. As we now know to be true, all

1   http://www.timeslive.co.za/business/article865852.ece/King-fights-huge-tax-ruling

2   http://www.moneywebtax.co.za/moneywebtax/action/media/downloadFile?media_
    fileid=582

was definitely not well in Rangers' parent company. The 2009 accounts for MIH revealed that it had effectively defaulted on its debt repayment and a debt-for-equity swap was required to prevent technical insolvency.

More recently, Lloyds' private equity arm has taken 160 million convertible preference shares in MIH, giving it what will likely amount to total control. The bank effectively owns MIH, and MIH owns 85% of Rangers.

Part of tidying up the mess at MIH involved getting rid of "phantom assets", such as the loan from MIH to Murray Sports Limited, a completely separate company created to collect investments to fund Rangers' spending binges of a decade ago. An essential part of any turnaround is establishing transparent accounts and realistic asset values. However, MIH's balance sheet cannot be fully transparent until the absurdity of the valuations applied by Rangers to Ibrox and Murray Park are also addressed. Every pound of net assets on Rangers' balance sheet will now show up as 85p on MIH's.

It is possible that the delay in publishing Rangers' accounts is related to a major write-down of asset values at the club. In their last annual report, the book value of Rangers FC's tangible fixed assets was listed as £121m.

Assets can be valued in a number of ways. Normally, the original cost is used and the value of buildings is reduced each year through depreciation to provide a conservative estimate of net worth. The current market value could also be used, and the independent experts I have consulted have estimated that the land value of Ibrox is somewhere between £2m and zero. Much is made of the Class B listed building that is the main stand at Ibrox – Class B listed buildings can be demolished, but there is a cost and time delay involved.

Rangers' surveyors provided a valuation based upon "depreciated replacement cost", which is supposed to estimate the cost of replacing the assets using currently available technology and subtract costs for wear-and-tear and lack of maintenance. It does look odd that Celtic were able to reproduce functionally equivalent assets in the same city that have a book value of £65m less than those of Rangers.

Industry insiders have noted Rangers' asset revaluations with raised eyebrows for some time. The increased valuations of Rangers' properties coincided, of course, with the need to support increased borrowing, which reached a peak of £81m in 2004. One wonders what Lloyds must make of a situation which it inherited when press-ganged by the UK government into taking over HBOS. If it could be demonstrated that these asset values were deliberately inflated, it could allow the bank and Rangers' other shareholders to "lift the corporate veil" and pursue individuals for any losses in the event that HMRC succeeds in having the full amount of its tax assessments against Rangers crystallise. Individuals afraid of this type of legal manoeuvring might be tempted to start placing their assets in offshore trusts.

Remind you of anyone?

Alastair Johnston fights to save Rangers

19.04.11

An excellent source today informed me that the power brokers at Rangers now view chairman Alastair Johnston as being dangerously off message. The North American-based businessman is doing all he can to block the purchase of the club by Craig Whyte. The bank is happy for the deal to go through and is confident that Whyte has secured the borrowing to meet Lloyd's asking price. This would also allow Murray to be shot of this turbulent company. The thing is Johnston DOES care about Rangers. Moreover, he fears that Whyte will probably be unable to bankroll the club in a fashion that supporters have become accustomed to over the years.[1]

Whyte also seems to be labouring under the illusion that the tax bill, should it ever crystallise, will be paid by Sir David Murray. This is contrary to all of the professional advice that Whyte has received. So what happens if Whyte buys Rangers? Good news for the bank as they get their money. It is also good news for Sir David Murray as he is finally rid of the club.

Now do the wise men on the independent committee have a Plan B?

Clear and present danger

07.05.11

Denial is the default setting for humans in trauma. I have written on this site and in other mediums for over a year about the impending

---

1 http://sport.stv.tv/football/scottish-premier/rangers/244372-rangers-takeover-board-want-whyte-to-ring-fence-25-million-investment/

for the club's benefit", or might have had his legal team insert a loop-hole in the documents that rendered "the pledge" null and void. He would then also be able to demand the first £18m from the sale of the club's assets in administration.

Rangers FC and its many supporters can consider themselves very lucky. In their vulnerable state, they were delivered to an owner who is both a shrewd businessman and a "keen Rangers supporter", Craig Whyte. It would be churlish to not acknowledge the good fortune of the blue half of Glasgow.

There is now truly light at the end of their dark financial tunnel.

Gordon Smith to return to Ibrox?

17.06.11

EXCLUSIVE
Could an Ibrox legend soon be walking up the famous marble staircase again, this time to assist the new owner and the rookie manager? My sources tell me that Gordon Smith will shortly return to the Ibrox club. The ex-chief executive of the SFA could soon be a permanent fixture in the Rangers boardroom.

For the record, despite having a very amiable and fairly lengthy chat with Gordon in the media centre at the Aviva stadium in Dublin last month, he never suggested to me that rejoining his old club was in the offing. One can only guess at the huge morale boost this will be for the club's inexperienced manager.

The sheriff is in town

08.08.11

EXCLUSIVE
I understand that HMRC have instructed a firm of sheriff officers to carry out an "asset evaluation" at Ibrox Park this week. It is expected that this visitation will happen either tomorrow or Wednesday, unless those in charge of Rangers can somehow stave off this embarrassing spectacle. These outstanding monies have nothing to do with the tax bill currently going through the tax tribunal system.

I have also learned that Rangers had a demand from HMRC served on them on 2 June by sheriff officers firm Walker Love, of Royal Exchange Square, Glasgow.

The sheriff's men at Ibrox

10.08.11

EXCLUSIVE

Two sheriff officers entered Ibrox this morning at 10.20 a.m. The two males arrived in a white Audi A3. They initially went through the main door but were then shown around the corner to Argyle House. One of the men was carrying a folder. They spent around ten minutes inside Argyle House at reception.

When asked by waiting press pack if they were indeed sheriff officers they did not deny it. One of the media scrum asked them, "Can we go home now?" The older of the two men nodded and everyone laughed.

I think it is fair to conclude that the sheriff officers have indeed been to Ibrox Park this morning, acting for HMRC.

Photographs you were not meant to see

10.08.11

These are the photographs that powerful people didn't want you to see. They were snapped this morning outside Ibrox stadium by a freelance photographer whom I had tipped off. I then contacted two people in Glasgow who move in the appropriate legal circles and I showed them these photographs. They both immediately identified these men as sheriff officers. One of them even pointed to the fact that the blue plastic folder held by one of them was of the type typically used to carry official documents and that he had seen its kind many times before.

Yesterday, the club was totally denying that there was any truth in the story that sheriff officers, instructed by HMRC over unpaid taxes, would be coming to the ground the following morning. A major daily newspaper was advised by the club that there was nothing in the story and not to bother. The visit is now reported as being "routine" and that the club is "calm" about the situation.

Anyway, a great deal of effort was expended yesterday so that these pictures would not be taken and you would not see them. In the PR trade this is called "fire-fighting". Everybody calm? Good.

Martin Bain's "race against the clock"

20.08.11

Martin Bain has expressed to several people close to him that his main concern about his case against Rangers is not the strength of the claim, but that he simply runs out of time. The ex-CEO certainly knows the parlous state of the Ibrox club's finances.

Bain is seeking over £1.3m from his former employers. On papers lodged with the Court of Session, he claims constructive dismissal as they broke his contract of employment.[1] Bain's lawyers have claimed that, although he knew he was suspended, he learned of his actual dismissal through the media when he was in the USA.

However, Bain's main concern is that Rangers will go into administration before his case can be settled. An insider said, "If this case doesn't get to court in time the company might not exist. This is a race against the clock."

Rangers failing to keep up to date with tax remittances

30.08.11

I am informed that administrative chaos and disorder has become the norm at Ibrox. Junior staffers have privately expressed dismay at what they have considered to be mismanagement for quite some time. However, under Craig Whyte's leadership, things have taken a more dramatic turn.

While Rangers fans try to reconcile the promises of lavish spending through media leaks during the takeover, the reality of the Whyte era is in stark contrast to the image of the billionaire entrepreneur who will calm the troubled waters of the latter half of the Murray era. Of

---

1   http://www.scotcourts.gov.uk/rolls/supreme/lists/r110729_003.htm

particular concern is the club's inability to stay on top of day-to-day bills. Not just any bills either.

You would think that, with potential bills totalling £54m related to the EBT scheme – currently in the tax tribunal system – and £4.2m plus a penalty related to discounted options, that Rangers would try to avoid inflaming relations with HMRC. Yet, amazingly, the club is often delinquent on its monthly and quarterly remittances to the tax man!

Mr Whyte is a man whose track record for the smooth administration of his businesses is available at Companies House for all to see. When one looks at the utterly inept attempts at spinning about the imminent visit from sheriff officers to Ibrox earlier this month then the picture of an organisation that stumbles from drama to crisis without a plan becomes increasingly clear. Has, perhaps, Mr Whyte placed too much faith in the hands of those who cannot see further than the next news cycle? If the same energy and cost was expended to stay on top of Rangers' bills, it might have done more to help Rangers' reality than to sustain the fantasy world portrayed in the mainstream Scottish media.

A failed attempt to censor an investigative journalist

01.09.11

Originally published on Scotzine[1]

The American writer Marshall Lumsden said, "At no time is freedom of speech more precious than when a man hits his thumb with a hammer."

Well, today someone hit my thumb with a hammer when they persuaded my web hosting company to suspend my account and close down my site. If I say the air turned blue, you will fully understand my thinking when you discover the people demanding the site be closed were Rangers "stakeholders". According to the system administrator at the hosting company, one Archie Ferguson MCMI, MIET, MBA, claimed to be the representative of a stakeholders' group.

We can forgive the member of staff at the hosting company in Australia. Perhaps he or she believed that Mr Ferguson represented Rangers FC and had threatened legal action against the company and me. According to Archie, I, Phil Mac Giolla Bháin, had "harmed the

---

1   www.scotzine.com

commercial standing and good trading name of this company", namely Glasgow Rangers FC plc. Archie and "his legal team" are considering legal action against the company.

According to Archie I had "shed doubt on the company's inability to run its financial affairs and implied that there was some impropriety on the part of the company with regard to its tax affairs". According to Archie I had written a "litany of . . . misguided suppositions".

How did the meeting with the HMRC team at Ibrox go today? Final score: Rangers 0–1 HMRC.

I have another question for Archie Ferguson MCMI, MIET, MBA. Who was the source of the story about the £9m "mystery bid" for Nikica Jelavić? Everyone in the Scottish press knows his identity, but will you read about it tomorrow? Probably not, so why wait? It was Gordon Smith.

You are a stakeholder so you will be able to ask your club's director of football.

Tonight on BBC Radio Scotland, Chick Young was sombre and dignified about the perilous financial situation at Rangers. Your club is staring into the abyss. Chin up now, Archie. Dunkirk spirit and all that . . .

Penny Blockade

03.09.11

The news that monies in Rangers' bank account have been "ring-fenced" by the Bank of Scotland after a court application by HMRC should come as no surprise to the many thousands of readers who frequent this site. At this stage, with an "arrestment order" in place, the situation at Rangers over this overdue tax bill becomes harder to spin in a positive light for the Ibrox club.

The arrival of sheriff officers last month was not normal practice. Yet the club said it was "calm" about the situation. It was, in fact, a sign that money was owed, was overdue and that a legal process was underway to get that money. The visitation yesterday by two HMRC staff was also a sign that everything is not in order. As far as HMRC is concerned, Rangers Football Club owes them money. Moreover, the court agrees with HMRC.

When I arranged for my snapper to be outside Ibrox to capture the sheriff officers visiting last month, I was informed by sources that a 21-day demand for payment was in force from that date and this would tie in with the timing of the revisit yesterday.[1] That period has now expired, hence the latest development, which means that HMRC has petitioned the court to arrest funds on the back of the unmet demand.

Developing story.

The Bain Papers

10.09.11

The revelations today on the Rangers Tax Case blog could not have come at a worse time for Rangers and their new owner, Mr Craig Whyte. The papers from Martin Bain's case against his former employers contain highly damaging facts about the new regime at Ibrox, especially its attitude to the ongoing disputed tax case with HMRC.[2]

If these court papers are, indeed, genuine then they are truly explosive. Some of the information contained within them has been doing the rounds for some time.[3] However, this is the first time that they have been laid bare in forensic detail from one side in this legal dispute. That includes the eye-watering sum being sought by Mr Bain: £1,308,853.50. This may be greater than Rangers' net spend in the summer transfer window. It is hard to envisage such an amount being paid by the current regime without some difficulty.

However, to see the facts in black and white does take it to another level. It states that Mr Bain's legal team, from Balfour & Manson, wanted the case processed with all appropriate haste because they feared that the defender, Rangers FC, might not exist due to insolvency. This is similar in tone to the concerns expressed by Rangers' former lawyers, Levy & McRae, when they clashed with Rangers over an unpaid legal bill of £35,000 in the Court of Session in Edinburgh last week. The Ibrox club's former lawyers stated that they had a "real concern about solvency" in relation to Rangers.

That is two firms of lawyers that have recently expressed a concern over the long-term solvency of the current SPL Champions in Scottish courts. The court papers refer to the Ibrox club's inability to pay bills on time. The "Bain papers" also shine a light on Mr Whyte's attitude to the

1 http://www.philmacgiollabhain.com/photographs-you-were-not-meant-to-see/

2 http://rangerstaxcase.c-9/10/martin-bain-his-lawyers-rangers-insolvency/

3 http://www.philmacgiollabhain.ie/martin-bains-race-against-the-clock/

tax case. It is stated that if the tax bill was over a certain amount "he was prepared to pay £10–15m. Beyond that he would let the company go under." It also questions the actual worth of Rangers' fixed assets, Ibrox stadium and Murray Park, if a "forced sale" was to go through.

Now that this information is in the public domain, it may be admissible to the tax tribunal when it reopens in November. I fear that some people at Rangers will have further explaining to do at the first-tier tax tribunal in November. Rangers Tax Case has consistently provided valuable forensic analysis since the blog first appeared. HMRC's legal team can now claim these papers to be admissible in evidence at the tax tribunal. If these papers are genuine, and I have no way of knowing if they are, then I am sure that HMRC will want their hands on the real ones lodged with the court.

Clearly, there will be legal hurdles to be surmounted before that can happen. However, this could be the piece of the evidential jigsaw that results in Rangers Football Club losing the tax case. That such a coup de grâce was administered by an anonymous, perhaps obsessed, blogger does indeed show the power and reach of this technology. The fact that these revelations, which could prove decisive in the tax case, involve a true Rangers man like Martin Bain makes RTC's exclusive all the more remarkable.

Rangers. The clock is ticking

12.09.11

When Rangers had its bank account legally impeded on Friday 2 September, a 14-week clock started ticking. The funds, on order of the court, were moved into a holding account. Rangers cannot access that money till then. The core amount of £2.8m has been arrested. It is also common practice for a sum 1.5 times the amount arrested to be set aside. This means that an additional £1.4m has been placed in the holding account. Therefore, the total cash currently arrested will be £4.2m. Therefore, £4.2m is currently beyond Rangers' reach. This is approximately three months' wages for the Ibrox club. This £1.4m – most of which will be returned to Rangers at the end of the 14-week arrestment period – is not to be confused with a penalty payment, which is also £1.4m.

To avoid another demand for immediate payment from HMRC

for the £1.4m penalty, Rangers should have filed an appeal within 30 days of receiving the penalty assessment. If they were late in filing an appeal, they would still be expected to have one granted should they apply now, given the consequences of enforcing payment at this time. The £2.8m bill cannot be appealed as Rangers' previous board signed an agreement to pay it. If they do appeal the £1.4m penalty then it will go into the tribunal system. This is where the "big tax case" is currently progressing in a separate process. That case resumes in November.

Rangers were successful in applying for the big tax case to be heard in private. That is why there have been no reporters present.[1]

> Public Hearings: Hearings before the tax tribunals are nor-
> mally open to the public. However, any party to the proceed-
> ings can ask for a hearing, or part of a hearing, to be held in
> private in certain circumstances. If you wish for your hear-
> ing to be conducted in private, you should write to us with
> reasons why. The fact that your financial affairs are personal
> is not enough; there must be a special reason such as it is in
> the interests of public order or national security or not do so
> would prejudice the interests of justice. Should you wish for
> your hearing to be heard in private, you should write to us
> as soon as possible. The tribunal will make the final decision
> on this.

Obviously, anything that could attract a crowd of Rangers support-ers can have a public order concern. However, I do not think that the inability to give free tickets to HM forces for Ibrox would seriously imperil the defence of the realm, so national security shouldn't be a concern here.

Despite getting a result on the big tax case for a private hearing, Rangers might not be successful a second time around in applying for a tribunal dealing with a £1.4 million penalty for late payment to be heard in private. When the clock stops ticking, RFC will get their arrested £1.4m back, minus costs. They have to get by until then with-out that money.

What state will Rangers be in on the 9 December when the clock stops? All of their current behaviour indicates a difficulty in paying even minor bills, e.g. the £35,000 to Levy & McRae. This requires an explanation.

There should have been more than enough working cash from the season ticket money at this stage of the financial year. However, at the

---

1   http://www.justice.gov.uk/guidance/courts-and-tribunals/tribunals/tax/index.htm

moment, Rangers are behaving like a company with very little ready cash and no access to credit. Now, for the blue half of Glasgow, that must be highly distressing.

Rangers in receivership?

14.09.11

When is a highly paid footballer not a highly paid footballer? Answer: when he becomes an unsecured creditor of a company under receivership – or administrative receivership, to give it its proper name.

Rangers players could soon have their contracts simply torn up by a court-appointed receiver. This could happen if Craig Whyte successfully applied for the appointment of a receiver. Whether or not Mr Whyte applied for receivership would partly depend on whether or not Rangers' parent company, Rangers FC Group Ltd, held the "floating charge" on RFC's debt.

Of course, had the journalists at this week's press conference been properly prepared, Mr Whyte should have been asked this question. Because he wasn't, a press conference that was meant to make things clearer has, in fact, left the situation as opaque as before. This is because the floating charge is the key to understanding what is in store for Rangers. It is perhaps useful to think of a floating charge rather like a mortgage on a house. It protects the interest of the lender. If you don't keep up your payments, the bank can repossess the property. It allows the interests of the holder of the floating charge to be placed ahead of the other creditors including, for the most part, employees.

Under Scottish receivership law, that would apply to Rangers. Employee contracts are a one-way bet that favour the major secured creditor, in this case the employer, Craig Whyte's Rangers. If Rangers went into receivership, the decisions over which players would remain employees of the new company, and who would simply have their contracts shredded, would be taken out of the hands of players. If a receiver, acting on Whyte's behalf, wanted to sell a player to another club, the player would be under severe pressure to agree to any deal or face being left out of contract.

Is it now possible to discern Whyte's plan for Rangers? If he was successful in having a receiver appointed on his behalf then he, as the major secured creditor, would be at the top of the pile. The receiver would then run the club on behalf of Mr Whyte's company, Wavetower. The receiver could, if he/she deemed it to be in the best interest of the main secured creditor, tear up players' contracts. The players would, in practice, only be entitled to statutory redundancy pay, which amounts to a sum unlikely to put petrol in Kyle Lafferty's Bentley!

With Rangers under the control of a receiver, the players would join the long queue of unsecured creditors and would receive nothing from this position. Now, with question marks over Rangers' future solvency being discussed in open court, it will become increasingly unlikely that any company will want to do business with Rangers on anything other than a "cash up-front" basis.

The timing of the press conference this week was not, perhaps, of Mr Whyte's choosing. If nothing else, the publicity over the last few weeks has helped to focus attention on the economic health of the club. The questions that should be asked in the coming weeks are:

– Does the company have enough cash to get by until January?

– Will the club have to sell players during the January transfer window?

The news that Martin Bain was successful in having £475,000 arrested means that Rangers cannot touch around £712,000 of their money for the next 14 weeks. With these cash flow issues building up, perhaps the timing of an application to appoint a receiver is really out of Mr Whyte's hands. Of course, this potential problem for Rangers players is something that should be exercising the players' union. I hope that they are already on the case and are fully aware of this danger to their member's interests.

As for the many unanswered questions about the Whyte regime, it is time for the hack pack in Scotland to realise that journalism means digging for stories and not forming an orderly queue for a press release and a free mutton pie.

Source material

03.11.11

This time last week, I was expecting some major news out of Ibrox. I had been told weeks before that the days 26 and 27 of October would be "historic for Rangers Football Club". This source has been consistently correct with many RFC stories for me over the past few months.

Therefore I had no cause to doubt his information. The one time I did so I had reason to rue my scepticism. It was he who told me that Mr Whyte was very serious about buying Rangers. I didn't believe him. That was the last time I made such a mistake.

When he told me of these important dates at the end of October I put it out on Twitter. Those sufficiently interested can scroll back through my tweets, but it must have been a month ago. As the month of October went on, we kept in daily contact and he used terms like: "They're going into meltdown. Situation rapidly deteriorating."

October 28 arrived and there was not a peep that anything was happening. I contacted another source. This man is a senior corporate lawyer, a staunch Rangers man and very "in" with people who had recently been around the Ibrox boardroom table. That lunchtime, he told me the following: "There is a big pow-wow going on at Ibrox right now. They are in a position where they are no longer able to trade." He stated this as an assertion. He was utterly convincing. I didn't think he was lying. I couldn't stand this up, but I did put out the quote on Twitter. It kicked off a firestorm.

People believed that this spelled the end for Rangers that afternoon. Of course, I did not say that or anything like it, but people put their own spin on it. When Rangers continued to trade, there was some crowing in the succulent lamb wing of the mainstream media.

We learned yesterday that Rangers, on 26 October, lodged paperwork with Companies House indicating that they have moved "the whole assets of the company" to the control of Close Leasing Ltd.[1] An excellent analysis follows here from the irrepressible Rangers Tax Case blogger.[2] (The online piece carries a link to the Rangers Tax Case blog.) What I try to bring to the readers of this site is newsworthy content that is the product of many hours of fact checking and good old journalistic "digging". At the end of it though, you have to trust your sources.

Throughout the month of October, I was confident that my primary source on this matter was correct. His belief was based on excellent access to crucial data. He consistently stated to me that Rangers were simply running out of money because they couldn't access a credit line with a bank and the owner would not bankroll the operation. All my secondary sources were saying very similar things. In the intelligence world, what they were providing me would be described as "chatter". What my primary source was giving me was real gold dust.

---

1 http://rangerstaxcase.com/2011/11/02/borrow/

2 http://rangerstaxcase.files.wordpress.com/2011/11/rangers-security-charge-change-11_11.pdf

We now know that Rangers FC have approached a company to access a line of highly expensive credit. They're on borrowed time, on borrowed money and, of course, the big tax case is due to resume this month. As I was preparing this piece, I called him to tell him I was setting the record straight for him. I said, "Fair play, you were bang on the money!" He gave a little chuckle. My source has been vindicated and so, dear reader, have I.

Rangers and their accounts

04.12.11

For the first time in the history of Rangers, their accounts are unaudited. A reasonable person might ask why this should be the case. The business experts I have spoken to say that the most likely reason for this strange turn of events is that the club's owner doesn't want a "going concern letter" attached to the audited accounts. Reputable firms like Grant Thornton couldn't sign off on accounts if they didn't think they presented the entire picture. If such a letter were attached to Rangers' accounts, the company would be forced into "quarterly reporting". This would mean we wouldn't be waiting for a year to see what the state of play was apropos the club's finances.

With quarterly reporting, Rangers' accounts – unlike Mr Whyte's personal wealth – would no longer be off the radar. Although I am told that the accounts released this week by Rangers are accurate, they don't tell the entire story. As ever in these matters, the irrepressible Rangers Tax Case blog gives more than the mainstream media. Here, RTC reveals not only the headline figures, but crucially, details not released by Rangers.[1] The RTC numbers show that Whyte had not made good on his promises of working capital investment by 30 June. If Rangers were forced into quarterly reporting, the accounts would give us a view into Whyte's handling of Rangers every three months. Almost certainly, the figures show that, despite assurances at the time of buying the club from Sir David Murray, the new owner has not injected £10m of working capital.[2]

This clipping from a Rangers internal memo in May 2011, published in the comments section of the RTC blog, indicates that the promised

---

1   http://rangerstaxcase.files.wordpress.com/2011/12/rfc_creditors.png

2   http://www.guardian.co.uk/football/2011/may/06/rangers-business

working capital was needed to pay the £2.8m "wee tax bill".[1] (The online piece carries a link to the Rangers Tax Case blog.) My understanding is that the old board effectively brokered a deal with HMRC, promising that the £2.8m tax bill would be paid very shortly after Mr Whyte took over at Edmiston Drive. What was paid was £500,000, out of the Rangers season ticket pot, to fend off punitive action by the taxman. This leaves £2.3m outstanding, plus penalties.

Business experts I have consulted have told me not to be surprised if Rangers decide to change their financial year very soon. This will buy them time, perhaps another six months, before having to have an AGM and publish fresh, audited accounts.

Craig Whyte. Some vital details

10.12.11

Did the directors of Rangers Football Club PLC mislead the PLUS Stock Exchange regarding Craig Whyte's disqualification? On 30 November 2011, Rangers' directors issued a statement to the PLUS SX.1[2] The statement read:

The Rangers Football Club plc

Director disclosure

The information in the paragraph below is disclosed pursuant to paragraph 18 of appendix 1 of the PLUS Rules. Craig Whyte was disqualified to act as a director of Vital UK Limited in 2000 for a period of seven years. The directors of The Rangers Football Club plc accept responsibility for this announcement.

That was the issue which had dogged Mr Whyte since Mark Daly's brilliant BBC documentary was shown in October. Mr Whyte had allegedly failed to declare this to the PLUS SX, the SFA and the SPL. He also, of course, had failed to mention this trifling matter to STV when he was interviewed before the BBC documentary was screened.

However, even in such a brief statement, there seem to be a couple of problems. First of all, any order disqualifying a director, in terms of The Company Directors Disqualification Act 1986, applies to all UK companies, not just a named one. There are circumstances where, for example, shareholders might try to remove a director, but that is

1 http://rangerstaxcase.com/2011/12/03/sources-close-to-whyte-in-economical-with-truth-shocker/comment-page-1/#comments

2 http://www.plus-sx.com/newsItem.html?newsId=1419480

different from a ban imposed by the court following an Insolvency Service investigation. The second issue is the name of the company referred to in the statement.

Vital UK Limited is a name used by more than one company in the past, so I thought I would have a look to see which one it was. Vital (UK) Ltd of Milton Keynes, company number 05123705, was incorporated in 2004 and dissolved in 2005, so it is not that one. Vital (UK) Ltd of Bristol, company number 05706268, was incorporated in 2006 and dissolved in 2010, so it is not that one. Vital UK Ltd of London, company number 02919664, was incorporated in 1994 and dissolved in 2003. This looks better, but (a) there is no trace of Mr Whyte having been a director of this company and (b) a liquidator ran the company from appointment in November 1995 until dissolution. Mr Whyte is listed, however, as having been a director of Vital Plant Services Ltd, company number 03122782 – dissolved as of 29 January 2002; Vital Holdings Ltd, company number 03099824 – dissolved as of 26 April 2005; and Vital Security Ltd, company number 03122730 – dissolved as of 18 April 2000.

Vital Security Ltd includes amongst its former directors Kevin Sykes, identified by the BBC *Inside Story* programme as a convicted fraudster, and in Companies House records as a disqualified director. Also listed as a former director is Kenneth McLeod, the former accountant alleged in the programme to have been struck off. Vital Plant Services Ltd and Vital Holdings Ltd also list Mr McLeod as a former director.

On the basis that a disqualification normally follows an insolvency investigation, this might suggest that it was, in fact, Vital Security that Mr Whyte's disqualification stemmed from. Does it therefore appear that Rangers Football Club plc has made an incorrect statement to the PLUS SX? If so, this would be a breach of the rules of the exchange, as well as, I am told, a breach of company law, and can be punished by the PLUS SX.

If the exchange decides its rules have been breached, the company can be punished by (a) a censure; (b) a published censure; (c) a fine of up to £100,000; or (d) a suspension or cancellation of dealing in the company's shares.

One would have thought that, bearing in mind the furore which resulted in the above statement having to be made, surely someone in Rangers should have checked to see if they had named the correct company, otherwise the statement that "Craig Whyte was disqualified to act as a director of Vital UK Limited" would not have been made.

Maybe this is just another mere "technicality", but I think we'll just put this one down to an honest mistake. I suppose when one is a billionaire with wealth off the radar then such details are left to the little people.

A new journalism

11.12.11

I chaired a seminar at the NUJ's biannual delegate conference in Dublin earlier this year. It was about new media and the future of journalism. Presenting was Donnacha DeLong NUJ President and Professor Roy Greenslade. You can listen to the entire event here.[1] (The online piece carries a link to an audio clip of the conference.)

Roy's CV is too long for a blog post, but anyone interested in the work of the fourth estate can't really afford to miss his *Guardian* blog. During that seminar, Roy offered his view of a "horizontalised" model as the future of journalism. He saw the future for journalists as sitting at the centre of online communities. He used the term "the hub" to describe the model he envisaged. I think I am starting to get my head round this. Moreover, he described what happened when the *Guardian* first comment-enabled a piece that had appeared online. Although the first comments were to the author, the author was soon sidelined as the people who read the piece started interacting with each other.

Roy also stated that it became apparent that the people posting at the bottom of the *Guardian* online piece knew more about the subject than the journalist who had written it. For someone like Roy, with a background in print journalism, this was a step into the unknown.

I finally realise that I sit somewhere near the centre of a new media community which is seeking to do the job on Rangers' new owner that much of my trade has shied away from. That cannot be said, of course, about Mark Daly and his colleagues at the BBC.

Yesterday I asked some questions about matters relating to Mr Whyte's disqualification as a company director in the UK.[2] My post was analysed on the Rangers Tax Case blog. Tip of the hat to poster Sorrynocando, who posted that, in fact, Mr Whyte had been disqualified for his actions relating to Vital UK Limited. So I'm happy to set the record straight on that.

---

1   http://www.nuj.org.uk/files/NewMediaWhole3.mp3

2   http://www.philmacgiollabhain.ie/craig-whyte-some-vital-details/#more-1816

The Rangers statement is still misleading as it states that Mr Whyte was disqualified from being a director of Vital UK rather than being disqualified from all companies. Also, he was a director with the struck-off accountant Kenneth McLeod in all three other Vital companies, and in one with convicted fraudster Kevin Sykes, as revealed by the BBC documentary.

I merely posed the question, and it still remains, that the statement made by the Rangers directors is misleading in regards to one of the two points I made. His ban covered ALL UK companies. If the statement meant to say that it was while acting as a director of Vital UK that he got his ban then that is different, but that is not what it said. The statement implies it was only Vital UK he was disqualified from. Of course, one could argue that the source of the confusion is Mr Whyte's refusal to discuss the past and his track record. I would suggest that this lack of transparency, combined with the liquidation of the other three Vital companies managed to confuse even the wise heads on RTC initially. So, tip of the hat to the RTC poster Sorrynocando for putting me on the correct trail.

Mr Craig Whyte could not have imagined the level of scrutiny and excavation that is currently being undertaken apropos his business background. My post yesterday set the RTC folks off with their spades. This story has legs and I'm happy to be part of the hub. This is, as Roy Greenslade stated in Dublin earlier this year, a different type of journalism.

A Mayan moment for Rangers in 2012

06.01.12

I wrote only yesterday of the importance of precision when reporting on a complex story such as the Rangers tax case.[1] One of the fantasies which has recently been doing the rounds of Scottish sports journalism, heard regularly on Radio Clyde's *Superscoreboard* over the last month, is that some "out of court settlement" will be reached between Rangers and HMRC. Therefore, the headline figures, broken by me in 2010, will not be in play and Rangers will only have to pay a fraction of that amount. Even for the low standards of the Scottish sports desks, this is illiterate.

Now we have the club's owner, Mr Craig Whyte, telling the fine fellows of the Rangers Supporters Assembly the inconvenient truth.[2]

1   http://www.philmacgiollabhain.ie/the-importance-of-precision-in-journalism/
    #more-1905

2   http://www.facebook.com/permalink.php?story_fbid=212245192197518
    &id=200509926704378

"No scope for negotiating a settlement with HMRC due to the criticism they have had from MPs and the media about some high-profile 'deals'. That means the case could take even more time to resolve as any outcome is likely to be appealed by either party. If the decision is adverse and the club appeals, HMRC can still seek to enforce the decision."

The first part is spot on. The explanation is not, because there never was any chance of an out-of-court settlement with HMRC, but some special circumstances have to be created to explain why there won't be. Pesky MPs . . .

The third part of Mr Whyte's statement is as unarguable as the first. HMRC, if they win the case, can push for immediate payment, even if Rangers appeal.

As for the future, the Rangers Supporters Assembly was told: "He [Whyte] hopes 'Rangers Football Club plc' could survive any administration event but feels it would not be the end of the world if it didn't."

Regular readers here will not be surprised at any of this, only the poor souls who rely on the output of Scottish sports desks will be taken aback at what Mr Whyte told the Rangers Supporters Assembly.

Scotland's establishment club is approaching its Mayan moment in 2012 and unless I haven't been paying attention properly, the owner just said as much.

Privileged information

31.01.12

The client–lawyer relationship is protected in law. What someone tells their lawyer is protected by a privilege that the legal system and wider society recognise.

The *Daily Record*'s piece today on Craig Whyte and Rangers carries a quote from Paul Murray, an ex-director of the club.[1] "HMRC asked for a meeting at the end of last week to find out what knowledge I, having been a director of the club at the time, had of these transactions prior to the takeover," Murray said. "I knew nothing about this and although I have been questioned by HMRC and seen some especially revealing documents which are in their possession, it is still very hard to take in

1 http://www.dailyrecord.co.uk/2012/01/31/rangers-owner-craig-whyte-
   admits-he-sold-four-years-worth-of-season-tickets-to-keep-ibrox-club-run-
   ning-86908-23728301/

what has been going on. Collyer Bristow were acting for Craig Whyte during the takeover and I have been shown their client account, from the opening of it until today. I've also seen all invoices from Ticketus to Rangers and Rangers to Ticketus supporting all these actions."

What legal instrument would allow HMRC to see private legal papers held by a solicitor? This information is protected by legal professional privilege. HMRC could not have been given this information unless either Craig Whyte or his company provided it voluntarily, or the fundamental legal professional privilege was overridden by such circumstances that Collyer Bristow was obliged to provide it. Would Mr Whyte have provided this information off his own bat to HMRC while he tries to keep his business afloat by allegedly withholding tax remittances? Possible, but unlikely. Remember also that this is an investigation, and Mr Murray saw the document dated this week, not last year.

Solicitors' obligations under legal professional privilege can only be superseded by such serious means as the Terrorism Act 2000, or the Proceeds of Crime Act 2002, specifically sections 327–329, 330 and 332, relating to disclosure of confidential client information. The Law Society of England and Wales' guidance is extensive in this area and presented within its professional practice note on anti-money laundering, dated 6 October 2011.[1] Assuming that this is not a terrorism issue, the implication would be that the Proceeds of Crime Act is at play, which covers various matters, including money laundering and similar activities. These rules empower the Serious Organised Crime Agency to obtain much of the information it needs to enforce the law.

The question for lawyers remains: "Under what circumstances would you be required to disclose details of a client's account to a public enforcement agency?"

Yours for a pound!

02.02.12

When Craig Whyte bought Rangers FC for one pound last May, he confided to an aide that the interest in him by the media would "blow over in a day or two". Yeah. Whatever.

What puzzled Rangers-watchers was how someone could borrow

1   http://www.lawsociety.org.uk/productsandservices/practicenotes/aml/4997.article

£18m to pay off Lloyds Banking Group for a company that was worth less than that, with potential liabilities of £50m, and still expect to make money.

Now we may have a clearer view. Maybe Craig Whyte didn't borrow the money, but the Rangers season ticket-holders, in effect, borrowed the cash. If that is true then he truly has bought Rangers for one pound.

We know that the bank was very keen on the deal as it wanted out of Rangers ASAP. If I can remind you, this was the time of banners declaring "Donald Muir the enemy within" and message board campaigns to close accounts at Lloyds. In the law of unintended consequences, the more belligerent among the Rangers support created an extreme urgency within the senior personnel of Lloyds Banking Group to get the hell out of Dodge.

We know from Alastair Johnston that the bank threatened to stop Rangers' credit line if they didn't agree to the Whyte takeover. Now, of course, Rangers have no credit line from any bank. My sources tell me that similar pressure was applied to Sir David Murray, as the bank also effectively controlled Rangers' parent company, Murray International Holdings (MIH). The bank got its £18m by the corporate equivalent of a payday loan.

The campaign against Lloyds by Rangers supporters effectively created the conditions where the club was delivered into the hands of someone without the cash to bankroll the operation. People in the Rangers-watching fraternity scratched their craniums when they tried to work out Craig Whyte's "angle" for buying the club. How could he make money out of Rangers?

Consider this. What if he actually did buy Rangers for only a quid? He immediately and perfectly legally could pay himself Martin Bain's salary. He is, after all, carrying out much of Bain's functions. So, right away he would be on £310,000 per annum for a mere one spot. Given it is his company, he could write up the bonus criteria for the job he was doing. Again, all perfectly legal.

I'm not saying any of this happened, but given the fact that the club might only have cost him a pound then anything he got by way of earnings or remuneration seems a smart move. However, Mr Whyte doesn't seem to have processed the emotional as well as he has the financial. What seemed on paper like a no-risk, no-lose deal has seen him stumble into a shit storm of dignity. Perhaps Mr Whyte just didn't get the extent to which many thousands of unstable people invest their fragile emotional wellbeing in Rangers Football Club. The only way out is to enter a witness protection programme and relocate to a nice country – somewhere pleasant that doesn't have any bears.

Too late to catch the ticket bus

07.02.12

Let's cut to the chase. Where is the Ticketus money?

The *Daily Record* alleges that the Whyte Knight tapped Ticketus – or "ticket bus" as big DJ called them on *Real Radio* – for £24.4m. During a choreographed interview with Tom English in *Scotland on Sunday*, the saviour of Rangers challenged the accuracy of the figures, saying it was "closer to £20m", so that is something else that is unclear. Until writs are issued or retractions are made, let's go with the *Daily Record* figures for now. So that's £24m and change. That's more than the club is worth borrowed on future season ticket sales.

What happened to it? Where is it? If he didn't use it to buy the club then Rangers are currently £42m in the hole. However, if he did use the Ticketus money to pay off the bank then he actually did buy the club for a quid!

A lot of the confusion over Craig Whyte's plans for the club and uncertainty over his intentions could be answered if we knew the whereabouts of this money. This could all be cleared up if audited accounts were published. Mr Whyte's reason for the delay in getting the accounts published is the uncertainty over the tax case. That uncertainty was there last year.

I believe it is his concern about the auditors having doubts about Rangers being a going concern that prevents publication.[1] I have been charting Rangers' impending financial catastrophe since 2009. That story cannot be told without reference to Sir David Murray and his indebted empire, but some of the mainstream media still seem intent on trying.[2]

I have been writing specifically on the Rangers tax story since April 2010. In that time, I have used outlets such as the *News of the World* and *Superscoreboard* on Radio Clyde to get the news of the tax story out there. However, it has been mainly on this blog that I have tried to keep the denizens of Planet *Fitba* up to speed.

1 http://www.philmacgiollabhain.ie/rangers-and-their-accounts/
2 http://www.philmacgiollabhain.ie/the-fall-of-the-house-of-murray/

Telling the story of the Rangers tax case and the wider financial problems of the club has been a victory for new media. This story is very much in the mainstream now. I have war-gamed various scenarios for Rangers with business analysts recently and there aren't any of them that end well for the Ibrox club (1872).

When I started this work, the response from the blue bit of Planet *Fitba* was to scoff derisively that such a fate could befall "the rainjurz" and that I was a fantasist. Those dignified British patriots may wish to revisit their opinion of my work.

One of the more enjoyable aspects of this story, for me, is that people who could have made a difference for Rangers didn't act to save their club despite being provided with top-class information. The reason for this, I suspect, was that the warning came from a Fenian in Donegal.

It is now too late for them to do anything.[1] All they can do now is brace for impact. Soon they will realise that the future of their club, like their season ticket money for the next four years, has probably gone.

Rangers. Preparing for the end

09.02.12

Preparing for the death of Rangers (1872) is now the most pressing matter for those who run the beautiful game on Planet *Fitba*. I have been informed by an excellent source that senior personnel in the Scottish Premier League now accept that an "insolvency event" for Rangers is inevitable. The denial phase should be over for Rangers fans. In the Kubler Ross model, the next stage is anger and, to be fair, I have always thought that to be the forte of the followers of Scotland's establishment club.

This morning I spoke to a good source in the tax consultancy world. In the past he has provided reliable information to me about the operation of employee benefit trusts. I was taken aback when he told me today that he wouldn't be surprised if Rangers (1872) were formally insolvent before the next match with Celtic next month. I asked him why he thought that would happen and he told me that this was the "scuttlebutt" going around the tax consultancy world, which has lines of information into HMRC.

In the intelligence world, all of this is categorised as "chatter" and sometimes it just disappears into the ether. However, sometimes it is

---

1   http://www.scotzine.com/2011/09/why-its-too-late-for-gers-for-change/

a harbinger of a major event. All of the available evidence points to Rangers being terminally ill with no Doctor Bunnet to rush to the bedside. This is death watch on Rangers and anyone who doesn't realise that is still stuck in denial.

Rangers. Too bigoted to fail?

14.02.12

So, it couldn't happen? I have been repeatedly told that Rangers going into administration was a fantasy. Well, the events at the Court of Session yesterday mean that the fantasy is almost here. Even the most cursory glance at my work here will testify that I should be allowed a "Told you so!" on full volume. However, that wouldn't be very nice to the many Rangers supporters who visit this site to find out what is happening.

It was on here that they found out that sheriff officers were about to cross the threshold at Edmiston Drive, and I provided the photographic evidence.[1] It was here they found out that their club was about to appoint a director of football, ex-SFA supremo, Gordon Smith.[2] Meanwhile, the mainstream media was telling its Rangers-supporting readers that all was well. It wasn't.

So what next for Rangers? Administration is a given, and I then expect Mr Craig Whyte to appoint a receiver who will protect his interests, as he is the holder of the floating charge.[3] During that period, administration is effectively suspended until the floating charge-holder can get all of his money, or as much as is possible. There is still some clinging to the hope that a "pennies in the pound" deal can be struck with HMRC and that all of this pain will go away. No chance.

The number that now becomes vital is the liquidation value of Rangers FC. I am reliably informed by insolvency experts working in the west of Scotland that the total value would be somewhere south of £14m. The HMRC bill could crystallise soon. I do believe that Rangers will lose the first-tier tax tribunal. The alleged underpayment is £24m. The interest on that is at least £12m. Penalties are also being sought of £18m, although they still have to be adjudicated on by another tax tribunal yet to be held. So, for now, the HMRC potential bill is

1 http://www.philmacgiollabhain.ie/photographs-you-were-not-meant-to-see/

2 http://www.philmacgiollabhain.ie/breaking-the-gordon-smith-story/

3 http://www.philmacgiollabhain.ie/rangers-in-receivership/

£36m. Then we have to add debts of – depending on what became of the Ticketus money – anything between £25–50m. With those debts against the combined assets, Alastair Johnston's angry primate in the corner of the room suddenly has an appetite that cannot be satisfied. Rangers will be gobbled up by the gorilla.

As I write this, I am taken back to my first journalistic entanglement with this, err, unique football club, four years ago. I was first asked to write about Rangers by a news editor for an Irish Sunday back in 2008. It was over a song about the Irish famine. I was told there was a tip that the department of foreign affairs was going to communicate with the Scottish government. I was asked to check it out as I had good DFA contacts and the story pertained to Scotland.

Initially, I had no idea what he was on about. The story ran and I then took it to the *Irish Post*.[1] Whether I wanted to or not, I was being pulled into the open sewer where Rangers supporters get their affirmation.

My father is from Mayo and his mother's uncle died as a young child during an Gorta mór. I found this out after doing some research in the summer of 2008, just before that story broke. The "Famine Song" choir danced on the unmarked graves of a million people.

I first heard the term "employee benefit trust" connected to Rangers in early 2010 during a geeky exchange between two cerebral posters on Celticminded. I contacted both of them to find out more. It was the start of a journey.

A group of Rangers "stakeholders" claimed to my web hosting company last year that my coverage of the club's financial troubles was hurting it as a going concern. If I have done anything to assist the demise of a football club that has been the gathering point for racist poison like the "Famine Song" then I'm quietly pleased. Former club chairman Alastair Johnston said that the publicity over the tax case made it impossible to find a buyer.[2] I recently learned that one genuinely wealthy Rangers supporter was about to make a bid in early 2010.

In life, timing is everything and the *News of the World* "splash" on 16 May 2010 made this prospective buyer go to senior people in charge of Rangers and ask tough questions, as was his right, caveat emptor and all that. His questions were duly answered and he got on the bus. The Monday after that front-page scoop I spoke briefly to a senior employee of Murray International Holdings. He didn't sound happy that day in May 2010, not happy at all. With that genuine offer parked, there

1   http://www.philmacgiollabhain.com/wp-content/themes/original/ip031008.pdf

2   http://www.bbc.co.uk/podcasts/series/scotfoot

wasn't anyone else until Mr Whyte turned up. The *Daily Record* said he was a billionaire. I didn't believe them, but the Rangers supporters did.[1]

With the HMRC case looming, the only thing that could have saved the day was a seriously wealthy benefactor or someone able to access a substantial line of credit. What Rangers got instead was an owner without any serious money and an engrossing business background. The rest has probably made Rangers history.

The Saint Valentine's Day Administration

14.02.12

This morning, HMRC decided that by close of business Rangers Football Club would be in administration. The revelation that the club was £9m behind in PAYE payments since Mr Whyte took over should not come as a surprise to readers of this site.[2]

The game plan for Mr Whyte is to get the administrator to put in place a Creditors' Voluntary Arrangement (CVA). This requires the creditors who are owed at least 75% of the total liabilities to agree a deal with the company. This will not happen, as HMRC are owed enough money to block such a deal. Hector wants administration to remain in place until the first-tier tax tribunal delivers the death blow to Rangers.

Once more, for the new reader, the bill will be £24m plus £12m in interest. The £18m in penalties will be ruled on by a future tribunal. The problem for Mr Grier, the administrator, is to keep the company going until that £36m bill crystallises. I am informed that the best legal advice strongly suggests that HMRC would win a court case should it oppose a CVA.

There is some spinning going on tonight that the wily Mr Whyte has somehow bested the tax man in court with the appointment of "his" guy. However, there are strict rules laid down for how an administrator operates. The bottom line is that this morning Hector wanted Rangers in administration by the close of play. Now who do think is happier tonight?

---

1   http://www.philmacgiollabhain.ie/the-first-rough-draft-of-history/

2   http://www.philmacgiollabhain.ie/
    rangers-failing-to-keep-up-to-date-with-tax-remittances/

The liquidation of Rangers

15.02.12

Some people think yesterday was the darkest hour in the 140-year history of Rangers. That's a matter of opinion. However, the days ahead are going to make yesterday look rather bright. I am informed that the cash flow situation at the Ibrox club is dire, and that in order to make the payroll commitments at the end of this month there will have to be some chainsaw trimming of the staffing establishment.

Now that the club is in administration, it does not mean that they don't have to keep the lights on. Rangers have no credit line from a bank. If they simply run out of cash, then liquidation will follow on very shortly afterwards. To the regular visitors here who scoffed at the idea of the Ibrox club being put into administration, you were wrong. Sometimes I approved their comments for viewing, but often they were too abusive and libellous to be allowed out onto the site. These same dignified British patriots have, of course, the freedom to dismiss the idea of this "great Scottish institution" (sic) being liquidated rather rapidly.

It is permissible to laugh off the very concept that this could happen. No, please, chuckle if you want to. I haven't stopped laughing in two days. Join me in the mirth. It is the best medicine.

Are taxes only for stupid people in Scotland?

16.02.12

A new term has entered the lexicon of Planet *Fitba*. Suddenly everyone knows about the "CVA" (Creditors' Voluntary Arrangement) and it is being discussed in pubs where the finer points of insolvency law are not usually a topic of argument. In hostelries where liquid lunches are better appreciated than liquidation, the reality is slowly sinking in that Rangers (1872) could die.

The CVA is Rangers' only escape route from the current state it is in. If the creditors who are owed at least 75% of the monies can agree with the debtor – in this case, Rangers – for some kind of write-down, then the CVA will go through. This would take Rangers out of administration and prevent the liquidation of the club. This comes down to a decision of the senior people at HMRC. If they agree to a CVA, then it will happen. If the first-tier tribunal (FTT) finds against Rangers, then the club probably owes Hector somewhere between £65–70m and change.

In a CVA, the club might be able to offer £2m. The message this would send to businesses in Scotland would be clear and would be that "taxes are optional!" Indeed, only the stupid would pay tax after the Rangers CVA. The political damage to HMRC's reputation would massively outweigh the relatively meagre amount that would be paid back into the public coffers. The recent public reversals of HMRC would be nothing compared to the loss of credibility if they were to let Rangers live.

Instead of a CVA (Cosy Venal Appeasement), HMRC needs this club to be liquidated. Hector may get his wish sooner than you may think, dear reader. Unlike in the USA, an administrator in the UK cannot borrow money to keep the company going. There is no British equivalent of "debtor in possession financing" under Chapter 11 Bankruptcy. If the administrator currently in charge of Rangers simply runs out of cash, the company will be liquidated.

Hector can legally block a CVA in court until the cash runs out, or the first-tier tax tribunal delivers the big tax bill. Even if the FTT were to find in Rangers' favour, HMRC would appeal and knock it to the upper tribunal. I am informed that there is now very little cash left in Rangers, and that time is not on their side. HMRC realise that there will be no money to be had out of Rangers. Why, then, go to all of this trouble?

What is of value at Ibrox, and worth far more than the monies owed, is the public spectacle of the awful consequences of non-payment to HMRC. When Rangers were formed in the nineteenth century, the first crowds flocking to see this new form of entertainment had almost certainly watched public executions. Some social historians think that the decision to ban public executions in Britain created a vacuum for public spectacle in the rapidly expanding industrial cities like Glasgow. Dr Edward Pritchard, a Glasgow medical practitioner, was the last person to be executed in public in Glasgow. In a famous trial of the time, he was condemned to death for murdering his wife and his mother-in-law, and he was hanged on Glasgow Green in 1865 only seven years before Rangers first took to the field of play.

The rotting corpse of Rangers (1872) dangling from a fiscal gibbet in 2012 will assist in the good governance of the realm. It would be appropriate in this instance to build their gallows high.

Deals and taxes

17.02.12

It is ironic that those who advocated the creation of the devolved parliament in Edinburgh wanted one with tax-raising powers. Their view was that it should have the ability to raise funds independently or it wouldn't be worth the effort. The legislature in Holyrood does indeed have tax-raising powers, although it has never used them. The Scottish executive exists on a block grant from Westminster.

I have today been reliably informed by two excellent sources close to the action in Holyrood that Scotland's First Minister would love to attract the glory of "the man who saved Rangers" and this can only be done with a Creditors' Voluntary Arrangement (CVA). That will only happen with the agreement of the major creditor in this equation, and that is HMRC.

As a long-time admirer of the political skills of Alex Salmond, I realise that all successful politicians have to be able to grasp a populist opportunity. I doubt very much if there is anything that leaves the First Minister's mouth in any interview that he has not thought extremely carefully about. The position he proffered on *Al Jazeera* bore all the hallmarks of a testing-the-water exercise to first establish if the survival of Rangers was essential for the public interest. The second part would then be to facilitate HMRC going along with a CVA. This would, of course, mean that Scotland's establishment club would not have to meet its full financial responsibilities to HMRC and to the British state. The First Minister would then be hailed as the man who prevented the liquidation of Rangers.

Now, I fully understand that Mr Craig Whyte may harbour a somewhat cavalier attitude to the paying of taxes, but it is surely not the stance of someone whose job it is to deploy those monies in the public interest.

HMRC bank limited

21.02.12

"We are not a bank" is often stated by HMRC when companies ask for easy terms to pay. If Rangers benefit from a sweetheart deal with HMRC, the club would effectively escape without any financial sanction. One of the tenets of HMRC is that an individual or company should not derive any benefit from not paying on time. If the big tax case goes against the Ibrox club then they will have been found guilty of operating an illegal tax evasion scam. This wheeze allowed Rangers to be the guy in the race on drugs.

The EBTs gave the Ibrox club a secret "war chest" of £24m during the Advocaat and McLeish years. If there is a CVA, then Rangers will have been rewarded for tax evasion. If they are allowed time to pay, HMRC will be providing a credit line to Scotland's establishment club. The knock-on effect would be, almost certainly, to provoke other SPL clubs into using this get-out-of-debt-free escape route and file for administration.

The pleas have been heard over the last week that Rangers Football Club is a "Scottish institution" and part of the "fabric of the nation". Well, the same could be said of the Royal Bank of Scotland. Is Heart of Midlothian Football Club not also an "institution" revered by many? It is certainly part of the "fabric" of life in the capital. Indeed, I believe that Scotland's First Minister is a Jambo.

I am aware that Salmond's own special advisers are privately uncomfortable with his intervention.[1] The agreed line from the "spads" when they have been asked about it is that this was nothing more than a kite-flying exercise with some soothing words from their boss. Their reasoning is that if Rangers die then Salmond can say that he tried, and if the Ibrox club is saved then he will bask in the glow a little. However, if there is a data trail from Salmond's entourage to HMRC asking for special treatment for them, it could blow up in his face.

I know of one colleague who is excellently placed to excavate this story and he's a Jambo, too! He thinks he has a fair chance of finding a spad with his spade. Pesky emails . . .

---

1   http://www.philmacgiollabhain.ie/deals-and-taxes/

Order, order . . .

23.02.12

There have been some strange manoeuvres in the mother of parliaments this week. That fine upstanding member, Central Ayrshire MP Brian Donohoe, secretary of the Westminster Rangers Supporters' Club, is calling for a parliamentary inquiry to grill Motherwell billionaire Craig Whyte. Along with Donohoe, this Westminster band of brethren has luminaries like regular Ibrox guest and Govan MP, Ian Davidson, as vice chairman and true blue Gregory Campbell, MP for East Londonderry, a lovely man who wants the return of capital punishment – though to be fair, not for fraud.

But why the need for an inquiry now? Did Brian Donohoe and the others from the Westminster Rangers Supporters' Club not see through the Motherwell billionaire when he was their guest at Westminster only a matter of months ago? As seekers of the truth and guardians of the public purse, did they not ask probing questions about the billionaire's future plans for Ibrox? Did they probe Mr Whyte's financial background? Were they not aware of the tax bill Mr Whyte's club owed HMRC? No, sadly not. I am told it was an occasion for handshakes and back slapping all around.

Some have rightly questioned the wisdom of statements from the SNP Government about Rangers and the tax bills.[1] However, they should digest at their leisure some of the thoughts from Scotland's red, Whyte and blue party. Shadow Scottish Secretary Margaret Curran wrote to the British Treasury, urging it to act in a reasonable way with Rangers and claiming that ongoing discussions between HMRC and Rangers were key to reaching a sustainable outcome for the club.

Were the Rangers' administrators who visited Westminster this week quizzed about the outlandish possibility that the taxpayers who elected Donohoe, Davidson, Campbell and Curran were ever likely to get their millions back?

---

1   http://www.philmacgiollabhain.ie/deals-and-taxes/#more-2129

Charity before dignity

28.02.12

Is Rangers FC a charity case? A basket case, certainly, but do Rangers now have charitable status? I only pose the question following the revelations that part of the proceeds from a charity match between Rangers legends and AC Milan legends scheduled for Ibrox on 30 March are to be given to the club, presumably through the administrators. Rangers FC manager, Ally McCoist, has billed this game as a fantastic initiative by Rangers Charity Foundation. The plan was that profits would be split between Rangers and AC Milan charities. Very noble, some might suggest dignified.

In today's papers, Connal Cochrane, Rangers Charity Foundation manager is quoted as saying, "The club and the Rangers fans have been tremendous to the foundation over the last ten years and now it's our turn to step up for Rangers. The Rangers Charity Foundation suggested the club should benefit from the match, and we were delighted that the AC Milan Foundation agreed."

There are very tight rules in place by the Scottish Charity Register stating quite clearly that you can't advertise an event as a charity occasion then redirect cash for another non-charitable project. I'm sure the Charity Commission could sort it out and advise the administrators if they are free to accept the money.

Dead club walking

07.03.12

Rangers are a zombie club. The statement by Duff and Phelps today is further evidence, if it were needed, that Rangers FC (in administration) will soon be no more. It has been clear to the well-informed readers of this site that Undead FC does not have long for this realm. With massive liabilities and limited revenue streams, there is only one dignified thing to do and that is to go out and heroically check the Antarctic weather. Instead, they have something of the night about them. Of course, the end of Rangers should have happened a long time ago, but the club cheated death by drinking the life blood of others.

Hearts, for example, will almost certainly never get their money for Lee Wallace. Rangers used PAYE remittances as cash flow, a practice that regular readers to this site were aware of last year.[1] The finely crafted Dave King statement today is the first shot in a war for the remains of Rangers.[2] There are two "conditional offers" being prepared. I understand that the condition is that the club wins the big tax case and that outstanding liabilities can be dealt with in a CVA.

The key to the success of NewCo Rangers would be access to Ibrox stadium. The team would play in the same colours, in the same stadium and the fans would be the same. However, they would have to deal with the owner of that asset and that is likely to be Mr Craig Whyte. I am sure he would only charge a modest rent. Liquidation would, of course, mean a break in the historical link to the founders of the club.[3]

I contacted an insolvency expert and I asked him for a brief explanation of the liquidation process:

Quick guide to liquidation

A liquidator can't be appointed whilst administration is in effect.

If administrators decide purposes of administration can't be fulfilled, i.e. they can't rescue the business as a going concern nor will it be better for creditors to stay in administration, the administrator can move the company into creditors' winding up (winding up equals liquidation).

This is by notification to the Registrar of Companies and the court, but not by court order. Or else, administration ceases and the company, the directors or a creditor ask the Court of Session to make a winding up order.

A provisional liquidator can be appointed when the petition is presented to court, especially if there are concerns regarding disposal of assets by the insolvent company. A provisional liquidator does not mean the company is in liquidation.

If a settlement is not agreed and winding up is granted (or the administrators appoint a liquidator) an interim liquidator is appointed. He has 28 days to investigate the company's affairs and will call a creditors' meeting.

The meeting appoints the liquidator. On a winding up order being granted, the liquidator has to complete, transfer or bring to an end all company contracts. This includes employment contracts.

---

1 http://www.philmacgiollabhain.ie/
   rangers-failing-to-keep-up-to-date-with-tax-remittances/

2 http://www.telegraph.co.uk/sport/football/teams/rangers/9129002/Rangers-in-administration-Dave-King-statement.html

3 http://www.philmacgiollabhain.ie/the-end-of-history/

Effectively they end on winding up.

The liquidator has to cease the company's business; settle legal disputes; sell any assets; collect money owed to the company and distribute funds to creditors.

Player registrations revert to the SPL.

The company is effectively dead at that stage.

Hope this helps!

It does, indeed. The only thing that can save Rangers from going into liquidation is a REAL billionaire. So far, only Tommy from Glasgow seems to be a player, which is a bit rich. I fancy having a stake in them myself.

Rangers still have to walk the green mile

10.03.12

Yesterday, in rather dramatic circumstances, Rangers were forced to live within their means. The administrators have imposed reality on Scotland's establishment club after a generation of financial delinquency. When they were appointed, Duff and Phelps said they would have to restructure the company so that income was greater than expenditure. This is a revolutionary new idea down Ibrox way. It is, of course, all too late.

The gorilla that troubled Alastair Johnston last April is still in the room. I have stated here repeatedly that, given what I know of the evidence presented to the first-tier tax tribunal, I believe HMRC will win the big tax case and I am confident that Hector will push for immediate payment.

The administrators bought themselves some time yesterday and there is much to do. They have to challenge the validity of the floating charge, and they also have to attempt to extricate Rangers from the Ticketus deal. That one may be complicated by the fact that the Octopus subsidiary appears to be backing "Blue Knight" Paul Murray. Mr Murray stated when he was on the Rangers board that it would be folly for anyone to buy the club while the big tax case was outstanding. Quite.

I have not seen any objective evidence that Mr Murray has wealth off the radar. Therefore, he has to raise the finance. This is exactly the situation that Mr Whyte was in last year. There is one interested party who COULD write a cheque for £100m, and ipso facto clear off Rangers' debts, and that person is Brian Kennedy. The question he would have to ask himself is whether or not he wanted to lose that money, because there is simply no chance he would get it back, let alone make a profit on that £100m. His time at Stockport County didn't end well, and the Ibrox club is a much larger money pit. Rangers are in administration, Mr Kennedy, that's a clue.

Of course, the massive debts that the club has are only part of the problem. HMRC gorilla has a new primate playmate. The second contract allegation made by ex-Rangers director Hugh Adam threatens to have massive ramifications for not just the club but the governing bodies of the game in Scotland.[1] There is also the regular remittance to HMRC from last month's payroll which is due on Friday 16 March. Unlike the rather relaxed regime under Mr Whyte, the administrators are now personally liable if those monies are not paid. Moreover, yesterday's deal does not repay the £16m outstanding from last May.

Finally, there is financial sanity at Scotland's establishment club, but it is, of course, all much too late. The wrecking ball of the big tax case is heading their way and the company cannot trade out of the position it is in. Anyone saying that they "know" that HMRC will take a haircut for these millions or allow Rangers decades to repay is either lying or they have been duped by some PR chappie. Given that these same people described Mr Whyte as a "billionaire" then I'll leave you, dear reader, to work out which.

Yesterday was a stay of execution. They were taken off the gurney at the last moment, but Rangers are still on death row. The mainstream media are spinning this as a pardon. It isn't. Liquidation day is coming.

Situation Vacant. Stupid billionaire required

11.03.11

If you were to believe the mainstream media then Rangers have been suddenly saved and all is well. They aren't, and it isn't. As stated previously, the deal with the players has only bought Duff and Phelps some time. They will have to draw up a plan and present it to the creditors and copy the court in by 10 April. They have to address three questions:

---

1 http://www.dailymail.co.uk/sport/football/article-2109233/Rangers-investigated-
   SFA-Hugh-Adam-claims.html

(1) Is the business a going concern?

(2) For the benefit of the creditors as a whole, is it better to continue in administration rather than liquidate the company?

(3) Should the company continue in administration to raise enough money to pay off the secured creditor?

If none of these options are possible, then it will be liquidation.

Option (1) is a non-starter really, as the company's debts are too large, even before the big tax case arrives. The next option (2) would be likely if the administrators could show that assets (i.e. players) could be sold in the summer transfer window. This will depend on what "escape clauses" the playing staff had written into the deals they struck for the 75% pay cut. Moreover, other clubs will know of the situation and make lowball offers. The last one (3) is, at the time of writing, clearly the best one for Craig Whyte. He currently holds the floating charge and is, ipso facto, the secured creditor. The administrators have indicated their intention to challenge the validity of this floating charge, so off to court we go!

An insolvency practitioner I contacted stated to me, and with a fair degree of confidence, that the courtroom wrangling over these various matters could go on into the summer – that is, next summer! As in the summer of 2013. Of course, my expert reminded me that a sure-fire way into liquidation was simply to run out of cash while in administration.

The cost of these legal battles will come out of Rangers' existing funds. As well as that, Duff and Phelps wouldn't be doing their job properly if they weren't keeping a close eye on their own billable hours and where those monies would come from. The consensus of the qualified and experienced people I have asked is that the company is likely to "bleed out" of money while still in administration.

The creditors must give their verdict on what Duff and Phelps will present on 10 April by 24 April. They have two weeks. The mainstream media that screamed that Craig Whyte was a "billionaire" are trumpeting that HMRC are ready to play ball, if only the current owner would leave the scene.

In January 2011, HMRC was approached by Rangers and offered £10m in settlement of the big tax case, but Hector flatly refused.[1] Why would HMRC, now owed another (circa) £16m and change, be willing to settle for, say, £2m? Mr Whyte offered to pay back the entire bill of the big tax case – approximately £50m – by offering £2m per year. That would have taken twenty years. Hector refused.

---

1   http://www.philmacgiollabhain.ie/rangers-board-desperate-to-settle-tax-case/

The big tax case is a wrecking ball swinging in the direction of Rangers. The only question that journalists should be asking is: what will kill Rangers first? Any prospective owner who the churnalists gush about must have around £100m to lose in this company in order to save it. Ain't going to happen, folks.

What is happening, in my opinion, is grandstanding by people who want to run a NewCo. What will kill Rangers (1872)? My money is on the bleeding out in administration as the cause of death before the big tax case hits. I could be wrong, as there are several variables. However, I stated many, many times on here that Rangers would go into administration, and they did. I now don't see any other option than liquidation. The condition is terminal. What is moot here is the likely cause and time of death. Recovery is off the table.

Rangers are a going concern the same way the *Titanic* is currently seaworthy at the bottom of the Atlantic. The death watch continues no matter what PR-generated fluff the churnalists throw at you. Expect breathless copy about mystery consortia "waiting in the wings" and hints of great wealth. If I can revert to the west of Scotland vernacular, the stories about impending takeovers by fabulously rich types will be utter pish. Only a stupid billionaire can save Rangers from liquidation and there are very few of them around.

The undeniable truth

05.04.12

Three days ago I stated that Duff and Phelps would publish a report after the Wednesday deadline and that it would clearly spell the end for Rangers. They have.[1] These figures mean one thing: liquidation.

No doubt the succulent lamb chaps will try and put a positive spin on these figures. Rangers' administrators have revealed the club owes at least £55m to 276 creditors. Duff and Phelps say that Rangers have been running at a "substantial cash shortfall" since going into administration on 14 February. In the period between 14 February and 30 March 2012, Rangers had a £2.5m trading shortfall. That means they spent £2.5m more than they brought in. The reality is that this company is finished.

Only a sugar daddy of Abramovich proportions willing to fund the

---

1   http://www.rangers.co.uk/staticFiles/fe/a8/0,,5-174334,00.pdf

club as a toy can save the day now.[1] So far, no one has applied for that job. Unless someone does then Rangers (1872) and all its "illustrious" history will soon be dead.

Scotland's Shameless

06.04.12

This isn't about owing lots of people money. This isn't about being insolvent. This is about morality. From Inverness to Austria, football clubs to newsagents and even the emergency services. No one seems to escape the Rangers contagion. The infection is out of control and this club is poisoning everything that it comes into contact with.

Among the 276 creditors are small businesses – some of them family-run – that could go to the wall because of the cavalier attitude of Scotland's establishment club to meeting their responsibilities. Rangers FC have behaved in a fashion that suggests that they believed paying bills was for lesser types and that everyone else had to pick up the tab for their indulgent lifestyle. Shameless!

The mainstream media today are trying to portray this as a damning indictment of Craig Whyte. Someone not aware of the history of this club would be forgiven for believing that if their only source of information on Rangersgate was the succulent lamb lads. Those who dined at Murray's table and obediently followed his orders now style themselves as investigative journalists seeking out the truth. Shameless!

However, I believe that an item scheduled for transmission on *Channel 4 News* tonight will put that one to bed for good. The headline figure of £134m does, of course, include the big tax case, which, of course, didn't happen on Craig Whyte's watch. The emphasis by the mainstream media on Whyte attempts to conceal the larger truth. This is a club that has sought, over more than two decades, to get any financial advantage possible over their rivals and to hell with the wider consequences. Did someone mention "unsurpassed dignity"?

Just asking . . .

---

1   http://www.philmacgiollabhain.ie/situation-vacant-stupid-billionaire-required/

Death watch on Rangers

06.04.12

There has been much anticipation of the decision on the big tax case on Planet *Fitba*. Everybody knows that this is the guided missile from Hector that will finally kill Rangers. There is just one point on this scenario and it is that Rangers (1872) is already bleeding out on the floor. The club went into administration in February because it had simply run out of money to continue operating. It was then confirmed that the club had been using the PAYE remittances as a useful source of ready cash for the business. Clever. Very clever. Dignified, too. Classy.

Of course, readers of this site would not have been surprised at this revelation.[1] Subsequently, after Mr Whyte bought the club in May 2011, Rangers built up another debt to Hector of over £15m. This is probably close to the liquidation value of the assets of the club and that is before adding the Ticketus cash and the other creditors. Duff and Phelps came in and, after a bit of apparent dithering, got the players to accept wages cuts of up to 75%. The wage deal is over at the end of May.

Yesterday's report confirmed the information that I had been previously given that the club, despite the wage deal, was still in a cash flow crisis. The trading loss since administration began means that the club is still insolvent while . . . err . . . being insolvent.

It is a moot point whether or not the club will limp over the line on the final day of the season next month. Moreover, it is difficult to see how Duff and Phelps will be able to make payroll in June for all of the existing staff once the temporary cuts are restored.

Of course, June is a month with no match day revenue. Given the Ticketus issue, there may well be a smaller "pot" of season ticket money than usual as fans are unsure of where their money will go. Of course, all of this is before the three judges in the first-tier tax tribunal hand down their judgement.

The big tax case is now about as necessary to kill Rangers as a precision-guided 1000lb bomb being dropped on Osama Bin Laden's house an hour after a Navy Seal put a couple of rounds of 5.56mm NATO into his head. It is over.

---

1   http://www.philmacgiollabhain.ie/
    rangers-failing-to-keep-up-to-date-with-tax-remittances/

Ally McCoist and the Rangers Supporters Trust (lovely dignified fellows) have both mentioned the "L" word in the past week. In fairness, the legendary Rangers manager has said that liquidation is "not his preferred option". However, he conceded that it might well make business sense. The Rangers Supporters Trust has said that no new owner by summer makes it "likely" that liquidation will happen.

The prospective owners want to acquire the ASSETS of Rangers rather than the current company because that is the way to leave the huge liabilities behind. Duff and Phelps have said Wednesday 4 April is (yet another) deadline for offers for the club. Presumably, this time they really meant it.

The stark reality now is that no one would buy Rangers as a going concern. The report from Duff and Phelps proves that there are enough fatal pathogens in Dignity FC without injecting them with the plague of the big tax case. What we have here is a terminally ill patient and we're just waiting for death to arrive. The specific cause of the final expiry is merely academic and of interest to the professionals.

These days I have my head jauntily cocked to one side, eagerly waiting for the sound of that distinctive death rattle from Edmiston Drive. Oh what a jolly little chap I am!

They're Rangers till they die

10.04.12

I am told that there was something of a strange vibe in the blue room at Ibrox on Saturday. Moreover, it didn't have anything to do with the carnival atmosphere at Rugby Park. My source said that the chat kept coming back to the possibility of a NewCo and whether or not these well-heeled Rangers men would pledge allegiance to it. The consensus among these corporate Gers was that they could not support the new club as if it was the current one.

I was surprised at this, but perhaps that just further proves that this graduate psychologist doesn't understand anything about human behaviour. Perhaps I have just been paying attention to the wrong Rangers supporters. There could be a class difference in how this NewCo is viewed. I simply don't know. When these chaps in the blue room take their seats in the directors' box they, or their companies, pay a lot of money for that privilege.

Personally, I think that once the blue jerseys run onto the field of play at Ibrox then the "New Rangers" will be supported like the old. The example of Airdrie has been pointed out to me and their fall in home crowds after the new club was formed, but I don't think that the same situation will play out at Ibrox. No matter how negative the view of such a scenario in the blue room, a NewCo is the most likely outcome of the current crisis. Every business journalist and insolvency expert I have spoken to has laid this out for me quite clearly.

The current bidders are most probably after the assets in a liquidation sale. The current company just owes too much money to make it viable. The ordinary fans continue to do what they can.

I believe that a cheque was handed over on Saturday for £15,000. This, of course, won't meet the cost of Duff and Phelps for a single day. Of the three bidders, only Paul Murray's Blue Knights are emotionally connected to Rangers. It is the denizens of the blue room that he needs to connect with if there is to be sufficient local corporate support to launch the new Rangers, for it is pretty much a racing certainty that the old Rangers will soon die.

Preparing for the end

22.04.12

A belief in life after death appears to be common to all human cultures. The strongly held conviction, taught from childhood, that physical death is not the end of a person is extant in all the religious belief systems I have studied. Therefore, it must be true. Well actually, no.

I am in that awkward evidence-based squad that says "Show me the proof!" What I am convinced of is that these ideas are adaptive. Those beliefs do a good job for us. They make us feel better about living. In common with other intelligent species, we have self-consciousness. We know that we exist as unique creatures. I know I am me, and you, dear reader, know you are you. This is the essence of being human.

Science has proved, to its collective sceptical satisfaction, that chimpanzees, dolphins and Indian elephants are aware of their own uniqueness. There may be other species with this cognitive ability; brain size seems to be the key determinant. When my dog looks in a mirror she sees another dog. When the crazy cat lady thinks that Tiddles is admiring its own feline beauty in the mirror then the old girl is clearly barking. When Tarzan's best buddy Cheeta looked at his reflection in a pool he saw himself and he knew it.

Some psychologists think that the knowledge of our unique existence was a huge evolutionary step forward. However, everything comes at a cost. Being aware of existence means having to cope with the knowledge that one day we will cease to exist. Ah, death and taxes. Did I mention taxes? Sorry.

Belief in life after death deals with the angst of our impending non-existence. Hence, the hereafter meme has a survival benefit. It allows us to be stoic in the face of huge odds, to be brave in battle and to achieve what Camus always considered to be THE existential challenge of any life: a happy death. Atheists like me just have to deal with the grim reality. I would love to buy into the wonderful fiction that death isn't the end, but I can't.

So it is on Planet *Fitba* that some can't deal with the end, with the finality of it all. For a football club there is no life after liquidation. That's it, finito, kaput, the end. Anyone selling ideas to the contrary may acquire a feeble-minded following. The typical adherent will still be in desperate denial. It will be just another cult for the fearful who can't handle the truth.

Now, where would one look for such a group in Glasgow?

Scrap value only

03.05.12

Bill Miller is a successful businessman. Unlike Craig Whyte, there is evidence of wealth. Not the billionaire off-the-radar variety, but he has been a success in the jungle of North American business. He has made his money out of car wrecks. Now he turns up to one of the biggest pile-ups in the history of British sport. I have yet to see any evidence of the mainstream media in Scotland doing their due diligence on Mr Miller.

I do recall the last time that a North American-based businessman declared an interest in Rangers.[1] (The online piece carries a link to an interview with Graham Duffy published in the *Herald* in 2009.) There

---

1 http://www.heraldscotland.com/sport/spl/rangers/exclusive-graham-duffy-outlines-his-plans-for-a-supporter-led-takeover-of-rangers-football-club-1.989026

are many questions that the guys on the Scottish sports desks should be asking.

- What exactly does Mr Miller plan on towing away from this pile of wreckage?
- How much scrap value is in Scotland's establishment club?
- Will he have to haggle over the registration documents from the current less-than-careful owner?
- Does he intend to put this jalopy back on the road?

Just don't expect the lads in the Scottish press to be looking under the hood. They will be too busy fingering the gear stick to notice that the big end has gone. As this wreck of a football club is towed away, some of those on board still think that it is motoring along nicely. Ah, bless.

Meanwhile, those of us at the side of the road can be forgiven for rubber necking at the entire macabre spectacle.

Open season on the bears

03.05.12

All things have their time.

The Tennessee black bear hunting season is over until early autumn, but don't be surprised to see bear traps being set for the new owner designate of Rangers FC, Bill Miller, in the next few weeks. Yes, while the black bears can sleep soundly in the Smokey Mountains, the blue bears of Snake Mountain are plotting through the knights to wreck the wrecker and tell the Tennessee trucker to truck off!

But what about the king of the Sharks, the trillionaire double-glazing salesman Brian Kennedy, the world's richest man since Keith Jackson met Craig Whyte – is he finished with his bid and set to head down the M74 at great speed? From some quarters there has been opprobrium poured on Craig Whyte, arguably Rangers' Player of the Year, and his dealings with Hector. Well, it could be Brian that will soon be like a bear with a sore head after hearing that HMRC are turning their attention to his tax affairs.

Double-glazing, double-speak, double-dealing – you couldn't make it up! After the Life of Brian, expect the Strife of Brian, starring Hector in the lead role. I hope he doesn't feel hunted.

The quiet man . . . take two?

08.05.12

I love the movies. One of my favourites is *The Quiet Man*, a John Ford classic film of the early fifties which starred John Wayne, Maureen O'Hara, Victor McLaglen and Barry Fitzgerald. It was a magical piece of escapism that told the story of a rich American, Sean Thornton, who came across the ocean with a fistful of dollars to spend. It is a comedy drama and love story with an epic fight that seems to cross three counties and lasts for hours.

What a pity the sequel has been scrapped. The main roles had been cast with Bill Miller playing the John Wayne role and his beauty queen partner, Becky Willard, playing the role of Maureen O'Hara. Why the sudden change of mind? As the tumbleweed blew through the sleepy town of Ooltewah, a young hotshot rode into town. Mark McGivern was fast with his laptop and caused quite a stir as he exposed, yes, perhaps that is the right phrase, detail after detail about former Miss Georgia Peach. Then, the *Daily Record's* hotshot McGivern ambled up to ol' man Miller's factory and upset the local cowboys to such an extent that the local boss, Hogg, called on the sheriff.

Those close to the deal saw red; in fact they saw red, white and blue. The one thing Miller hadn't signed up for was the exposure and microscopic analysis of his affairs, including his one with Georgia Peach's finest.

There is a certain irony that Scotland's finest, who had ensured David Murray and Rangers could flourish for around two decades, might have been one of the main reasons that Bill Miller did indeed 'truck off'. What now?

Probably we can expect more spin, more Blue Knights and more Brian Kennedy. Stand by for more bidders to appear on the horizon, only to disappear before our very eyes like a blue mirage. *The Quiet Man 2* would have been great, but all we are left with now is *Apocalypse Now*!

The horror, the horror . . .

Bear necessities

09.05.12

If I didn't know any better I would think that this entire Rangers saga was an exercise in cruelty. When you look at the almost daily shenanigans of declarations of interest, preferred bidders, CVAs and no CVAs, then it is difficult to discern a clear pattern. You could be forgiven for thinking that the king of the spinners, some Govan VIP, was merely toying with the emotions of the inhabitants of Ibrox.

Now the man himself, Craig Whyte, is back in the frame. A year ago he was hailed by the Ibrox klan as a hero, a saviour. Ah well . . .

I know from my survival training that the average person can survive three weeks without food, three days without water, in Arctic conditions three hours without shelter, but only three seconds without . . . without hope.

The Rangers klan need hope, desperately. The SPL chaps need to get to the end of the season, and Duff and Phelps need to appear competent. When Bill Miller was announced as preferred bidder, the administrators said that a stand-alone CVA was a nonstarter.[1] The American was the saviour!

I, ahem, took a slightly different view.[2] And so it came to pass. A CVA would require the agreement of HMRC and Ticketus. Oops . . .

The next few days and weeks will be agonising for the bears of Ibrox to endure. They are now in the bargaining phase of their grief. Moreover, they tell themselves that liquidation isn't really the end of their beloved Rangers. They need to believe, they need to hope that their club can survive this nightmare.

I don't.

Deadline day?

10.05.12

In the world of journalism there is no term more important than

---

1   http://www.ft.com/intl/cms/s/0/a18422b8-953b-11e1-8faf-00144feab49a.
    html#axzz1uNQwdety

2   http://www.philmacgiollabhain.ie/open-season-on-the-bears/#more-2558

"deadline". When people saunter across the office for a chat it means they have filed their copy. If they are met with a quick stressed-out glance then they usually know that their colleague is "up against it" and needs to be left in peace.

The hour before a paper "goes to bed" is really, really crazy. The bottom line is that those printing presses must roll at a given time. In the broadcast world the feed goes live and you're on air.

Today, there is another deadline in the Rangers saga. I would doff my cap to any journalist or interested observer who could take me through a timeline of the dates when Duff and Phelps have said that "This is the day!" At this stage I've lost count.

If there is a deadline set for offers and, say, someone comes in with an offer two hours after, will that bid be refused? Quite.

Many NUJ colleagues have cheerfully confessed to me over the years that they wouldn't do a thing without a deadline. The trade seems to attract people prone to procrastination. A joke within journalism is the one about writing a novel. Two journalists meet in a bar (I know this sounds far-fetched, but it is based on a true story) and one says, "I'm writing a novel." The other hack replies, "Neither am I!"

Novels, unlike newspaper articles, aren't written to deadline. Don't expect the guys at Duff and Phelps to start behaving like editors. What started as a tight news bulletin has grown into a sprawling Russian novel with no end in sight. Reality will intrude at some point, but not because Duff and Phelps say that a deadline has been reached. The outside world will call a halt to this pantomime, but not today. I gave myself a deadline of midday for this post. Made it!

Quantum of Sorrow

11.05.12

Paul Murray could not have been clearer today. There is no more time. The Blue Knights/Brian Kennedy CVA is now off the table. According to their expert legal opinion, it is no longer achievable within the available time frame. Therefore, liquidation is now the only option.

At the press conference, Paul Murray's face said it all. He looked ashen, crushed and defeated. Brian Kennedy was more in-your-face, but then he isn't a Rangers supporter. He's annoyed, but he isn't hurting. Paul Murray is hurting.

In the weeks ahead there will be so much more hurt to come. If anyone wants to know what is going to happen to Rangers, they can use the search function on this site. For some, that will be a sorrowful journey.

The final performance

12.05.12

Tomorrow in Perth, Rangers will take to the field in the final SPL match of season 2011/2012. I believe it will be the last time that this club will play a competitive professional football match. I am convinced that Rangers (1872) will soon be liquidated.

There are several players interested in acquiring some or all of the assets with a view to trading under the Rangers franchise, but the club will be no more. Companies House will record that the company established in 1872 and incorporated in 1899 will have ended in 2012. It will say "liquidation" beside that company. "The Rangers" will be over, done with, a thing of the past.

Contrary to the increasingly desperate spin from the hack pack this week, Scottish football will not "die" when Rangers expire, quite the opposite, in fact. The Ibrox club introduced financial doping on an industrial scale and this choked off a career route for young, native talent. It also forced Celtic into a borrowing-fuelled arms race in the first decade of the millennium. Celtic bought off-the-shelf senior pros and put it on the card. There was little space for youth to blossom in the Hoops. Now, the Parkhead club is financially healthy with home-grown players like James Forrest and Dylan McGeouch figuring in the first team. Hopefully this trend will continue.

Moreover, I believe that the country as a whole will be the healthier without the toxic pathogen at Edmiston Drive. Ibrox stadium has been a theatre of hatred for generations. The employment policy of Rangers wrote a permission slip for anyone in Scotland who harboured a hatred of Irish Catholics. When football historians examine this club post mortem, will they finally establish that there was also a "policy" for Republic of Ireland players similar to the one for Catholics pre 1989?

Scottish society will undoubtedly benefit from the absence of a club that has provided a gathering point and a source of affirmation for social poison. Ibrox stadium was the hedge school that taught the mob that wrecked Manchester in 2008 and socialised the man who murdered Mark Scott. Anyone wishing to establish a NewCo and trade on the Rangers franchise may wish to examine the unique selling proposition of the brand. If excising anti-Irish racism alienates the Ibrox customer base then any prospective owner must address their own social responsibility. Is it acceptable in 2012 to have a business plan based on the bigot pound?

As the Billy boys gather at Perth tomorrow, the locals may wish to point out that Muirton Park, the original ground of St Johnstone, was sold to the retail giant Asda. Of course, St Johnstone FC will still be alive at the start of next season. Rangers won't.

The stealth consortium

14.05.12

There are perfectly legitimate reasons for wanting to stay out of the public eye. I get that. Some people cherish their anonymity, just as others yearn to be famous. Most people who want to own a football club fall into the latter category. No one could accuse Sir David Murray of shunning the limelight. These days, I suspect, he may want a lower profile when it comes to matters Rangers.

A friend of mine recently interviewed the son of one of Mr Charles Green's consortium. The man, who is in business with his father, is no stranger to the craziness of English football fans and rather enjoyed the notoriety. However, he was convinced that his dad didn't want his name out there on this one. He explained, "We don't want to be known as part of this because of the angry people around Rangers."

I was surprised to hear this. Mr Green's consortium is about to save the wonderful old institution, woven as it is into the fabric of Scottish life, by investing serious money into Rangers. Given that fact, I would have thought that these fine fellows would want to take all the plaudits from the Ibrox faithful for their sterling work. Apparently not. Ah well.

The boys in blue at Ibrox?

27.05.12

That was the week that was for Duff and Phelps. In just seven days, Duff and Phelps managed to alienate the BBC, FIFA, UEFA, the SFA and the Insolvency Practitioners Association. It just couldn't get worse – or could it?

I am sure that Strathclyde's finest ringing the front door of the Big Hoose to speak to Paul Clarke and David Grier about their role over the last few months could well make it a lot worse. A defining moment? Well, I think they would have to step aside if the police were formally involved.

The plight of Rangers has been debated in clubs and bars throughout the world, but I am told their financial predicament and their questionable tax strategies have reached the ears of the powers that be at UNICEF. Their worry is that the global children's charity may have accepted tainted money from the disgraced club.

When the SPL gathers this week to decide (no laughing at the back there), expect newly promoted Ross County to have more insight into the Rangers EBT scandal than most. George Adams, now director of football at Victoria Park, was given the sum of £30,000 through an EBT when he was Rangers head of youth development. I am sure his input in the decision making process will be very valuable.

Charles Green asks the Blue Knights for help

06.06.12

I have to admit that I am developing something of a liking for Mr Charles Green. For a start, the man does think big! If you are to succeed in life you need the vision thing. Before he got the keys to the White House, Barack Obama published his book, *The Audacity of Hope: Thoughts on Reclaiming the American Dream*. It was about the power of having a dream and of thinking things can be better. Certainly, the young Obama had a dream! So, it would appear, does Mr Green.

I am reliably informed that just before the Jubilee bunting went up, Charlie and the boys went soliciting some members of the Blue Knights consortium to get on board. I understand that the response was less than chivalric. He was forced into this course of action because promises of cash from other parties have all but dried up and Charlie appears to be in a bit of bother raising the readies. That he thinks it is OK to approach the opposition for financial backing makes me warm to the guy. It really does. I hope he makes it.

It would be a great pity if he stumbled at this stage. Charlie owning NewCo Rangers would be simply wonderful. Sweat the dream, Charlie. Sweat the dream.

The hinge factor

07.06.12

The pre-season friendly between Rangers and Le Havre has an interesting aspect of the Ibrox club's recent history.[1] One would have thought that the one name Rangers would try to avoiding thinking about in their current terminal state would be that of Jean-Alain Boumsong. The big centre-half started his career at Le Havre before joining Auxerre and then onto Rangers in 2004. The French defender joined the Ibrox club as a free agent and signed a five-year contract. When he went to Newcastle in the 2005 January transfer window for £8m it looked like a shrewd bit of business on the part of David Murray.

Rangers got the services of a top-class defender for the first half of the season for free and then sold him on for a massive profit. However, historians may well look back and conclude that the Boumsong transfer was the hinge factor in the club's downfall. This was one of the player sales that figured in the Stevens inquiry. Ibrox was raided and all sorts of goodies were confiscated by plod.[2] What the City of London police found was information that they thought would be of interest to their colleagues in HMRC. It was. Very, very interesting.

It turned out that Rangers had been naughty. Ever so naughty. HMRC then had an armoury of smoking guns. They knew about how the EBTs were being administered and because of the Boumsong raid on Ibrox, they could prove it.

A hinge factor can only be discerned as such after the fact. That such momentous events can turn on an unforeseen and unconnected minor

1   http://www.rangers.co.uk/news/football-news/article/2803802

2   http://www.dailymail.co.uk/sport/football/article-468810/Police-raid-clubs-corruption-investigation.html

event is an uncomfortable thought. Conspiracy theories are a comfort blanket, a quasi-religious belief for those who cannot face the chaos of the universe. However, without the seizure of that data by the City of London police, HMRC would not have had the strong case that they presented to the first-tier tribunal.

Both Rangers and Le Havre have been in existence for 140 years this year, but because of that ill-fated transfer, it is the French club that has a future. The British club that Jean-Alain Boumsong joined in 2004 will soon go out of existence.

Helping the police with their enquiries?

08.06.12

It would appear that Strathclyde's finest are not best pleased with Duff and Phelps. The guys looking into the Whyte takeover of Rangers believe that the administrators have failed dismally to provide Strathclyde police with the documents they require to complete their investigation.

My source believes some vital paperwork that they have requested cannot be currently located by Duff and Phelps. Some of the documentation that the cops do have has been scrutinised by a Home Office handwriting expert. Police insiders consider the preliminary report to the Crown Office to be seriously incomplete. The canteen chat inside Strathclyde police is that Duff and Phelps' conduct on this has been "unprofessional and unhelpful and verging on the obstructive".

Oh dear . . .

Paying a tribute to Rangers

13.06.12

Do you believe in life after liquidation?

There are certain states where there is no equivocation, no ambiguity, nor shades of grey. Death is like that. You can't be a little dead any more than a woman can be slightly pregnant.

With companies – and a football club is a company – liquidation is similarly final. Yesterday on Twitter it was fun to see the succulent bambs take a pasting. Some of them took it personally. I tried to tell them it was just business, but they took it very personally.

In the age of new media they can't insulate themselves from inter-acting with those who consume their product. Often, it has been the hacks who have been badly informed and it is the "consumers" of old media who have been able to put them right. The credibility test for the mainstream media in Scotland over the next few weeks is whether or not they fall into line with the fantasy that liquidation does not mean the end of the club.

When the death certificate is formally written for Rangers (1872) then that will be that. Some people will want to pretend that things haven't changed and will want to dress up like the old days when Rangers were alive. There are, I am reliably informed, entire conven-tions devoted to who is the best Elvis impersonator. Sigh . . . However, no one outside of a locked ward is pretending that Elvis Aaron Presley (1935–1977) is in the building in corporeal form.

What will now emerge is a Rangers impersonator. A tribute band. Of course, in European competitions they will be, for three years, a tribute banned.

The marketing fantasy that Rangers still lives is vital to the financial health of the tribute club. The risible idea that Rangers are not dead needs to take hold so that the roadies who trashed Manchester and turned beautiful Barcelona into a urinal will still part with hundreds of pounds for season tickets. Charlie himself said that if a CVA didn't succeed, the club's history would be gone.[1] Mr Green was bang on the money.

If Rangers fans want to be in contact with the club they love next season then I suggest they invest in a ouija board rather than a season ticket for Ibrox.

Richard Gough, to be fair to him, acknowledges that the club he captained is now dead.[2]

As we know with Elvis, no matter how much the deceased is missed, no one comes back from the grave.

Rangers have left the building.

---

1   http://www.bbc.co.uk/sport/0/football/18373399
2   http://www.thescottishsun.co.uk/scotsol/homepage/sport/spl/4369672/Culprits-must-pay-price-after-killing-off-my-club.html

Rangers are dead!

13.06.12

ORIGINALLY PUBLISHED ON *VAVEL*[1]

Yesterday the British tax authorities signed the death warrant for a football club that many thought would last forever. They were wrong. Hubris and hatred made Rangers self-destruct.

Rangers are dead. I will not pretend that writing that sentence did not give me great pleasure. It did. I am glad that they are dead.

All of my life, this "Scottish institution" was a powerful symbol that I was, by accident of birth, born into a country where I was not wanted and not valued. If city rivals Celtic are an iconic manifestation of the existence of Glasgow's Irish community then Rangers came to symbolise xenophobia and hatred of my people.

By the early twentieth century, the Ibrox club had brought in a signing ban on Catholic players. Indeed, Rangers legend Sandy Jardine recently said that when he joined the club in 1964 there wasn't a single Catholic member of staff employed there. Although that signing ban was publicly lifted in 1989 when they bought ex-Celtic player Maurice Johnston, another "policy" remained in place. Since the Football Association of Ireland was recognised by FIFA as a separate entity in 1949 there has not been one single Republic of Ireland player to play in the Rangers first team. During the last twenty years, a Republic of Ireland international – full or under-21 – has played for EVERY other senior professional football club in Britain. Yet this is not challenged by the media in Scotland.

The death of Scotland's "establishment club" could not have been scripted any better if it had been written by a Celtic supporter working for a movie company. For over a decade, Rangers scammed the British taxpayer while proclaiming that the club loved the country more than anyone. During that time, Britain fought two wars and troops died because of inadequate equipment. Yet this club invited soldiers in uniform to watch matches for free to make a PR point to the Irish club across the city. It would have been better for the troops if they had paid their taxes, like everyone else.

Rangers, under their owner, Sir David Murray, brought financial doping

---

into Scottish football. The country had a tradition of developing players who would go and play for bigger clubs in England. Celtic won the
European Cup in 1967 with an entirely home-grown team. Being the first
team from Britain to win Europe's highest club trophy inflicted a deep psy-
chological wound on Rangers. Murray wanted to replicate the success of
the Lisbon Lions, but he knew he would have to spend money that couldn't
be generated within football. His business model, based on borrowing,
brought in the plague. Other clubs were forced to borrow to keep up.

Young Scottish players had little chance to break through as the
league was deluged with foreign players on high salaries that they often
didn't deserve. There is now an inquiry into whether or not Rangers
fielded players in contravention of the football rules.

The Ibrox club operated a "dual contract" system to thwart the taxman. Although Rangers' history is now concluded with liquidation,
they may still lose some of the honours that they won under Murray.

In May 2011 Sir David Murray sold the club to shady businessman,
Craig Whyte, for a single pound. The mainstream media called Whyte a
"billionaire" with "wealth off the radar". They were effectively acting as
secretaries for Whyte's PR people and failed in their duty as journalists.

As first written by this journalist in June 2011, Whyte had used
future season ticket money to pay off the bank debt and acquire the
club. He used the money from Rangers' own fans to buy their club!
Whyte wasn't even a millionaire and ran the club by withholding taxes
from the government. This was in addition to the huge potential tax bill
that had been accrued under Murray. That case has still to be judged.

The reporting of the death of Rangers has been a victory for new
media. Bloggers have been ahead of the game throughout. Finally, serious journalists from the mainstream got in on the act. Mark Daly from
the BBC and Alex Thomson from *Channel 4 News* started to investigate the Rangers scandal. Throughout this saga, sports journalists in
Glasgow remained obedient and "on message" that everything would
be OK at Rangers.

Yesterday, as news came through of the club being liquidated, well-
known sports reporters were derided on Twitter for their cowardice.
There is now a plan to have a new company using the assets of the
deceased club. It is not clear what league the new club will play in.

However, the main thing is that Rangers are dead and in my opinion,
Scottish society will be the better for it. The Ibrox club has provided
a gathering point for the most toxic elements in Scottish society for
generations. Being a Rangers supporter was to be given a permission

slip to hate Catholics and Irish people. In 2008, the supporters came up with a song that mocked those who had died in the famine of 1847 in Ireland. One million people died in that catastrophe. One of them was my grandmother's uncle. The "Famine Song" was ruled racist and illegal by the High Court in Scotland in 2009.

People in cities all over Europe shuddered when they knew that supporters of the Ibrox club were about to visit. Now, at least, those fans will not have an interest in European competition. They will not be missed.

It is not just Europe that the new club might be absent from. It is now a distinct possibility that the new club calling itself Rangers will not be registered in time to play professional football in Scotland in the season starting in August. An absence of a season will ram home the reality to those still in denial.

For some it is too big to take in. However, it is a fact. Rangers are dead.

Links

http://www.philmacgiollabhain.ie/the-fall-of-the-house-of-murray/
    11.01.2009
http://www.philmacgiollabhain.ie/taxing-times-for-rangers/   07.06.2010
http://www.philmacgiollabhain.ie/
    rangers-offer-to-settle-with-hmrc/   23.01.2011
http://www.philmacgiollabhain.ie/rangers-board-desperate-to-settle-tax-case/
    23.01.2011
http://www.philmacgiollabhain.ie/what-tax-experts-are-saying-about-rangers/
    03.02.2011
http://www.philmacgiollabhain.ie/
    the-real-value-of-rangers-fixed-assets-may-soon-be-known/
  09.02.2011
http://www.philmacgiollabhain.ie/will-sir-david-murray-pay-the-tax-bill-for-
    rangers/ 11.02.2011
http://www.philmacgiollabhain.ie/another-tax-case/   14.02.2011
http://www.philmacgiollabhain.ie/rangers-mid-term-accounts-delayed-why/
  06.03.2011
http://www.philmacgiollabhain.ie/
    alistair-johnston-fights-to-save-rangers/   19.04.2011
http://www.philmacgiollabhain.ie/clear-and-present-danger/   07.05.2011
http://www.philmacgiollabhain.ie/

rangers-strike-it-lucky-with-their-new-owner/   07.06.2011
http://www.philmacgiollabhain.ie/
    gordon-smith-to-return-to-ibrox/   17.06.2011
http://www.philmacgiollabhain.ie/the-sheriff-is-in-town/   08.08.2011
http://www.philmacgiollabhain.ie/the-sheriffs-men-at-ibrox/   10.08.2011
http://www.philmacgiollabhain.ie/
    photographs-you-were-not-meant-to-see/   10.08.2011
http://www.philmacgiollabhain.ie/
    martin-bains-race-against-the-clock/   20.08.2011
http://www.philmacgiollabhain.ie/
    rangers-failing-to-keep-up-to-date-with-tax-remittances/   30.08.2011
http://www.scotzine.com/2011/09/a-failed-attempt-to-censor-an-investiga-
    tive-journalist/   01.09.2011
http://www.philmacgiollabhain.ie/penny-blockade/   03.09.2011
http://www.philmacgiollabhain.ie/the-bain-papers/   10.09.2011
http://www.philmacgiollabhain.ie/rangers-the-clock-is-ticking/   12.09.2011
http://www.philmacgiollabhain.ie/rangers-in-receivership/   14.09.2011
http://www.philmacgiollabhain.ie/source-material/   03.11.2011
http://www.philmacgiollabhain.ie/rangers-and-their-accounts/   04.12.2011
http://www.philmacgiollabhain.ie/
    craig-whyte-some-vital-details/   10.12.2011
http://www.philmacgiollabhain.ie/a-new-journalism/   11.12.2011
http://www.philmacgiollabhain.
    ie/a-mayan-moment-for-rangers-in-2012/   06.01.2012
http://www.philmacgiollabhain.ie/privileged-information/   31.01.2012
http://www.philmacgiollabhain.ie/yours-for-a-pound/   02.02.2012
http://www.philmacgiollabhain.ie/too-late-to-catch-the-ticket-bus/
    07.02.2012
http://www.philmacgiollabhain.ie/rangers-preparing-for-the-end/
    09.02.2012
http://www.philmacgiollabhain.ie/rangers-too-bigoted-to-fail/   14.02.2012
http://www.philmacgiollabhain.ie/
    the-saint-valentines-day-administration/   14.02.2012
http://www.philmacgiollabhain.ie/the-liquidation-of-rangers/   15.02.2012
http://www.philmacgiollabhain.ie/
    are-taxes-only-for-stupid-people-in-scotland/   16.02.2012
http://www.philmacgiollabhain.ie/deals-and-taxes/   17.02.2012
http://www.philmacgiollabhain.ie/hmrc-bank-limited/   21.02.2012
http://www.philmacgiollabhain.ie/order-order/   23.02.2012
http://www.philmacgiollabhain.ie/charity-before-dignity/   28.02.2012

http://www.philmacgiollabhain.ie/dead-club-walking/   07.03.2012
http://www.philmacgiollabhain.ie/
    rangers-still-have-to-walk-the-green-mile/   10.03.2012
http://www.philmacgiollabhain.ie/situation-vacant-stupid-billionaire-
    required/ 11.03.2012
http://www.philmacgiollabhain.ie/the-undeniable-truth/   05.04.2012
http://www.philmacgiollabhain.ie/scotlands-shameless/   06.04.2012
http://www.philmacgiollabhain.ie/deathwatch-on-rangers/   06.04.2012
http://www.philmacgiollabhain.ie/theyre-rangers-till-they-die/   10.04.2012
http://www.philmacgiollabhain.ie/preparing-for-the-end/   22.04.2012
http://www.philmacgiollabhain.ie/scrap-value-only/   03.05.2012
http://www.philmacgiollabhain.ie/open-season-on-the-bears/   03.05.2012
http://www.philmacgiollabhain.ie/the-quiet-mantake-two/   08.05.2012
http://www.philmacgiollabhain.ie/bear-necessities/   09.05.2012
http://www.philmacgiollabhain.ie/deadline-day/   10.05.2012
http://www.philmacgiollabhain.ie/quantum-of-sorrow/   11.05.2012
http://www.philmacgiollabhain.ie/the-final-performance/   12.05.2012
http://www.philmacgiollabhain.ie/the-stealth-consortium/   14.05.2012
http://www.philmacgiollabhain.ie/the-boys-in-blue-at-ibrox/   27.05.2012
http://www.philmacgiollabhain.ie/
    charles-green-asks-the-blue-knights-for-help/   06.06.2012
http://www.philmacgiollabhain.ie/the-hinge-factor/   07.06.2012
http://www.philmacgiollabhain.ie/
    helping-the-police-with-their-inquiries/   08.06.2012
http://www.philmacgiollabhain.ie/paying-a-tribute-to-rangers/   13.06.2012
http://www.vavel.com/en/uk-football/scottish-premier-league/glasgow-
    rangers/170300-rangers-are-dead.html   13.06.2012

Part II: Media Section

Introduction

I am proud to be a journalist. Functioning journalism is essential to a functioning democracy. In fact I cannot think of any democratic society without a free press. Some of the best people I have ever met are journalists, while some of the most odious specimens of humanity are also in this trade. I look around the table when I am at a meeting of the Irish Executive Council of the NUJ and it is a fine ensemble of bright, charitable, difficult, opinionated and tenacious sods. I'm proud to be one of their numbers.

I have the New Media seat on the council and I am also the Irish representative on the union's New Media Industrial Council. This voluntary involvement is all the more fascinating because this is a time of huge change for media. The digital revolution, like all such paradigm shifts, is no respecter of tradition or reputation. Revolutions are by their nature convulsive events, releasing such a torrent of pent-up energy that they destroy that which had previously seemed timeless and immovable.

The story of Rangers' downfall is also a cautionary tale about the modern media. One of the most baffling aspects of this tale is the fact that the greatest story in the history of British sport was sitting there waiting to be told. Over several years I experienced, to say the least, a certain reticence on the part of the guys on the sports desks in Glasgow to go after it. As a freelancer living in another country I established my credentials as being unhealthily interested in this subject over several years. I called people incessantly either to elicit information or, if they were in a position of influence in the media, to take up the story properly. I was simply the pest!

I caught a break in early 2010 when I was able to take the story of the "big tax case" to the *News of the World* Scottish edition. The editor, Bob Bird, and his guy on the news desk, Craig Jackson, just saw it as a damn good story. Scotland's establishment club was about to be hit with an unpayable tax bill. They rightly saw it as front-page material. I thought that the rest of the mainstream media would run with the story and develop it. I was wrong.

I couldn't understand this; the Rangers tax case was a huge story. The usual response when a newspaper has been "scooped" is to go after the next strand in the story. A chase develops and that's how the public is informed. The media is a highly competitive world. Yet there seemed to be very little interest in this story from the mainstream media after May 2010. Even as far back as early 2009 there was evidence that, following the banking crisis of 2008, Sir David Murray's business empire was in serious trouble. When I wrote "The fall of the house of Murray" in January 2009 I didn't have access to any secret information. I wasn't doing anything that couldn't have happened in the offices of any newspaper or broadcast organisation in Scotland. When Walter Smith revealed on live radio to the BBC's Chick Young that the bank had taken control of the club, the journalist said "Thanks, Walter" and terminated the interview . . . It was a scoop, but not, perhaps, one he was entirely comfortable with.

Here was the bizarre situation where the reigning champions of the SPL had effectively been taken over by the bank. Lloyds TSB had their guy on the board and a bank-driven austerity programme was being imposed. I continued to work on the story with little or no visible end product. In late 2009 I heard the first rumours that the financial problems facing the Ibrox club were much bigger than the much written-about bank debt. However, I was still going down the road of trying to ascertain the exact extent of the hands-on nature of the bank's control of the club. In early 2010 I first had it confirmed that the other financial problem that Rangers faced was the tax man. Through various sources I was able to piece together the story that the *News of the World* would run in May 2010 on their front page. The big-selling Sunday would run a series of pieces from me on the story in the succeeding weeks. Editor Bob Bird called time on the story after four editions in a row. However, it had been the best mainstream media coverage of Rangers' potentially fatal financial problems ever seen in a Scottish newspaper. Despite that, even a year after the *News of the World*'s "big splash" on Rangers' tax troubles the mainstream media seemed oblivious to the reality of the situation.

The people who frequented my site and social media sites that were associated with Celtic were very well informed about Employee Benefit Trusts and the entire lexicon of tax evasion and fiscal rectitude. However, the good plain folk of Planet *Fitba* were still largely in the dark. It was as if the *News of the World* coverage of the Rangers tax case had been scrubbed from the collective memory. The response to the *News of the World* coverage on Rangers message boards was pretty universal. It was generally known that I was behind all of these stories although they appeared under the *News of the World* house by-line of James Douglas. Because I was the journalist involved it was easy for Rangers supporters to dismiss the stories as made-up nonsense. This was a fatal miscalculation by anyone well disposed towards the Ibrox club. These *News of the World* articles were warnings that should have been heeded.

It had always been my intention to put the impending financial catastrophe at Ibrox into the mainstream. In the meantime, I used my own site to put out information about the biggest story in Scottish football history. As I researched further I was convinced that unless a bluenose billionaire turned up, the Ibrox outfit was finished. In January 2011 I tried again with the mainstream media – this time, radio. I broke the story that Rangers had offered £10m in settlement of the tax case and that HMRC had refused it. It was a genuine scoop and the fitba internet went mental.

Several callers to the Clyde 1 *Superscoreboard* wanted to know more so I obliged and called the show the same night. Jim Delahunt was the anchor and Darrell King was in the studio. Once more I stated, slowly and clearly, the basic arithmetic of the problem that was threatening to put Rangers out of business. The response among the Rangers folk of Planet *Fitba* in the next twenty-four hours appeared to be one of shock. Yet this was almost a year after the *News of the World* front page and still the news had not penetrated into the collective consciousness of the mass of Scottish football.

Again I was baffled that this story didn't take up more of the mainstream media's focus. As Rangers continued to win on the field it didn't seem to be a priority for the sports desks. In May 2011, on the anniversary of Celtic's finest hour in Europe, I was in the AVIVA stadium in Dublin to see Scotland take on Wales. The tournament was a flop and as I looked at an empty stadium I remembered what Jock Stein had understood – football without fans really didn't amount to much. I mingled with some of the Scottish sports journalists who I thought should have been onto this Rangers tax story like bloodhounds. I spoke with Graham Spiers, then of the London *Times*. We had spoken several times on radio phone-ins over the years and in the immediate aftermath of the Dallas email story he was aware of my work. Our chat quickly turned to the big tax case, as it had become known among the press pack. I opined that this was a bill that would kill Rangers unless they found themselves a very rich owner who was willing to bankroll this huge contingent liability. Graham disagreed. I was interested to hear his take on it.

"David Murray will pay the bill," he said.

"Really?" I couldn't believe what I was hearing as we stood beside a small, round table in the media centre. Graham thought that David Murray would be "morally compelled" to pay it or his reputation would be in tatters. At that point in the conversation I didn't have an answer; I'm always like that when I interact with an exponent of Pollyanna's Glad Game.

As I took my seat for Scotland against Wales, I looked over at the boisterous Tartan Army and wondered how many of them would think that the Rangers owner could be "morally compelled" to pay the tax bill from his own pocket. Quite. Yet this conclusion was from one of the more erudite sports journalists to be working in Scottish football.

Spiers had enjoyed Murray's hospitality in the Channel Islands along with Darrell King, Andy McInnes and James Traynor just before the term "succulent lamb" entered the irreverent lexicon of Scottish fitba on 19 November 1998. James Traynor wrote a piece for the *Daily Record* headlined: "SECRET FEAR THAT DRIVES ME TO WIN 10 IN A ROW". It detailed an interview that Traynor had conducted over a meal with David Murray during that trip to the Channel Islands. The usual suspects from the hack pack had gone to the Guernsey home of the Rangers owner. This was part of a festival of puff pieces celebrating Murray's first decade at the helm of Scotland's establishment club. A close associate of Traynor told me that the *Daily Record* man saw this piece as an opportunity for him to show his prowess as an expressive writer. The piece has become famous, but not perhaps in the way that Traynor would have wished, as this extract demonstrates:

> If the past ten years have taught Murray, who is one of Britain's wealthiest individuals, anything it is how to win and he believes Rangers will continue to grow and prosper. "I look upon these last ten years as having been a great era, but it is over and Rangers are about to head on into a new era," he said over a glass of the finest red. He was about to take in another mouthful of the most succulent lamb – anyone who knows Murray shouldn't be surprised to learn he is a full-blooded, unashamed red-meat eater – when he put down his knife and fork. It was like a statement of intent and looking

directly across the table to make sure I hadn't yet succumbed
to the wine, he said: "Bring on the next ten years, there's
more to come for Rangers."

The journalists on this trip were house guests of Murray. The Rangers
owner also invited a small group of sports journalists to his son's wedding celebration at Gleneagles Hotel. This select bunch included
Andy McInnes of the *Express* and James Traynor of the *Daily Record*.
Journalists are regularly invited on PR-generated junkets to be sold a
message, but being invited to a family wedding is something that is for
family and close friends. I know mine was.

Such personal closeness makes it more difficult to maintain a professional distance. In fairness to Graham Spiers, he had pointed out the
inconvenient truth of the growing debt in the Advocaat years and had
been exiled from the tent. He also persistently tackled the Rangers fans
over their bigoted chanting. Graham was also happy to go on camera
for Alex Thomson and Channel 4 and put his hands up to the succulent
lamb culture, but that was this year, after the catastrophe was undeniable. During the same tournament I spoke to several other Scottish
hacks. It is fair to say that none of them were in Graham's intellectual league and they were fully credulous of the credentials of the new
prospective owner of the Ibrox club, Mr Craig Whyte. I told one of
the journalists that I had tried my best to ascertain the nature of the
"Motherwell-born billionaire's" wealth but had been stumped. I made
reference to various sources in the City of London (without naming
them) who had turned up very little on him. I saw from this that the
extent of this excavation surprised the Scottish press pack. Later on,
it was revealed that the journalists had been given their orders by Mr
Whyte's PR people. "We were told to call him a billionaire" was one
amazing revelation by the *Daily Record*'s Keith Jackson once the Whyte
regime had crashed and burned. One would have thought that having a
father as a detective in the CID would have prepared the young chap to
be more of an investigative journalist rather than an obedient regurgita-
tor of PR fairy tales.

Around the time I was chatting to the cream of Scotland's Fourth
Estate in Dublin, Carter Ruck, the legal firm favoured by Mr Whyte,
had communicated with Andy Muirhead of Scotzine.com. The student journalist and blogger had uploaded a well-researched piece
on Mr Whyte when he had first come onto Planet *Fitba*'s radar in
November 2010. The letter would request that the piece be taken
down or legal action might be the result. Young Andy agreed to take

the piece down. He was good enough to share his research with me and I was grateful for that. It was the start of a collaboration that continues to this day.

I had registered the appearance of the new saviour of Rangers back in November 2010 but little else as I was still working on the Dallas email story. I knew that anyone buying the Ibrox club at that point would have to be prepared to bankroll them and budget to pay the big tax bill if they lost the case to HMRC. It had to be an emotional investment, not a business one. Therefore Mr Whyte's credentials as a Rangers supporter were material to the case. One would have thought that this would not have stretched the investigative powers of Scottish football journalists. Ah well. Maybe I was playing the Glad Game by this time.

The man with "wealth off the radar" duly acquired the Ibrox club in May 2011 and the hacks were in blue heaven. After all, good news stories about Rangers are what it's all about on the Glasgow sports desks. I sketched out a likely scenario for Mr Whyte and, mindful of Carter Ruck being on the job, made it satirical. On 7 June 2011 I had sketched out a clear enough picture, if anyone cared to look beyond the ribaldry, that Ticketus had shelled out to Mr Whyte on season ticket futures. A freelance colleague ran with the story and was warned off by a PR chap working for the reclusive "billionaire". My buddy, who had worked with me on the *News of the World* story, was told that Mr Whyte's lawyers, Carter Ruck, were on my case. It was darkly hinted that writs were imminent so he dropped the story. For the record, I never received as much as a Post-it note on the rear end of a carrier pigeon let alone a letter from the London-based litigation lawyers.

A year later the text of the email makes for hilarious reading. One day I'll occasion upon the PR guy and let him know that there are no problems between us, it's just business. A month after I had told Rangers fans how lucky they were to have Craig Whyte as the club's new owner I had extracted my tongue from my cheek with surgical assistance and I was back at the AVIVA. The Dublin Super Cup was a pre-season tourney involving Celtic, Manchester City, Inter Milan and the best that the League of Ireland could muster in a select. Once more, the Scottish press pack landed in Dublin.

I spotted veteran sports journalist Hugh Keevins. I helped him find his way around the AVIVA set-up and made sure he had a pass for the mixed zone. At some point in the competition we bumped into each other in the media room where once more I was discussing the

Rangers tax case with a senior member of the Scottish press pack. As I outlined for the umpteenth time the basic numbers of the case, Hugh's eyes widened.

"£36m? Well, that means closure!" He appeared to be genuinely surprised. This was the journalist who had said on his breakfast slot in May 2010 that Rangers were consulting their lawyers over the *News of the World* front page with exactly those numbers.

I then became aware that handpicked hacks were receiving briefings from the same PR folks. My claims had to be dismissed. I was a "fantasist" and a "chancer", and my allegations about Mr Whyte's use of future season ticket money were preposterous and actionable. While the mainstream media were on message about Mr Whyte I knew that it would be difficult to break through.

In movie scriptwriting courses they teach students to show, not tell. I was using words, as they were all I had. In August 2011 I got a chance to use pictures. An excellent source inside Rangers contacted me and said that the guys in charge were in a panic about the impending visit of sheriff officers. It was about the "wee tax bill". If sheriff officers were due to arrive then clearly that HMRC bill hadn't been paid. I knew immediately that, if at all possible, I needed to capture this event.

I contacted the NUJ office in Glasgow and asked them to recommend a freelance photographer that I could hire. I caught a break. They put me in touch with a very experienced snapper who had just been made redundant from a major title. He knew his way around the city and was highly competent. He accepted the commission over the phone.

I had already told my readers that the visit by the sheriff officers to Ibrox was imminent. That had sent the club's PR into fire-fighting mode. Journalists were briefed that this was just more fantasy from the "chancer" in Donegal. It is my firm view that my location and stated Irish ethnicity made it easier to sell a negative message about me to many of the chaps on the Glasgow sports desks.

The visit didn't take place on the day it was meant to although I knew from an HMRC source that the papers had been issued and sheriff officers had been instructed. I even knew the specific firm. A contact in the legal trade in Glasgow, an ex-police officer, was invaluable in finding out that the visit would happen the following morning.

My guy was in place. The sheriff officers were snapped. Although I wanted the scoop on the pictures I also wanted the greatest possible mainstream coverage. I tipped off another freelance colleague in central

Scotland. We had worked together on the Rangers finance story and he had done the introductions to the *News of the World* for me. It was time to pay him back. I knew he was freelancing for the *Sun* so I suggested that he take this to the news desk in Glasgow.

In fairness to the "soar away *Sun*" they had stuck with the story after the first no show from the guys with the court papers. On the morning it happened my freelance snapper was there alongside a staff photographer from the *Sun*. It took me a couple of hours to get a positive ID on the sheriff officers pictures from a source inside that small paralegal world. That night the pictures were on my site.

I allowed my snapper to take other images and sell them to the *Daily Record*. The following day, both the *Sun* and the *Record* led with the story. It was the Kodak moment for Rangers. However, on the fans' message boards the denial continued. One inventive chap dismissed the pictures as "two surprised men photographed after leaving Ibrox stadium after trying to book a function room". Oh dear. I wonder what he thinks now . . .

That was August 2011, and still the Rangers fans didn't want to believe that anything was amiss at their club, which was now owned by Mr Whyte, the enigmatic billionaire. The sheriff officer story led to my being on Clyde 1 *Superscoreboard* – as it transpired, for the last time. I called the show to clarify a couple of points. Jim Delahunt, as always, was gracious and professional. Graham Spiers was on the panel and it became a tetchy exchange because I claimed the scoop. When he thought that I could not make this claim because the *Sun* were also lying in wait for the guys with the court papers I didn't have the heart to tell him who tipped them off.

The important thing for me from the entire episode was that, for the first time, it was in the mainstream that all might not be well with the new regime at Ibrox. The bought-in PR people had suffered a major reverse in stating categorically that I was completely wrong about the impending visit to the stadium by sheriff officers. It wasn't a bad day's work for a "chancer", I thought.

I knew from several sources that it was only a matter of time before the Whyte regime ran out of money. It was conceded that the club didn't have a credit line from another bank since Lloyds Banking Group had got their £18m. I couldn't see how Rangers under Whyte could avoid administration. Once the insolvency event occurred I couldn't see HMRC allowing them out. I knew that the HMRC game plan was to liquidate the club and put their head on a spike. I was fairly sure that Mr Whyte and his clever people were also aware of this reality. Moreover, I could not see how they could make enough money in the short term just to keep going.

I asked a business analyst who had been a great help to me throughout this story. My question to him was simple enough: "If you were Craig Whyte, what would be your next move?" He said, "Oh, that's simple. I would have you killed." At that point he had my full attention. Only after a pregnant pause did he laugh. He continued to explain: "You're stopping them getting credit. This coverage, especially those pics, it's killing them". It was the first time I had considered that I was playing a role in events. Of course at no time did I think, nor did he, that Mr Whyte wished me any ill will. However, the point was well made. The negative coverage of the financial health of Rangers as a business was bad for the Whyte project.

I closed that month of August 2011 by breaking another story about the club's failure to honour their regular tax remittances. It was this that would finally put Rangers into administration in February 2012. For some in the Rangers camp it was the last straw. I had to be taken offline.

At the time I had an account with an Australian company called Flexihostings. They received an email from a man called Archie Ferguson who claimed to represent "stakeholders" in Rangers. Basically, Mr Ferguson alleged that I was fabricating stories about Rangers being in financial difficulty and because of this I was damaging the club as a going concern. He had letters after his name and he hinted strongly at legal action. Flexihostings suspended my account. Given the time difference I had no idea until I awoke to a fine Donegal morning to find that it had happened.

Once the nature of the issues was established I immediately used my author rights on the Celtic Network (TCN) to tell the online Celtic community of what had happened. Andy Muirhead of Scotzine graciously allowed me to publish a piece about why I was offline. The very day I was offline, HMRC applied to have funds frozen in Rangers' bank account. It was a massive PR own goal for Archie and his "stakeholders". It also coincided with the closing of the summer transfer window and, as I had predicted, the billionaire had not delivered the Barcelona first team for training at Murray Park.

Utilising Scotzine I broke the story that the club had not turned down a "mystery bid" of £9m for Nikica Jelavić. In fact it was a fantasy that had emanated from Rangers' director of football, Gordon Smith. My web hosting company could not give me any guarantee that if there were similar unfounded complaints that they would not do exactly the same again and suspend the account. Despite having recently paid for another year of service I quickly found a new hosting company.

The day Rangers went into administration I got an email from the young entrepreneur who looks after my server needs these days. His email was a simple one liner: "Rangers. Looks like you were right!" I was. Maybe that made the guys on the sports desks that wee bit tetchier.

The inhabitants of Planet *Fitba* increasingly voted with their fingers and migrated to the new media outlets for their news on what was actually happening at Rangers. The day that the BBC broadcast the second Mark Daly documentary, the Rangers Tax Case blog won the Orwell Prize for political blogging. It was brilliant timing. The view of this writer and "RTC" was that the story was out there about Rangers but the mainstream media was, err, hesitant about going after it.

When football supporters ranted about the inadequacies of Scottish hacks they in fact meant sports journalists. When I had been writing about the "Famine Song" in 2008 and 2009 I was very clear that I wanted the story in the news pages and not in the sports section. I had long suspected that the sports guys in the big Scottish titles had been over mighty subjects at their papers. They could claim to be the main reason for the circulation and therefore anything in the news section that infringed on their turf might hit sales. It was always a winning argument. The sports desk rules supreme. It was another fatal pathogen in the Rangers story. It was the reputation of Scottish sports journalism that died.

The simple truth is that much of the material about Rangers' financial fiasco was above the pay grade of the basic football writer. Hugh Keevins admitted that on Radio Clyde when they had Alex Thomson of Channel 4 News in the studio. Despite pleading ignorance about matters relating to "corporate governance", they did not get a pass from Mr Thomson because they couldn't answer him on the question of why they didn't go and ask someone about this financial stuff.

I have witnessed the clubby, back-slapping nature of the Glasgow sports lobby. That they tugged the forelock to Rangers and their alpha male owner David Murray is beyond debate. However, this docility towards the people they were writing about was also evident across the city at Kerrydale Street. I attended the Celtic AGM in 2011 as a shareholder. I asked for press accreditation from the PR people at Celtic. There was an interesting exchange of text messages with the Celtic press officer about my being allowed entry to the post-AGM press conference. Perhaps there was a concern that I would ask the wrong type of questions. They were right about that.

By the time I had run around the stadium to the main door and got into the boardroom the usual suspects were all in place. I sat beside Hugh Keevins just as the new Celtic chairman, Ian Bankier, was being paraded to the hack pack like a nervous deb at the Palace. He had described himself to the AGM as a "lifelong Celtic supporter". However, my sources had informed me that the self-made man wasn't that interested in association football, never mind the Hoops. As a young man his main interest had been rugby and there were sound business reasons for having someone with Mr Bankier's CV replace Dr John Reid on the Celtic board. Someone in the Parkhead hierarchy thought it necessary to fabricate a past as a Celtic supporter for the new chairman. In the intelligence community this is called "a legend". Among fitba supporters it's called "pish".

I asked the new guy about his first Celtic game and his first Celtic hero. On planet soccer, never mind Planet *Fitba*, these are the two questions that are industry standards when establishing the credentials of any supporters of any team anywhere. The answer wasn't immediately forthcoming from the new chairman and I remember the Celtic press officer looking a touch nervous; may have been my imagination though.

After some stumbling, Mr Bankier, perhaps to establish his Celtic-supporting credentials, informed the press conference of the name of the Catholic school he went to. I had asked what his first Celtic game was and the name of his first Celtic hero, not about his schooling. It was embarrassing stuff.

When I arrived at the press event a softball question was being lobbed at Dr John Reid by Hugh Keevins for him to smash out of the park, along the lines of "Do you think the Celtic fans realise how lucky they are to have Dermot Desmond as a major shareholder in the club?"[1] Oh, this was tough stuff. I then asked a question of the Celtic CEO. I put to him a scenario where Neil Lennon came to him in the January transfer window and asked for two players that, in the opinion of the Celtic manager, were required for the Parkhead club to win the SPL. In that situation would the Celtic board authorise borrowing to purchase the players? It was exactly the question that had been buzzing around the AGM. Lawwell stated some figures about how much the club had spent on players. I asked a secondary question. "Was that a net spend?" "It doesn't matter if it's a net spend," countered the Celtic CEO. An

---

1   http://www.philmacgiollabhain.ie/the-invisible-owner/

awful realisation fell on me that Mr Lawwell actually thought that this was a credible answer.

At the start of that season the Parkhead club had just sold their star player, Aiden McGeady, a product of their youth academy, to the Russian team Spartak Moscow, for £9.5m. It was excellent business and it had helped fund Neil Lennon's rebuilding of the squad. However, one did not need to be a football expert to know that with McGeady gone the squad had been weakened. That the Celtic CEO possibly thought that his initial answer would be sufficient told me more about the assembled hack pack than it did about Peter Lawwell. As on the sports field, you can only beat the opposition that is put in front of you.

It really wasn't going well for the PR guy who was looking increasingly like a *consigliore* who had just realised that his family had pissed off Michael Corleone. Lawwell offered up a wonderful prize as he tried to bat away my pesky question: "We're not fixated on zero debt." I hadn't asked that question, but it was gratefully received.

The vignette is worth relating here because it shows that the tame lobby system in Glasgow didn't operate solely for Rangers' benefit. My enduring memory of the press conference were the glances directed my way from the hacks in the room. It was clear that I didn't know the rules. These guys in the room knew that what you do is throw softball questions and get easily digestible bytes. That usually suited everyone nicely.

One of the terms that I still recall from my early days as an undergraduate sociologist is "common sense inventory". It is what outsiders do in a situation, just by dint of not knowing the form. I was, and remain, outside the Glasgow football lobby. This gave me a freedom to ask questions and go after stories that someone working there full time could not.

Martin O'Neill said that the people who matter in the game are those who play and those who pay. The latter have been consistently shortchanged by a press pack that has been too close and too chummy to the people they should have been investigating. When I first wrote of impending financial implosion at Ibrox I started at the top, the very top.

Sir David Murray has led a charmed life with the Scottish press, best summed up when he split from his wife, Louise. In a media with a voracious appetite for personal scandal and tittle-tattle not one line about the couple's split graced the pages of the tabloids. Murray spent years engaging and wooing the Scottish press. He ensured Endell Laird, *Daily Record* editor in the late 1980s through to the mid-1990s, travelled in five-star style with the Rangers board to a Champions League tie in France. That cosy relationship with *Daily Record* editors continued with Bruce Waddell, editor of the paper until 2012. Bruce, brother of columnist Gordon Waddell, was a guest of Mr Murray in France; there are those who claim he was so exceptionally close to Mr Murray he received almost daily calls from the Rangers guru offering advice on editorial matters.

Murray's relationship was certainly cemented when Sir Angus Grossart became chairman of the Scottish Daily Record and Sunday Mail Ltd and main board director of Trinity Mirror plc (formerly the Mirror Group). He resigned from both Trinity and the *Daily Record* boards in 2007. Sir Angus McFarlane McLeod Grossart, to use his Sunday name, is a former vice chairman of the Royal Bank of Scotland and his connections with David Murray are plentiful. Sir Angus was, until 2008, a director of Murray Sports Limited and a director of Murray Group Holdings Limited until 1999. In the 2005 Murray International Holdings Limited annual report it is noted that Sir Angus, a director and co-founder of Noble Grossart Investments plc, then owned 5.5% of the issued share capital of Murray International Holdings Limited.

In the 1990s there were few voices that questioned Mr Murray or Rangers. One was Alf Young, an award-winning financial writer at the *Herald*. Over three pages in robust terms the *Herald* questioned the financial state of the Murray empire. One phrase that was taken out of the story through financial and legal pressure was "trading insolvently". Alf Young recalled in *Scotland on Sunday* that Rangers' descent into oblivion can be traced back to the late 1980s. He said:

> When the news came through that he [Murray] was buy-
> ing Rangers, I was as astonished as everyone else. Some three
> years on, with the early 1990s recession beginning to bite,
> my editor called me into his office. "I've heard there are seri-
> ous problems with David Murray's property interests. Could
> you check it out?" he suggested. I talked to my contacts
> and checked out the relevant company accounts. It rapidly
> became clear there were problems. They were big ones . . .
> And this was happening at the same time as a recently
> acquired Rangers overdraft had tripled in the space of a year.
> All in all, my editor's whispers had substance. This was a
> story of considerable significance for both the bank and for
> the credibility of David Murray's growing business empire.
> When the stories on what I had found appeared, he went
> ballistic. There were demands I be sacked.

I have never spoken to David Murray from that day to this. I once found myself in his company, tried to broker a peace and was right royally snubbed for my pains. I'm telling you all this because it illustrates how the events of recent days – plunging one half of the Old Firm into ignominious administration and threatening its very existence in its present form – have been incubating for a very long time indeed.[1]

But did the Murray empire claim an even higher media-profile victim? Jim Cassidy, the editor of the *Sunday Mail* for around ten years, was sacked in 1999.[2] Cassidy had a highly volatile relationship with Murray from the moment they first met. Minutes after their first meeting, at lunch with Graeme Souness, Walter Smith and the *Record* editor, Endell Laird, David Murray stormed to colleagues: "That Cassidy doesn't like me."

Perhaps Murray was being astute, as Cassidy, one of the first Catholics to edit a national paper in Scotland, believed his paper should have no friends except the readership. Jim Cassidy once famously hired a hearse to be pictured outside Celtic Park when he thought the club was about to die. Interestingly, many close to the "rebels" who took over Celtic claimed it was the turning point that forced the Kellys and Whites out and opened the door to McCann and Dempsey. Although Celtic fans saw the hearse stunt as gleeful hand rubbing by a hostile media, Cassidy is, in fact, a huge Celtic fan and wanted to sound a warning that the club was about to die.

In a series of rows with Murray over the paper's coverage and analysis of Rangers, Murray went over Cassidy's head to complain. Sir Angus Grossart would pass on the "anger" to David Montgomery, chief executive of the Mirror Group. Montgomery, a unionist from Northern Ireland, warned Cassidy but backed him knowing that the *Sunday Mail* was, relatively speaking, the best performer in the Mirror stable. It was not until Montgomery was dismissed and Trinity took over that Cassidy was fired.

Those close to the fraught relationship between Cassidy and Murray recall a phone call Cassidy took from Murray on an open line during an editorial conference. Murray ranted and shouted for several minutes before Cassidy replied, "David you may shout at Rangers players, you may shout at Rangers directors, you may shout at Rangers managers, you may even shout at Rangers fans but never come on here and shout at me. Do you understand? Do you understand 100%?"

1 http://www.thedrum.co.uk/news/2012/02/20/
   scottish-journalist-alf-young-reveals-former-rangers-chairman-sir-david-murray

2 http://www.guardian.co.uk/media/1999/sep/20/mondaymediasection.comment1

Murray replied that he had never been spoken to like that before, to which Cassidy replied, "Well, phone back any time, David." The line went dead and Cassidy's editorship would soon follow. When Cassidy was removed there weren't many in the Glasgow media village who didn't put two and two together. The lesson was clear: stay in the tent, stay on message and you'll do OK.

Murray had a hand in launching quite a few media careers in Glasgow. From 2000 to 2006 Murray had another ally on the *Daily Record* and *Sunday Mail* board, Steve Sampson.[1] Sampson was a brash and boisterous journalist, who had for a time edited David Murray's doomed paper, the *Sunday Scot*. When the paper sunk without trace Sampson remained close to the Ibrox leader. He was the founder and CEO of First Press Publishing, which he co-owned with David Murray until they sold it to Trinity Mirror in 2000. First Press published *Rangers News* for a time and, much to the consternation of many in Scottish media circles, *Celtic View*.

When he bid farewell to Trinity Mirror in 2006, sweet talking Steve persuaded Scottish Enterprise to part-fund a new venture called TalentNation to the tune of £1m. The ebullient Steve was nowhere to be seen at the Court of Session in September 2011 when the company was placed in the hands of liquidators Grant Thornton. It was explained that Scottish Enterprise was keen to discover what they described as "misappropriated sums".[2]

Other keen and fresh-faced youngsters also had their careers launched on the doomed Murray Sunday, including the present *Daily Record* editor-in-chief, Allan Rennie, the former editor, Bruce Waddell, and several others, but it was on the sporting side that the *Sunday Scot* boys really blossomed. Ian King, for many years the voice of Scottish football on the *Sun*, worked on the ill-fated title as did Mark Guidi, who joined the *Sunday Mail*, and George Cheyne, who became sports editor at the *Sunday Mail*. Another junior in the *Sunday Scot* ranks was Keith Jackson, step-brother of *Desert Island Discs* presenter Kirsty Young. Their father, Joe Jackson, once head of Glasgow's CID, was a fabled figure in the police ranks. He abandoned Kirsty and her mum when she was a baby.[3]

Like many powerful men Murray sought to control the flow of information about himself and his activities. The reticence to go after

1   www.linkedin.com/pub/steve-sampson/b/27a/5b1

2   http://www.thedrum.co.uk/news/2011/09/13/
    scottish-enterprise-succeeds-liquidating-steve-sampsons-talentnation-over

3   http://www.express.co.uk/posts/view/64862/Why-I-abandoned-my-daughter-Kirsty

Murray as he sent Rangers and Murray International Holdings into a debt spiral was down to a combination of factors. Firstly, the experience of Jim Cassidy of the *Sunday Mail* was never far from anyone's mind in the Glasgow newspaper world. That's what happened if you crossed Murray. In the late 1990s it looked like his reign at Ibrox would last forever as he openly spoke about establishing a family dynasty at Rangers.

As well as the manifestation of his power there was also Murray's legendary generosity to quiescent members of the media. Favoured hacks could enjoy free holidays in France, the Channel Islands and in the Highlands. Professionally he kept his domesticated journos in "exclusives". There is, of course, no such thing as a free lunch, let alone a free vacation.

There were certain subjects that were off limits. Graham Spiers found this out when he started to do his job. The Rangers debt was becoming potentially fatal and the fans were showing no sign of abandoning their birthright to go wading in Fenian blood. Spiers, the chief sports writer on the *Herald*, went after Murray on the debt and the Rangers fans for their bigotry. Spiers has been open and honest about the realities of being frozen out.

However, there is life beyond the lobby and actually it isn't too bad out here. This book is about what can be achieved when you deliberately place yourself outside the tent and, using new media, go after the story that the guys in the tent aren't allowed to go near on their own terms. When Rangers went into administration a good friend, a veteran Scottish political journalist, joked with me on the phone and said, "I suppose the world is beating a path to your door." When I told him that I had not received a single media request about the Rangers administration story he was shocked. He asked me if I considered his surprise to be a manifestation of his naiveté apropos the realities of Glasgow sports journalism. I couldn't disagree. I told him that as he was a denizen of Holyrood and a political correspondent he clearly had no idea. We've been friends for too long for him to have taken it personally.

It reminded me of the furore over "Dallasgate" in late 2010. I had broken the story, on Saturday 6 November, that on the day of the Pope's state visit to Britain the SFA's head of referee development had passed on an email insinuating that His Holiness himself was a danger to children. I broke the story and developed it over the next three weeks. My work drew praise from the likes of Roy Greenslade, the *Guardian* media blogger and professor of journalism at the City University in London. Even as Hugh Dallas was sacked there wasn't a single mention in any Scottish title of the journalist who had got the scoop and run with the story. Senior people in the NUJ said to me that it was very poor form.

If I didn't know any better I would swear that these guys on the sports desks were taking it personally. A professor of journalism, an award-winning war correspondent and the president of the National Union of Journalists have endorsed this book and, ipso facto, my work, without hesitation. Yet the people who were asleep at the wheel of this story now actively ignore a fellow NUJ member who was on the story three years ago and hasn't left it alone since.

When I was interviewed in June 2012 by veteran Scottish sports journalist Kevin McKenna for a *New Statesman* feature about the demise of Rangers, he noted that despite being consistently ahead of the game my work was being disregarded by the mainstream media in Scotland. This was in stark contrast to organisations like Channel 4 News and the *Guardian* who had both hired me to work on the Rangers story and the Lennon letter bomb trial respectively. Kevin said to me over a lengthy telephone interview that he was glad I wasn't taking it personally. I told him that there was little chance of that as only the people in my family and very close friends elicit that response from me. As with Hugh Dallas, it wasn't personal, it was strictly business.

The material in this section should convince any reasonable person that the greatest scandal in the history of British sport was largely left to bloggers and citizen journalists by the guys on the Glasgow sports desks. This happened on their patch and on their watch. There is now a considerable amount of unedifying, mutual alibi-providing going on as history is rewritten about who did what with the Rangers story. There is embarrassing, get-your-story-right stuff going on among the hacks about how they were on this one from the start. However, the people who matter – the public – now know that the sports hacks took freebies and easily digested morsels of safe info wrapped up as exclusives from the man who owned Rangers for two decades.

Addicted to succulent lamb, provided free of charge, their journalistic sinews atrophied so much that when they were told to call Craig Whyte a billionaire in 2010 they meekly complied. The public paid for their free lunch. There were genuine exclusives to be had but the Scottish hacks were too craven, fearful, tribal and venal to go after them. Instead, they became PR flunkies for Murray's vanity project, an ego trip that poisoned the national game in Scotland. They should have been investigating the set-up at Rangers instead of enjoying five-star junkets. They failed their trade and they failed the national game. That's why they are Scotland's other shame.

What is your point, caller?

28.12.10

Consider this, dear reader. Completely hypothetically of course. During a live radio phone-in a major story breaks. Moreover the subject matter is of great interest to the radio show's listeners. It's breaking news! That is a term that all journalists, whether they be in print, broadcast or online should drop everything to attend to. The broadcast journalists know from the callers that the story has broken. The guys in the studio know that they haven't broken the story, but their show then gets a call from the journalist that did break the story. He identifies himself as the journalist that broke the story and offers to speak on air, for free, to further elaborate on the story so far. This should be good news for the radio station. Actually it IS good news for any radio station.

He gives his number and waits for a call back. He waits and waits. Wouldn't you think that the radio show, with a duty to its listeners, would give them that on air exclusive – which was being offered for free – and call the journalist back? You would, wouldn't you?

This is a freebie for the radio station from the guy (an NUJ member) that broke the original story and has been lauded by a professor of journalism in a quality newspaper for his role in doing so. Now he is offering this new development, a fresh scoop, to the radio show. If the journalists on the radio show considered that their primary duty was to the listeners then I think they should have called that journalist back.

Of course if the said radio show, hypothetically speaking of course, is part of a lobby system that doesn't want their listeners to be fully informed then the journalist might be silly phoning them in the first place.

Clyde 1 Superscoreboard

27.01.11

I am genuinely surprised at the furore that my call into Clyde 1 *Superscoreboard* about the Rangers tax case has caused in certain circles. I am a bit surprised at this because I said very little on air that was new.[1]

For the most part what I stated in my short call to *Superscoreboard*

---

1   http://www.youtube.com/watch?v=cynMmAXFBuw

had been in the public domain apropos Rangers outstanding tax case with HMRC back in May 2010. The figures published by the *News of the World* (a piece I worked on as a freelancer) were as stated on Clyde. I then published a fuller account of my interview with Martin Bain on this site.[1] As stated then on this site and in the *News of the World* the "core amount" of tax that HMRC claim they are owed by Rangers is £24m. Interest accrued at that point was £12m (the meter is still running on that, but that figure was accurate in May last year), with the figure for the tax penalties being around £25m. However, penalties are negotiable. The core amount (the £36m) is not.

So the first-tier tax tribunal is debating whether or not RFC owe this £36m circa. It will resume again in May. It is scheduled to take three weeks to conclude its business. The three judges will then retire and consider their verdict. The penalties will be decided in a further tribunal. This is a split that RFC have asked for and their request was granted. Perhaps their reasoning is that should they lose the case on the core amount they may be able to finance that. That is merely my conjecture. Most companies get it all over with at once, which reduces the hefty legal bills. Why do it this way with double the legal bills?

Essentially Rangers would have to find someone willing to lend them £36m to pay HMRC. Perhaps the brouhaha after my appearance on Clyde 1 *Superscoreboard* was that these figures and the seriousness of the tax case faced by Rangers FC are slowly starting to sink in to people who, heretofore, have been in denial.

Finally let me record my thanks to the lads at Clyde 1 *Superscoreboard* for taking the call. The most important asset of any football club is the supporters. This is as true for Rangers FC as it is for any football club. The supporters put their hopes, dreams, passion and disposable income into the club. The people that own and run football clubs should be mindful of that and, at all times, level with the fans.

Rangers tax case. Questions that deserve an answer

12.03.11

I find the almost complete lack of journalistic "digging" into the Rangers

---

1   http://www.philmacgiollabhain.com/taxing-times-for-rangers/

tax case among the press pack in Scotland utterly fascinating. This is a huge story yet only Darrell King in Scotland seems intent on unearthing the truth. For example a rudimentary study of published figures throws up very relevant questions that have, so far, not been answered.

The following amounts were contributed by Murray International Holdings (MIH) to the Murray Group Management Limited Remuneration Trust. This is the same trust into which Rangers FC funnelled player salaries and contractual bonuses. It is the use of this trust that has landed RFC in the tax tribunal. Here are the figures:

MIH Contributions to Employee Benefit Trusts (EBTs)

2009 £3,211.00
2008 £2,849.00
2007 £6,874.00
2006 £9,663.00
2005 £3,892.00
2004 £2,951.00
2003 £2,721.00
2002 £1,233.00
Total: £33,394.00

The only explanation of these expenses (which appear under Staff Costs in the Notes to the Accounts in MIH's Annual Reports) is: the "Murray Group Management Limited Remuneration Trust" was established as an independently administered trust, to provide incentives to certain employees. Contributions to the Trust are charged to the Group profit and loss account in the year incurred.

These figures inevitably lead to some fairly pressing questions. Which "certain employees"? I asked Martin Bain in May 2010 during an interview about the Rangers tax case if he himself had been paid through an EBT. His answer was "that is a matter for me and the tax office". When I asked him if it was only players that had been paid though the EBT he stated that it was "employees of the trust". When pressed several times to state that it was ONLY players he restated his answer "employees of the trust". So who did financially benefit from this trust? Was Sir David Murray one of them? If so, why did Sir David Murray not declare a conflict of interest to Rangers' shareholders?

The UK Directors' Code states that directors should avoid conflicts of interest, and where they cannot be avoided, they should be declared. No conflict of interest in signing off on Rangers' tax affairs was disclosed to Rangers' shareholders.

Was Sir David Murray's judgment in fulfilling his responsibilities as a company director clouded by potentially huge personal withdrawals through the same Employee Benefit Trust which has landed Rangers in so much trouble with HMRC? Could Sir David's actions 'lift the corporate veil' and expose him to personal liability following an administration filing by Rangers FC?

Based on the numbers above, Sir David could be looking at a very substantial tax bill related to his own withdrawals from the EBT. Is Sir David's decision to transfer ownership of 95% of his MIH shares (and therefore his controlling interest in Rangers FC) to an offshore trust directed by Declan Kenny, an Irish born accountant, an attempt to avoid personal responsibility for any financial disaster that might befall Rangers after the tax tribunal returns its final answer?

Supporters of Rangers FC deserve answers to these pertinent questions.

The failures of lobby journalism

15.03.11

A source of mine was on the plane to Holland last week with the official Rangers party and the attendant hack pack. He noted with interest that despite having Rangers chairman Alastair Johnston and influential director Donald Muir on the plane not a single journalist made an approach to these two men. Yet these two are the main players in THE major Scottish football story since Celtic were rescued by Fergus McCann in 1994.

At one point Walter Smith more or less snapped his fingers and he had eager hacks around him gasping for his wisdom and his fatherly approval. Meanwhile the two movers and shakers at Rangers weren't troubled by a single question. This is lobby journalism in action.

How the Rangers tax case went mainstream

01.04.11

It is a year since I started working on the Rangers tax case. I initially took the story to the *News of the World* Scottish edition. They were very interested. As part of standing the story up I contacted Martin Bain, the

Rangers CEO. I had two telephone conversations on the morning of Saturday, 15 May 2010. I put the basic facts of the story that we were going to run with the following day. He was courteous and helpful.

The following day the *News of the World* published the figures on the tax case that I had secured for them. This was the first time that these figures had been in the mainstream media. Those published figures were a genuine scoop. The "core amount" that HMRC considered was owed to them in unpaid taxes was £24m. Added to that was £12m in interest payments with potentially £25m in penalties. The entire bad news was ballpark, £60m.

The *News of the World* in typical style had the headline "Simply the bust!" At the time the blue half of Glasgow simply didn't believe the news. The following morning Hugh Keevins said on Radio Clyde that Rangers were consulting their lawyers about the story. No writs were issued to the *News of the World*, not even a stiff letter.

With the passing of the last 12 months it has been interesting how the tax case has gone mainstream from that weekend. It is now not contested that Rangers are in tax court facing HMRC on the other side of the room. Moreover the figures of the case aren't contested either. I got to restate the facts of the case, this time on Radio Clyde on 26 January this year. After that the story went viral.

I was invited onto the show as a journalist because I had broken the news on this site three days earlier that the club had made an approach to HMRC to settle the case for £10m. It was another scoop. Jim Delahunt and Darrell King listened in silence as I calmly stated the realities of the case, the facts and the figures.[1]

Since late January it has been obligatory to insert at least one sentence on the Rangers tax case in any piece regarding the financial situation of the club. Since then there hasn't been anyone in sports journalism in Scotland or anyone associated with the Ibrox club that has contested the basic facts of the case that are currently in the public domain.

Think back a year when this story was broken. Consider the incredulity, the anger, the denial. Denial is the default setting in most humans when faced with bad news. Dr Elisabeth Kübler-Ross would recognise the collective grieving of Rangers fans on this one.

There is more to come on the Rangers tax case and when it is released into the public domain I expect a similar "no it can't be true" response. After "Denial" comes "Anger" and there has been plenty of that. There has also been some evidence of the next stage: "Bargaining". When I spoke to a senior Scottish sports journalist in the AVIVA stadium in

1 http://www.philmacgiollabhain.com/rangers-board-desperate-to-settle-tax-case/

February he accepted the reality of the tax case, but said that Sir David Murray would be "morally compelled" to pick up the tab from the tax-man. The next stage is "Depression". It's OK, that passes in time into "Acceptance".

Today of all days the club chairman Alastair Johnston, no one's fool, admitted that the club could go bust of the tax case is lost and he isn't joking.[1] When asked if the club's very existence was under threat if the case went against Rangers, he said: "The reality is that 'is it possible?' Yes. There could be a judgment . . . and at the point the club can't pay. There is a point in time you can't pay and accessing all the resources, yes, you couldn't pay." Asked if the club could go bust, Mr Johnston nodded.

Finally the penny will drop. The tax case is real.

Paul Baxendale Walker

05.04.11

I have recently had reason to look over interview notes I made last year. The notes were made when I was preparing an article on Mr Paul Baxendale Walker for a Scottish Sunday newspaper. He is the man that provided the expertise to construct the tax efficiency strategy of Sir David Murray's empire. That empire, of course, includes Rangers FC.

I had first seen his name mentioned apropos Rangers tax case on the Rangers Media website. When I contacted him last autumn he was very happy to speak On The Record about his work, and confirmed his role in helping to establish Employee Benefit Trusts for Rangers. He graciously afforded me his time with two lengthy telephone interviews. The second interview was me going back to him to fact-check and ask layman's questions for clarification on this complex area of taxation law. He was courteous and helpful. He did make one remark that I found very interesting. He told me that I was the first journalist to contact him about the Rangers tax case.

I was surprised by this because by this time the story about the Ibrox club's potential taxation difficulties and Mr Baxendale Walker's role as the club's tax expert had been in the public domain for several months. I have written before that there has been an element of denial among the Rangers fraternity about the seriousness of this tax case. Of course that

---

1   http://news.stv.tv/scotland/west-central/240551-rangers-debt-rises-to-29m/

fraternity stretches into the media in Scotland. Potentially the news is so bad for Rangers FC that people simply don't want to think about it. Now with the "second half" of the first-tier tax tribunal about to start this month the "Denial" phase of Rangers tax grief is no longer tenable.

This vignette reveals far more about the professional standards of sports journalism in Scotland than it does about the fiscal difficulties currently afflicting Scotland's establishment club.

A question of life or death for Rangers

10.04.11

I would imagine that by now the spat between James Traynor and Chick Young on BBC Scotland which happened live on air last weekend has probably gone viral on Planet *Fitba*.[1]

As in life it is ambiguity that causes most of the misunderstandings in journalism and the nod of the head delivered by Rangers chairman Alastair Johnston to an imprecise question left the way open for confusion. The USA-based businessman was apparently asked by STV, in a press conference for the broadcast media, if he thought that the club "could go bust". Mr Johnston, we are told, nodded in answer to the question.[2]

What precisely does "bust" mean in this context? What was Alastair Johnston nodding in agreement to? I have written here consistently that should RFC lose the tax case against HMRC then I see no alternative but to go into administration. Does that mean "go bust"? Of course administration can, in some rare circumstances, be a route into liquidation. Planet Third Lanark. So what did Alastair Johnston nod his head to? What was he asked?

It pains me slightly to agree with James Traynor, but the lack of clarity in the question and the failure to seek clarification does render the "scoop" rather inert. Had the "A" word been used in the question about the prognosis for the club if HMRC win then that would have been a story for sure. Had the chairman in expanding on his answer also conjectured with the "L" word then that would have been a real story lead. In the end the RFC chairman was asked an ambiguous question couched using an imprecise word. OK, he nodded, but what was he nodding to?

---

1 http://www.scotzine.com/2011/04/radio-scotland-descends-into-civil-war/

2 http://news.stv.tv/scotland/west-central/240551-rangers-debt-rises-to-29m/

This confusion was the author of confusion and this was played out; live on air, between Traynor and Young. Sorry to bring precision into this, but that is what journalism is meant to be about. People may dislike Mr Traynor's abrasive style, but his critique of Chick Young's "story" is spot on. There is no way I would have gone back to an editor with such an important scoop based on the nod of a head. Having nodded and then spoken about the difficulties that the club would face in paying the tax bill Alastair Johnston should have been asked if his nod of the head meant that he foresaw administration or administration which would lead to liquidation. The former is a racing cert should the club lose the case against HMRC, but the latter scenario is not impossible.

Asking important questions

06.05.11

I recently wrote on here about the on-air spat between James Traynor and Chick Young about the importance of asking precise questions. In that much listened-to tiff I came down on the side of the *Daily Record* man despite his abrasive ad hominem style on BBC Radio Scotland. James Traynor was, I thought, correct to observe that had Chick Young brought him a story based on a nod of the head he would have sent him back to the Rangers chairman for spoken clarification, but also to put a specific question to him. The term "go bust" was simply too ambiguous as it could mean administration or liquidation.[1]

However, similar questions can be put to Mr Traynor over the same story. How many times, for example, since last October has James Traynor had the opportunity to ask Martin Bain about the tax case? I don't know the answer to that. However, the following I do know.

When Rangers were called to the first-tier tax tribunal last October they were in possession of three important documents. The first one is called a "Citation Notice". It is, in effect, the summons to attend the tax court. On the Citation Notice there is the "Amount of Underpayment". That is non-negotiable. A Citation Notice without that amount on it would be legally incompetent. The Amount of Underpayment is the "Core Amount". It does not include interest accrued or possible penalties, just the tax that should have been paid in the first place according

---

1 http://www.philmacgiollabhain.com/a-question-of-life-or-death-for-rangers/

to HMRC. So as of last October Rangers senior personnel and their legal team have known how much the tax man thinks he is owed.

However, since the tax story broke last year the spin has endured that "no one knows how much the tax bill really is". This is nonsense. The amount on the Citation Notice served on Rangers is £24m. As well as the Citation Notice the club would have received two other important documents. The "Skeleton Arguments" and the "Statement of Case" would leave the Rangers top men in no doubt about what HMRC was going to put to them in the tribunal. The term "Disguised Remuneration" is how HMRC have characterised the Rangers use of the Employee Benefit Trusts. That is in the pre-tribunal paperwork.

So there isn't any doubt about the amount of tax underpayment in the minds of the top people at Rangers. They also knew what HMRC were going to allege in the first tier tribunal once it got under way. The following information apropos the documentation of tax tribunals would be known to any journalist on a business or finance desk in any major title. So a sports journalist could have been assisted with these facts by a colleague quite simply. That is why newspapers employ different specialists on different desks.

Interestingly I have not read any of these facts in Mr Traynor's copy. I can only conjecture that this is because he does not know, because if he did know these facts he would share them with the public as that is his duty as a journalist. So if Scotland's major sports journalist is not aware of these facts it is because either: (1) He has not asked Martin Bain these questions; (2) He asked and Mr Bain refused to answer. If it is (2) then he should be telling his readers that he put these important questions to Martin Bain and he refused to answer.

I put a series of tough questions to Martin Bain about the Rangers tax case back in May 2010. He was courteous and helpful. Some questions he did refuse to answer and I noted a "no comment" to my question. The bottom line was I WAS asking appropriate questions of public interest.[1] If James Traynor came back to me from an interview with Martin Bain and had not pressed him on these specific questions apropos the tax case then I would send him back to do the job again.

I focus on Mr Traynor because, in my opinion, he has the best "news nose" of any sports journalist in Scotland. Now when you consider these facts think of the questions that journalists in Scotland could have put to Mr Craig Whyte over the past few months . . .

1 http://www.philmacgiollabhain.com/taxing-times-for-rangers/

Breaking the Gordon Smith story

18.06.11

A month ago I was informed by an excellent source that "Alistair McCoist may not be the manager of Rangers by Christmas. This will be irrespective of on-field events." Obviously I wanted this bold statement backed up. Given the position of the source I knew he was in a position to know and I wasn't dismissing it as hot air. My source knows, likes and considers Alistair McCoist a friend and the emotional content of his voice signalled deep unease at what he was telling me. I pressed him for some details. He told me the situation was fluid.

Yesterday my source spoke to me around 10.00 hrs Irish time and said to be near my laptop later in the day. The phone rang around 15.15 hrs and the story came through. "Remember what I told you a couple of weeks ago about Alistair? What I am about to tell you will not help the situation, in fact it could speed up my prediction." He then proceeded to tell me about plans to appoint Gordon Smith in a senior position, possibly as a director. I quickly wrote up some copy. The piece was uploaded around 15.30 hrs.

Then the intrepid investigative journalists from the BBC were onto it. They had an excellent source – this website. Well, actually I got someone to phone them and tell them about it. I like to help.

The chaps at the Beeb called the Rangers FC press department and asked them if the story was true. Now why didn't I think of that? Rangers denied the story.

A BBC source was emailing me as late as 19.59 hrs saying that "both RFC and Whyte's PR people are denying the story". Finally, despite the denials, the BBC had the story on their website by 20.25 hrs. Just after 22.00 hrs it was on the club's official website.

I think it is fair to say the timing of this statement about the appointment of Gordon Smith as director of football was not of Rangers' choosing. Once more, just like the Dallas story, there is no acknowledgement by the old media in Scotland of the journalist who broke the story.[1]

Don't mention the Irishman.

---

1   http://sport.caledonianmercury.com/2010/12/06/
    opinion-dallasgate-and-the-man-with-no-name/00728

Telling the truth about Rangers

07.07.11

Apparently some people have been telling lies about Rangers Football Club. However, I was disappointed that Jack Irvine (of Media House International, Rangers' PR firm) was reported to have not identified these purveyors of untruths about the Scottish champions in this excellent piece by Michael Settle in yesterday's *Herald*.[1]

Liars should be faced down, whoever they are and wherever they may be. Anyone fabricating untruths about Rangers FC should be named, shamed and brought before the courts for defamation. As regular readers of this site will know I have written quite extensively on Rangers FC over the past couple of years. Here is a brief summary of some the stories related to Rangers that I have broken on here:

Murray International Holdings (MIH) – then RFC's parent company – was likely to default on its loans to the bank. The subsequent debt for equity swap and convertible preference share issue in favour of Lloyds' private equity arm proved that this conjecture was well founded.

This site told you that Lloyds Banking Group had effectively taken control of Rangers FC.

Walter Smith, the Rangers manager, later told Chick Young on live radio that the bank was indeed running the club and Alastair Johnston's exit interviews revealed the extent of that control.

This site reported the amount of underpayment in tax being sought from the club by HMRC. I also revealed that Rangers FC had already been billed by HMRC for penalties related to how the club had conducted its tax affairs (and provided the amount).

More recently, of course, I was first to bring Rangers fans the news that Gordon Smith would be the club's new director of football.

Obviously if I had fabricated any of these stories or had erred in any material way Rangers should have issued specific denials. All of these stories have been on the money, and while some were vaguely dismissed (in a "non-denial denial" fashion) by the club at the time of publication, they have all been proven correct with time. (Remember the widely reported misconception that MIH would be responsible for Rangers' tax bills?)

---

1   http://i.imgur.com/Inokd.jpg

Moreover, had these untruths impugned the club's reputation then legal action would surely have ensued. Rangers fans deserve to know exactly what lies have been told about their club and who is telling them. I look forward to the follow up interviews. I can only hope that Mr Irvine gets a bit more specific next time and names names.

It shouldn't be allowed? Shining a light on the financial situation at Rangers

15.08.11

Sometimes a simple choice of words can betray a greater truth. Listen to the exchange between James Traynor and Tom English (4.51 minutes) on BBC Radio Scotland's *Your Call* on Saturday 13 August.[1]

JT: The pictures. These are embarrassing. Aren't they?

TE: They are embarrassing. I don't doubt that Rangers have the money to pay this bill. Right? But it's allowing that picture. You know it was . . . I thought it was mortifying to be honest, to see it.

An interesting choice of words from Tom English: "allowing that picture." This, perhaps, shines a light on the unconscious understanding of the press pack in Scottish football.

Tom English is one of the most respected and experienced journalists working in Scottish football and he certainly knows the basic topography of the SPL. His words hint at an implicit acceptance that Rangers usually get the press coverage they want in Scotland. Well, they didn't last week.

I know that Rangers' PR people fought very hard to prevent those pictures being taken and finding their way onto the front pages of the tabloids in Scotland. The *Sun*, acting on my tip, had their snapper there on Wednesday morning. Taking a belt and braces approach, I also had a freelance photographer there, just in case. I knew there would be just one chance to capture the moment sheriff officers entered Ibrox with the demand from HMRC. He was able to sell his snaps to the *Daily Record*, where he used to work. I only asked that he give me two images for my site for use on the Wednesday – the day the pictures were taken. I was delighted that he sold his pictures because it meant that Scotland's two biggest-selling daily newspapers had the pictures that Rangers didn't want on their front pages.

---

1 http://www.bbc.co.uk/iplayer/console/b0138w3x

Dear reader, this is rare. This is very, very rare.

With the *Record* running the story and the *Sun* "going big" then it wasn't surprising that Sky had a guy outside Ibrox the same day. This was not the media coverage that Rangers wanted on Thursday 11 August. The PR plan since then has been to minimise the significance of the visit of the sheriff officers going into Ibrox. This strategy is aimed primarily at Rangers' own supporters. Perhaps that is why Rangers' director of football went onto Radio Scotland the same day to be interviewed by Traynor and Richard Gordon. The Rangers fans listening, I am sure, would have been looking for reassurance.

The interesting revelation for the listeners would have been the fact that Gordon Smith does not have a hands-on role in transfer negotiations. This is surprising given his knowledge of the game and his previous work as a football agent. Why is he not centrally involved in transfer matters?

I met Gordon in Dublin at the Carling Cup earlier this year (just before he was appointed director of football at Rangers) and had a long chat with him. He certainly knows what it takes to be a Rangers player. He also knows the soccer marketplace inside out. So his non-participation in Rangers' transfer dealings is puzzling. There is definitely a story worth pursuing here for some determined journalist in the Scottish press pack.

Rangers' supporters, especially those who bank roll the club with season ticket money, have legitimate concerns and their questions need to be answered. The primary function of Scottish sports journalism is clear: find the stories that are of public interest and publish them without asking whether powerful institutions will "allow" them or not.

How to defeat churnalism

25.08.11

An excellent piece by Michael Cross in the latest edition of NUJ in-house magazine *The Journalist* (Journalists under the spotlight) mirrored several conversations I have had recently about the onward march of "churnalism". This is a term coined by Nick Davies of the *Guardian* and it means the practice in media organisations of recycling press releases rather than doing original reporting.

With cutbacks in the print sector in Britain continuing to

diminish the quality of the product then those journalists left are increasingly vulnerable to being turned into churnalists. In churning out copy almost wholly based on press releases the journalist becomes a mere secretary of the PR professional. This is not in anyone's interest. It devalues and deskills good decent journalists and it diminishes the product. Subsequently churnalism must be exposed where it appears.

I would therefore commend the following website set up by the Media Standards Trust – www.churnalism.com.[1] The site's "churn engine" claims that it can match a segment of text from a press release to articles published across the web by national newspapers in the UK. So I'm crowd sourcing this one. My tekkie guy informs me that the regular visitors to this site continue to grow exponentially. I will be interested to learn what examples of churnalism that you all can find in your favourite newspapers.

The first rough draft of history

09.09.11

We journalists are a competitive bunch for sure, but there is respect too. Sometimes a piece comes along that, with hindsight, just stuns you when you gauge its courage and prescience.[2] (The online piece carries a link to the famous *Daily Record* article, penned by Keith Jackson on 18 November 2010, which described Craig Whyte as a billionaire.) In the age of the press release churnalist it is heartening to see one of my trade be bang on the money with a story. Check the date. Back in November . . .

Journalism is the first rough draft of history. It's just that some journalists have a better grasp of the historical moment than others. It would be churlish of me not to acknowledge that. It was also a brave piece. It would have been easy to simply stay on the negativity bandwagon. I was a doubter, a sceptic, perhaps blinded by my own club allegiance I failed to see the facts that were staring me in the face. So I have to be big enough to admit that I got it wrong about the Whyte revolution. Totally wrong.

---

1   http://churnalism.com/
2   http://www.dailyrecord.co.uk/football/spl/rangers/2010/11/18/craig-whyte-profile-the-scots-billionaire-on-the-brink-of-taking-over-the-club-he-loves-86908-22722617/

Now with the transfer window closed there have been seven, yes SEVEN quality acquisitions. Not only that, but a £9m offer for Rangers' star striker Nikica Jelavić was contemptuously rebuffed. Only a club in rude financial health would be able to refuse such an advance.

I am even hearing that a major sponsorship deal could also be in the offing. Details are sketchy, I am only guessing (I certainly don't have Keith Jackson's excellent sources that's for sure!), but perhaps a major business from one of the tiger economies of East Asia would be interested in the Rangers brand of Britishness, fair play and dignity. Obviously I have no certainometer and I'm just hearing snippets, but the Rangers brand is rightly attracting corporate suitors. Obviously with the club now on such a sound financial footing any minor cash flow difficulties won't present any problem. In fact with Mr Whyte as owner it is almost as if Rangers are owned by a bank. Indeed as Keith wrote in his piece on Mr Whyte: ". . . in charge of a vast business empire, his wealth is off the radar."

I'm afraid that the Rangers' city rivals will just have to get accustomed to this new economic reality in the Old Firm duel. I should have seen that sooner. I really should.

My questions for Craig Whyte

13.09.11

Yesterday at an unknown location, in an unknown universe I was invited to attend a press conference with the largely unknown owner of Rangers, Craig Whyte. OK, OK, I made that bit up. However, here are the questions that I WOULD have put to him. As a little media exercise, dear reader, see if any of those questions were put to him by the handpicked hacks at Ibrox yesterday.

(1) You say that you have purchased Rangers' debt in full. Can you unequivocally state that the floating charge on Rangers assets that secured the £18m debt has been assigned to you (or RFCG Ltd) without any encumbrances?

(2) A search of the public records for your business history reveals no transactions or business sales that would have yielded you a sum close to £18m. How did you finance the purchase of Rangers' debt from Lloyds?

(3) During and shortly after the takeover period it has been widely reported that you and your media representatives were briefing anyone who would listen that:
   – You are a billionaire or a man with off-the-radar wealth
   – That you would be investing £20m over four years
   – That £15m would be front-loaded
   Do you deny that such claims were made?

(4) You claim that the recent legal cases over payments were just part of good financial management to ensure that you do not pay for bills unnecessarily. This strategy resulted in you paying an extra £10,000 in court costs (before your own legal fees) on a £35,000 bill. On what planet is incurring an extra 29% on a bill a measure of good and conservative financial management?

(5) Lastly . . . how much of a funding gap has been revealed during your cash flow projections until the tax case process is over? In other words, can Rangers fund itself from operations or does the club require a cash injection? If there is a funding gap, how much is it and how do you propose to "fill the hole"? Will this funding gap be met by you contributing additional funds or will player sales in January be necessary?

Yesterday, in an unknown universe, all of these questions were answered in full.

And in the blue corner . . .

28.09.11

I have to admit that I find the world of PR companies horribly fascinating. For example it may seem just a tad ironic to some that the PR firm employed by Rangers' owner Craig Whyte to try and hold back the marauding hordes of journalists wanting to know the grisly details of monies owed to HM Revenue & Customs by Rangers are also hard at work for a controversial true blue who wants to be a crucial part of HM government. In the strange world of PR such conflicts are hardly worth a passing thought, it would seem.

The firm riding the two white horses is none other than Hay and McKerron. While not quite wearing the Queen's colour, the gallant duo released a press release on behalf of their new "true blue" client Ruth

Davidson, the lady who wants to be the leader of the Conservative and Unionist Party in Scotland. According to their release, bookies Stan James had their client Ruth as 11/10 favourite to win the Scottish Conservative leadership race. Perhaps not surprisingly they had no odds on their other client, Craig Whyte, paying the Rangers' tax demand if it becomes due after November.

Job done

18.10.11

As the BBC documentary on Rangers is about to be broadcast this week I feel that my work on these matters is largely over. When I started on this my objective was to put the story of Rangers and the likelihood of the club going into administration out there in the mainstream Scottish media. I realised that this would not happen overnight because of the craven venal nature of the average Scottish sports hack when faced with the cultural power of Rangers. Succulent lamb is a hard habit to kick.

This would be a story, like the campaign against the "Famine Song", that would have to happen in the news pages before the sports desks would get involved. Going back to early last year the main response from Rangers supporters was that this tax case thingy was all a terrible lie about "the Rangers" and that I would soon be found out as a Fenian fantasist. Ah well . . .

It was also alleged that I had an agenda. This was true. I had a clearly stated aim of getting this story out there into the mainstream. I had rock solid sources and since I started to work on it I have acquired others.

I had initially taken the Rangers/HMRC story to the *News of the World*. The news editor of the Scottish edition, after consulting his boss, commissioned me to write a series of pieces on the subject. Martin Bain spoke to me on the record when I contacted him as a freelancer for the *News of the World*. I spoke to him on Saturday, 15 May 2010. As I have stated before on here he was very helpful. Little did either of us know that day that his own employment with the club would come to an end and that his compensation claim would shed further light on the state of the club he loves. The *News of the World* went with the story.

I wrote my own feature-length piece about the story a few weeks later.[1] Once more the first response of Rangers supporters was to disbelieve what was being reported. First they didn't believe that Martin Bain had spoken to me. He did. Secondly many of them thought that his views had been misrepresented. They weren't.

I noted earlier this year how the story had gone mainstream.[2] In August I learned that sheriff officers acting on behalf of HMRC would visit Ibrox apropos an unpaid tax bill.[3] However, some people don't believe words, they need pictures.[4] Arranging that "Kodak moment" by having my own freelance snapper and tipping off the *Sun*, through a colleague, probably broke the final barrier to it becoming safe for the Scottish hack pack to start to look, however faintheartedly, at this story.

Now Rangers and the words "insolvency" and "administration" are in the mainstream. Funds are ring-fenced by court action by former employees and unpaid creditors. Eminent judges accept that the club is in danger of going bust and find against them. The most recent case involving Rangers in the Court of Session with ex-finance director Donald McIntyre saw the perhaps unprecedented event of the club not being legally represented in court.[5]

For the past few weeks the BBC investigations unit's researchers have been discovering, to their amazement, facts about Rangers' finances that were on this site over a year ago. Today the club withdrew cooperation from the BBC, claiming that the national broadcaster had an anti-Rangers bias.[6]

Yesterday Rangers' legend John Greig resigned from his post as non-executive director, claiming he was frozen out of the running of the club by the new regime.

As I have stated many times on here I DO believe that Rangers will go into administration and not necessarily because of the tax case currently in the tribunal system. The club doesn't, by their own admission, have a credit line and the Malmo debacle may turn out to have been the hinge factor that scuppered a very sketchy business plan. Without access to bank borrowing the negative cash flow inherent in the current

1   http://www.philmacgiollabhain.ie/taxing-times-for-rangers/
2   http://www.philmacgiollabhain.ie/how-the-rangers-tax-case-went-mainstream/
3   http://www.philmacgiollabhain.ie/the-sheriff-is-in-town/
4   http://www.philmacgiollabhain.ie/photographs-you-were-not-meant-to-see/
5   http://www.bbc.co.uk/news/uk-scotland-glasgow-west-15353713
6   http://news.stv.tv/scotland/
    west-central/275198-rangers-withdraw-cooperation-with-bbc/

season will choke them. In that scenario administration would follow very, very quickly.

As I've been finishing this piece I have had Clyde 1 *Superscoreboard* streaming and the Rangers fans have been screaming. There is very little denial around now. The "A" word is now common currency when Rangers are discussed. It's just the truth.

Mission accomplished.

The new BBC

23.10.11

We truly live in strange times on Planet *Fitba*. I awoke recently to a fine crisp Donegal morning with the sun streaming in my window across the top of Muckish Mountain, welcoming me to a brave new world. In this new dispensation the BBC comes out of the box with an institutional bias . . . towards Rangers FC. I know, I know . . . Presumably this is a different BBC that was extant when I had retired to a peaceful sleep the night before. It must be a new BBC because the old BBC employed James Traynor and Chick Young.

Listen again to this gloriously public spat on who loved Rangers more.[1] (The online article carries a link to a YouTube clip of an on-air disagreement between Chick Young and James Traynor)

When there is an institutional bias in an organisation then that is usually manifested in the workforce by an absence of the out group and in the attitudes held by most of the employees, especially in the upper reaches of the organisation. Earlier this year I bumped into Gordon Smith at the media centre in the AVIVA stadium in Dublin. We were both there for the Carling Nations Cup, an international football tournament for the countries of these islands minus England.[2] I had a lengthy chat with Gordon on just about everything, but mainly about Scottish football and especially his beloved Rangers. A few weeks later he was announced as director of football at Rangers. The club he played for, the club he supported as a boy. He was at the AVIVA working as a broadcaster. For the BBC . . .

Truly the world changed when I was asleep. It's all very confusing.

---

1   http://www.youtube.com/watch?v=I4G-3Vbv7X4&feature=related

2   http://www.philmacgiollabhain.ie/gordon-smith-to-return-to-ibrox/

Nikica Jelavić

22.11.11

I have to admit that this story in the *Sun* about Nikica Jelavić made me smile.[1] (The online article carries a link to a piece in the *Sun* by Derek McGregor on 21 November 2011 claiming Leicester had told Rangers they intended to make a £7.5m bid for Nikica Jelavić in the January transfer window.)

It reminded me of the last time the Croatian striker was the subject of "interest" from Leicester City FC.[2] At the time of the last "bid" from Leicester I stayed silent. I knew there was no substance to it. However, one should never interrupt your enemy when he is making a mistake. This bravado in the Scottish sports pages at the end of the last transfer window about Rangers rebuffing a multi-million pound bid for Nikica Jelavić was a serious own goal. One can only imagine the anger in senior HMRC circles at a company that they were taking legal action against for £2.8m in unpaid taxes publicly flaunting the fact that they had refused to realise an asset worth £6.5m! Oh dear . . .

Therefore I was quite content for this to go unchallenged at the time. Then of course there was the £9.5m bid at the same time from the unknown agent in another universe. Even the laptop loyal agreed with Peter Lawwell that the idea was risible. They all laughed. Although, I suspect, the taxman was not smiling at Rangers turning down a "real" bid from Leicester back in August. The £2.3m arrested in the "wee tax case" is still frozen.[3] That particular day of reckoning is in two weeks.

Of course Mr Whyte and his associates could attempt to access funding from other sources to keep the show on the road.

Rangers and STV

28.12.11

I reacted with more than a little surprise to the new commercial

---

1   http://www.thescottishsun.co.uk/scotsol/homepage/sport/spl/3950827/This-time-Gers-cant-say-no-to-Foxes.html#ixzz1eO7q0744

2   http://www.scotzine.com/2011/09/a-failed-attempt-to-censor-an-investigative-journalist/

3   http://www.philmacgiollabhain.ie/rangers-the-clock-is-ticking/

hook-up between Scottish Television (STV) and Rangers.[1] For me this immediately flagged up some ethical issues that will have to be faced by members of the National Union of Journalists at STV, especially on the news desk.

These problems are succinctly nailed by Roy Greenslade in his *Guardian* blog today.[2] There is an ongoing problem with the ownership of media organisations impacting on editorial autonomy. However, this new relationship between STV and Rangers is on another level. Rangers and their tax problems is a major news story in Scotland. Will the STV news journalist, employed by a media company now commercially conjoined with Rangers, be able to continue to cover that story adequately? The NUJ members employed by STV are blameless in this situation. The forensic examination of new owner Craig Whyte's business past by Mark Daly of the BBC showed what can be done. There are fine news journalists at STV and I hope that this new business relationship with Rangers does not hamper their freedom to dig in the appropriate places.

The importance of precision in journalism

05.01.12

If journalism is about anything it's about precision. It doesn't matter the platform the journalist is providing content for. Whether it is the print media or for broadcast. Ambiguity is the enemy of good reporting.

I was sent this by a Facebook buddy. It is from Clyde 1 *Superscoreboard*, 4 January 2012. You will note that he added some special effects to give weight to Hugh Keevins' words.[3] (The online article carries a link to a YouTube clip featuring material from Clyde 1 *Superscoreboard*, 4 January 2012.) I can't disagree with his insertion of the sound effects. "Until Revenue and Customs tells Rangers how much they owe we're shooting in the dark."

I am simply amazed at the import of this short piece of radio. I spoke to Mr Keevins at the AVIVA stadium at the start of the Dublin Super Cup in July of last year. I gave him the basic figures surrounding the tax case currently going through the first-tier tax tribunal. He appeared surprised to hear me disclose the figures to him. I was surprised that HE

---

1   http://www.rangers.co.uk/articles/20111227/
    gers-in-stv-agreement_2254024_2559000

2   http://www.guardian.co.uk/media/greenslade/2011/dec/28/stv-group-rangers

3   http://www.youtube.com/watch?feature=player_embedded&v=V1Tt_pJBE1E#!

was surprised! I had supplied the same information to his Radio Clyde colleagues, live on air, back in January 2011.[1]

For the record, Rangers FC have known the sums involved in the "big tax case" since early 2010. The paperwork sent to them by HMRC would have stated the assessment of the underpayment very clearly. That figure is £24m. The people running Rangers were also aware then of the interest payments on that sum at that time being in the region of £12m. The penalties sought by HMRC were £15m. So Rangers DO know what Revenue & Customs (sic) think they're owed. The club, of course, have appealed that and are now going through the first-tier tax tribunal.

These figures were put into the public domain in the Scottish edition of the *News of the World* on 17 May 2010. I know because I wrote that story. In the studio with Mr Keevins on 4 January 2012 was Graham Spiers. I provided these details to him personally at the Carling Cup on 25 May 2011 in Dublin, a full year after the *News of the World* "splash". Graham didn't believe that the tax case, should Rangers lose it, would threaten the club as he was of the opinion that Sir David Murray would be "morally compelled" to pay the bill from his private funds! I found this Pollyanna assessment to be staggering. So what are we to believe? What is the memory span of a pundit on Clyde 1 *Superscoreboard*?

This piece of broadcasting infers that the figures are a mystery. No, they're not. What IS in dispute is whether or not Rangers owe them.

Another bit of loose talk I have heard from some radio pundits recently is that "Rangers will know in January what the tax case result is". The tax tribunal will conclude this month then it will be time for the three judges to consider their verdict. Piece of string estimate, but it would be unlikely if there was a deliberation given before March.

No one expects a sports journalist to be fluent in the technicalities of UK tax tribunals. However, they do have colleagues on business desks and they do know this stuff. Having met both of these men I instantly liked them. They're both intelligent, insightful and clearly love what they do. However, I have a question. Almost two years on how is it possible for any sports journalist in Scotland to be apparently so badly informed about the biggest off-field football story since Fergus McCann saved Celtic from going out of business? When you're following a story of such importance it is vital that people are precise with their words and their utterances.

---

1   http://www.youtube.com/watch?v=cynMmAXFBuw

Ignoring the story

24.01.12

In recent weeks a few close colleagues have proffered the opinion to me that there is a book in how the mainstream media in Scotland covered the story of Rangers' financial problems over the past three years. These conversations happen almost every time you get a group of journalists in a room for any length of time. Most of these book ideas are worthy rather than worthwhile. They usually never get past the discussion stage. However, James Traynor's blog in the *Daily Record* yesterday suggested to me that there might well be legs in such a project.[1]

From my perspective it has been a long tortuous process to get the Rangers financial story, particularly the tax case, into the mainstream. There have been times in the past when I thought we were finally over the last hurdle.[2] Last April saw the famous nod of the head from Rangers' chairman Alastair Johnston and the spat between James Traynor and Chick Young on live radio.[3][4]

There are two powerful forces at work against the full truth coming out. The first one is a basic human emotional response to bad news. No one wants to believe an inconvenient truth. Despite the basic facts and figures of the Rangers tax case being published in the *News of the World* Scottish edition in May 2010 many Rangers fans have remained in denial. The second one is connected to the first and it is about the basic commercial interests of the major titles in Scotland. Quite simply their readership is mainly of a Rangers persuasion and they don't want to be fed a daily diet of bad news about their club. These titles, once with almost total market penetration, operate now on very narrow margins. Any significant dip in circulation could spell the end.

Quite simply "going big" on the Rangers tax case story could have cost them readers. Darrell King of the *Evening Times* stands out as the only journalist in a major Scottish title to have followed this story at every opportunity. He deserves much praise for this.[5] For the most part his colleagues have been asleep at the wheel on this one. Into this vac-

---

1 http://blogs.dailyrecord.co.uk/jimtraynor/2012/01/ibrox-on-the-brink.html

2 http://www.philmacgiollabhain.ie/how-the-rangers-tax-case-went-mainstream/

3 http://www.youtube.com/watch?v=rN3rEcwC41M&feature=related

4 http://www.youtube.com/watch?v=378qoB8j_tw&feature=related

5 http://www.youtube.com/watch?v=cynMmAXFBuw

uum has stepped new media. The Rangers Tax Case blog has unpicked the minutiae of this complex story and has regularly scooped the mainstream media.[1] RTC has also been a gathering point for engaged, knowledgeable posters who have interacted with the anonymous blogger and, crucially, with each other. I have had a foot in both camps in reporting on this story by filing copy to titles like the *News of the World* and blogging on this and other sites.

There is a story to be told about how this story, without new media, would have been largely ignored by the major titles in Scotland. I believe that the mainstream media's squeamishness on this story has been a factor in the absence of any major grassroots movement by Rangers supporters to secure new ownership for the club.[2] There is a glint in the eyes of most Rangers supporters these days when the HMRC case is mentioned. It is the reflection of headlights.

Oh dear . . . Now, someone should write a book about that.

The Daily Record catches up

31.01.12

Today's "revelations" in the *Daily Record* about the parlous state of Rangers' finances should certainly spell the end of the denial phase for those who are emotionally attached to the Ibrox club.[3] Regular readers here should not have gasped in horror at the idea that Scotland's establishment club have mortgaged future season ticket sales just to keep going.[4] Also the "scoop" about the non-payment of VAT will come as no surprise to regulars here.[5]

A recurring theme of my coverage of Rangers' financial problems is that the story was always out there for the mainstream media if they wanted it badly enough. Mark Daly's documentary for the BBC on Craig Whyte's business history is proof enough that there is a great story in the Whyte takeover. Despite threats of legal action by the club's

1 http://rangerstaxcase.com/

2 http://www.scotzine.com/2011/09/why-its-too-late-for-gers-for-change/

3 http://www.dailyrecord.co.uk/2012/01/31/rangers-owner-craig-whyte-admits-he-sold-four-years-worth-of-season-tickets-to-keep-ibrox-club-running-86908-23728301/

4 http://www.philmacgiollabhain.ie/rangers-strike-it-lucky-with-their-new-owner/

5 http://www.philmacgiollabhain.ie/rangers-failing-to-keep-up-to-date-with-tax-remittances/

"billionaire" owner no writs have been issued to date. It is the print media that has been behind the curve on this story.

When Craig Whyte became the new owner of Rangers they seemed quite happy to take press releases and file it as copy. When you do that you stop being a journalist and it is always a course of action that can come back and bite you.[1] The Scottish tabloids, dependent in the main on a Rangers readership, feared a loss in sales that would tip THEM into insolvency. I know I know . . . Anyway, better late and all that.

Welcome aboard, guys.

When journalists forget
which team they are on

04.02.12

When you're playing up front you know and understand that their centre half has a job to do. He is out to stop you and your job is to make sure he fails.

Some of my closest colleagues in the NUJ work in public relations. Some of them work as press officers for government departments and others are freelance, mainly working for big companies or celebs. Collectively they are known as "PRs" and many of them started in newspapers. When I occasion across them professionally I instinctively understand that I'm the attacker and they're the defender for the other lot. There are boundaries and there is a professional respect that I'm trying to do something that might not fully tie in with their client's interests.

In the poacher/gamekeeper analogy the journalists who become PRs are seen to have "crossed over to the other side". It isn't an act of betrayal, but it is a change of role. When you become a PR you're playing for the other team. What a journalist should never do is accept what a PR firms tells them without any corroboration on matters of major importance. If you don't seek out independent verification of what the PR is telling you then you effectively become their admin worker.

Here we have a piece from Keith Jackson this week explaining how the *Daily Record*'s readers were told last November that Mr Craig Whyte was a billionaire. The day after Keith Jackson was told to describe Craig

---

1   http://www.philmacgiollabhain.ie/the-first-rough-draft-of-history/

Whyte as a "billionaire" the readers of the *Daily Record* were treated
to this nonsense masquerading as news.[1] (The online article carries a
link to the famous piece in the *Daily Record* written by Keith Jackson,
published on 18 November 2010, which described Craig Whyte as a
billionaire.)

The following February I spoke to a Scottish journalist who was
over for the Carling Cup in Dublin. We chatted about Mr Whyte and
specifically about the extent of his wealth. I detailed to the reporter,
a staunch Rangers man who has authored a book about the club, the
extent of my investigations into finding the truth about Mr Whyte's net
worth. I told him that despite calling in every favour with every business reporter I knew that I hadn't found any evidence to back up the
description of Mr Whyte as a billionaire. He then confided to me that
the PR company representing Mr Whyte had told reporters what to
write about the new prospective owner of the Ibrox club and they had
obeyed. This, dear reader, is not journalism.

Nick Davies of the *Guardian* has another name for the type of
breathless, gushing nonsense about Craig Whyte being a billionaire –
churnalism.[2] By the close of the summer transfer window it was clear
that the only "frontloading" that Mr Whyte would be doing was to his
washing machine. So last September it seemed an appropriate juncture
to return to those November days and satirise the output of one of those
journalists who had loyally and unquestioningly reproduced information from Mr Whyte's PR company.[3]

I recall that I had one tetchy phone call with one of Mr Whyte's PR
people not long after the Motherwell born tycoon had bought the Ibrox
club. He said: "I don't know what you're up to and that gives me a problem!" What I was "up to" was trying to get to the truth of the situation
apropos his client's wealth because the official narrative seemed like a
fiction. He was the centre half and I was the striker, therefore giving him
a problem was at the core of my job description. I doubt he had much
of a problem with most of the compliant chaps on the Scottish sports
desks. Some of those producing this rubbish about Craig Whyte's "off
the radar" wealth are members of my union. They really should take a
minute to read what they've agreed to abide by.[4] (The online article car-

1   http://www.dailyrecord.co.uk/football/spl/rangers/2010/11/18/craig-
    whyte-profile-the-scots-billionaire-on-the-brink-of-taking-over-the-club-he-
    loves-86908-22722617/

2   http://churnalism.com/

3   http://www.philmacgiollabhain.ie/the-first-rough-draft-of-history/

4   http://media.gn.apc.org/nujcode.html

ries a link to the National Union of Journalists (NUJ) code of conduct.)

Now as the Rangers situation becomes even uglier they have another opportunity to finally put the ball in the net.

The future of journalism is bright

08.02.12

The inhabitants of Planet *Fitba* could be forgiven for having an extremely low opinion of my trade. However, that would be like thinking that you knew everything you needed to know about Celtic strikers because you had seen Wayne Biggins in the hoops.

I spent most of the month of January marking essays from students at the prestigious City University in London. They are reading for an MA in International Journalism. Most of these postgraduate students were from the UK, but some were from countries as diverse as Brazil, France, Germany, India and Spain. The questions put to them covered issues like the protection of sources, the right to privacy and the use of subterfuge in investigative journalism. The succulent lamb-fuelled churnalism of the laptop loyal and the stuttering waffle of the football phone-ins should not be taken for best practice in my trade. I am particularly impressed with the "next gen" of journalists. The authors of these essays provided ample evidence of a firm grasp of the skills, and crucially the values, that will make them fine reporters.

They know that they are coming into an industry at a time of turmoil. The writing is on the billboards for the print sector, and traditional broadcasting organisations are also facing challenges, but any democratic society needs a free press and an unshackled media will always need reliable journalists. Although I didn't detect anything distinctively Caledonian about any of my essay writers I know through this window on the world that there is a bright young crop emerging in Scotland.

I was recently contacted by a journalism student in the West of Scotland asking me about where her next step was in this evolving craft. It is heartening for an old stager like me to be holding impromptu tutorials late at night through Face Tube, or whatever they call it . . .

When the Rangers financial story is finally put to bed I intend to look back over the coverage of the demise of Scotland's establishment club by the mainstream media. In the main I will be surveying cowardice, incompetence and venality. If the Scottish hack pack was a football team, then it would be appropriate to use well-worn clichés like "dead wood", "clear out" and "major surgery" in any story about them. Why did the biggest sporting story in Scottish history have to be dragged into the public consciousness by bloggers and citizen journalists while the sports desks played safe?

It might even be a subject worthy of an essay question for those fine students.

Too cowardly to report. Too bigoted to believe

18.02.12

Suddenly Scotland is remarkably well off for brave journalists. The studios are full of dogged reporters who are calling out Mr Whyte. The man described as a "billionaire" by Keith Jackson of the *Daily Record* back in November 2010 is now a legitimate target for dogged reporting by the Scottish sports desks.[1] As well as rewriting their own role in this story, they are also attempting to alter the narrative of the origins of the Rangers fiasco.

The basis of Rangers' terminal illness is not the nine months of Mr Whyte's stewardship, but Sir David Murray's two decades in charge. With the arrival of the assessment for £24m in unpaid taxes in early 2010, the club was on borrowed time. That calculation from HMRC added £12m in interest charges. They also sought penalties of £18m. The total bad news of £54m was several times the liquidation value of the club. It was also double the much publicised bank debt that had forced Lloyds Banking Group to take effective control of Rangers.

Throughout this time, it was a constant battle to get any coverage of this into the Scottish media. In early 2010 when I had the forensic facts of the "big tax case" I took it to the news editor of the *News of the World* Scottish edition. A Cumbrian lad, he immediately saw the news value in the story and his editor, also an Englishman, agreed. The front page splash on Sunday 16 May of "Simply the bust" was classic *News of the World* stuff. I now know that these headlines caused the only serious bidder to withdraw from talks to buy the club. After that, moneyed

1   http://www.dailyrecord.co.uk/football/spl/rangers/2010/11/18/craig-
    whyte-profile-the-scots-billionaire-on-the-brink-of-taking-over-the-club-he-
    loves-86908-22722617/

Rangers supporter pulled out, it was only chaps like Mr Ellis and Mr Whyte who were interested.

The sixteenth of May 2010 was, in hindsight, "job done". It was also National Famine Memorial day here in Ireland. Which is where I came in . . . The *News of the World* stories in May and June of 2010 are worth mentioning because they are atypical of the coverage of this story throughout the period. The main impulse of the sports desks of the major titles in Scotland was to play down the significance of this tax case thingy. Any time a sports hack was pressed on this story by a gleeful Celtic fan or a concerned Rangers fan the stock response was to claim ignorance and have a side swipe at online cranks.

The main objective of the sports desks is to have a steady diet of good news to satisfy their main demographic, Rangers supporters. The tax case was not just bad news, but a death warrant for the club and meaning almost certain administration and possibly liquidation.[1] Had the back pages been full of this on a constant basis then there might have been an impulse for Rangers supporters to organise. Of course they didn't, preferring to wait on a new sugar daddy. When they were told of Craig Whyte's stealth wealth by Keith Jackson they believed what they wanted to believe.

Whyte's time at the club was plagued by an anonymous blogger who deconstructed the spin often within hours of the PR guys handing out the back page headlines to the obedient hacks. It gave me a smile to see a newspaper of the standing of the *Guardian* acknowledge the role of the Rangers Tax Case blog today.[2] Craig Whyte referred to the RTC blog as "99% crap", although usually the Rangers owner is much better at numbers. The success of RTC is a case study in what Professor Roy Greenslade of the City University calls a "horizontalized journalism", although he concedes that it is an awful word! Apart from the catalysing blog posts, often scooping the mainstream media in Scotland, RTC was and remains a gathering point for the inquisitive and the qualified. From the original wakeup call in the *News of the World* in 2010 to the excavations of RTC, the information was all there and, of course, on here too.

Rangers supporters could have been very well informed. Today they will flock into Ibrox to show their support and their defiance, but it is all too late. They cannot alter events, they are merely helpless spectators. Their culture of deference and an addiction to Herrenvolk hubris made

1   http://www.philmacgiollabhain.ie/taxing-times-for-rangers/

2   http://www.guardian.co.uk/football/blog/2012/feb/17/scotland-media-rangers

them easy targets for the fantasies being peddled by on-message sports hacks. The people they said were lying to them were actually telling them the truth.[1]

The irony was that the Rangers support was very well informed about the danger to their club. However, they had issues in that the information was coming from an anonymous blogger who is a self-confessed Celtic fan and by an, ahem, in-your-face-head-totally-above-the-parapet-Fenian in Donegal. Rangers supporters had the information to save their club. However, the sources of the information made them recoil from the narrative. Instead, they believed the fairy stories about billionaires.

Scotland DOES have very fine journalists. News reporters and political correspondents shake their head at the antics of the denizens of the sports desks. I spoke with one veteran "Pol Corr" yesterday and he jauntily assumed that the Scottish media would be beating a path to my Donegal door. When I told him that I had not received a single media request from Scotland he was genuinely shocked. "That's bizarre," he said. I told him that I wasn't in the least surprised. When Celtic fans lambast Scottish journalism I always insert a caveat that the journalists they have experience of aren't the cream of the crop.

Today in the Debt Dome the Rangers support will once more manifest a trait of their subculture that was a major part of their undoing. Uncomprehendingly loyal they believe that the status quo will always deliver for them. The trailer trash of a dead empire, they aren't the stuff that rebellions are made of. This could be the last time that the club formed in 1872 plays at their home ground. Only a CVA can save them and that is in the balance. There is not a ticket to be had and I would not be surprised if we hear of Fenian blood and Famines at Ibrox today. However, as their club bleeds out it was a Fenian with Mayo DNA who warned them. They couldn't allow themselves to listen.

Little wonder that I allow myself a small smile today.

Two very different conversations

20.02.12

I was speaking to two young Scottish journalists this week about the significance of the Rangers in administration story. One of the

---

1   http://www.philmacgiollabhain.ie/rangers-strike-it-lucky-with-their-new-owner/

reporters works on the sports desk for a UK daily and the other for a small regional title. The guy from the big-selling tabloid wanted to discuss with me how the mainstream media had missed what he called "the biggest story in Scottish football in his lifetime", and he was genuinely perplexed about this. The other journalist wanted to share her observations on how Rangers going into administration had authorised people to reveal their feelings about the club. She said that over the week in her rural local pub people of an older generation were "opening up" and saying what the end of Rangers would mean for them.

This clearly wasn't about sporting rivalry, but a longstanding cultural wound. Repressing feelings about the decades of discrimination, taunting, threats and occasional physical attacks had taken their toll. The real possibility that Rangers could "die" had acted as a releaser cue for people who were the targets of the Ibrox crowd because of their religion and their ethnicity.

At the last home game against Kilmarnock, the paying customers demonstrated their love for Rangers by singing about being up to their knees in Fenian blood. Once more Ibrox was the gathering point for those who define themselves by what they hate rather than what they love. This is a culture of ethnic hatred, Herrenvolk hubris and a crass sense of entitlement. Is it any wonder that many of the victims of the Rangers sub culture do want this "institution" to go away?

Humour has always been a main weapon in the armoury of Scotland's Irish community when faced with the racist hostility from followers of this magnificent Scottish "institution", and last week was no different. Social media was deluged with satire at the expense of Rangers and their supporters. Tabloid man had called me and he made it clear that he had been stung by my allegations in this post.[1] Although he wasn't named in the piece he took it to heart. At the end of the conversation he accepted my explanation for why the sports desks in Scotland had failed on this story. Moreover, they had failed their readers, ironically mainly comprised of Rangers supporters. The cowardice and venality of the sports desks prevented the necessary information getting out that could have facilitated a grass roots movement by the club's supporters. I was making a generalisation about the occupants of the sports desks at the big titles and in the major broadcast organisations. The generalisation held as it was generally correct.

---

1   http://www.philmacgiollabhain.ie/too-cowardly-to-report-too-bigoted-to-believe/

I thought that these two separate conversations from very different journalists told the same tale. The same venal tabloids that had withheld the distressing news from Rangers fans also allowed them the licence to continue to have it in for the "Fenians" and anyone who would challenge their birthright. I hope the death of Rangers, if it finally comes to that, is a watershed moment for the media in Scotland. Through their venality and cowardice, the fourth estate didn't cover a story of national significance. They now play catch up and tell the world that they were on it from the start. Few were prepared to break ranks in this fiction because they knew they wouldn't work again.

A mention and tip of the hat must go to Darrell King of the *Evening Times* who was on the tax story from the start and saw the significance of it. Both the journalists I talked to were young with decades in the trade in front of them. Tabloid guy is a decent human being, but it was the other reporter who demonstrated a lighter touch and more nuanced grasp of the significance of the entire saga. If she is typical of the future of journalism in Scotland, then the trade will be OK.

On the Record

01.03.12

What does Keith Jackson of the *Daily Record* think of Craig Whyte?

Is it this?[1] (The online article carries a link to the famous piece in the *Daily Record* written by Keith Jackson and published on 18 November 2010, which described Craig Whyte as a billionaire.)

Or is it this?[2] (The online article carries a link to an audio clip of Keith Jackson on talkSPORT radio on 1 March 2012, in which he claims Rangers are heading closer to liquidation and a new owner is their only hope.)

Clearly he cannot believe both as they are clearly mutually exclusive. It is, of course, perfectly acceptable to change your view of someone, that is part of life. However, it is unedifying to pretend that you were right all along when in fact you described Mr Whyte as a "billionaire" back in November 2010. If a journalist meekly accepts the word of a

1 http://www.dailyrecord.co.uk/football/spl/rangers/2010/11/18/craig-whyte-profile-the-scots-billionaire-on-the-brink-of-taking-over-the-club-he-loves-86908-22722617/

2 http://www.talksport.co.uk/radio/richard-keys-and-andy-gray/blog/2012-03-01/jackson-rangers-are-getting-closer-liquidation

PR on a matter of substance about their client then they are in danger of being duped.[1]

These are the end of days for Rangers and although it was the tax strategies authorised by Sir David Murray that created the crisis, the reign of Craig Whyte has also been a factor. For those who grieve and for those who celebrate the passing of Rangers they should be mindful that Mr Whyte had the benefit of a local media. The local press didn't question the good news that the Ibrox club had finally been delivered from the clutches of the bank. Indeed, during the protracted negotiations with the bank Mr Whyte appeared to have leading Scottish sports journalists on his side.[2] Overall from November 2010 until a few weeks ago Craig Whyte had an easy press from the Scottish sports desks. Even after the BBC documentary in October 2011 they remained on message and played their part in the Nikica Jelavić charades in the January window.

The only questions being asked about the source of finance to buy the club and Mr Whyte's plan for Rangers as a going concern were on here and the Rangers Tax Case blog.[3] Note the date on the post. The real Craig Whyte story was always there if the mainstream media in Scotland had truly wanted it. Now that they're finally on the job, regular readers of this site will not be fooled that guys on the sports desks were always with the programme because they weren't.

All right on the Knight

12.03.12

It is heartening for this commoner to see that the ways of chivalry are not dead. The ennobled are a different breed to the rest of us. Whyte knights, blue knights and of course the knight to end all knights, the one and only Sir David Murray.

You may have noticed that the bile, freshly brewed in Larkhall, Govan and Belfast has been poured over Craig Whyte to such an extent that some have a degree of sympathy for the Motherwell billionaire. However, once the odium has eventually seen off the Whyte Knight, which will be a long time coming, look out for the guns finally turning

1 http://www.philmacgiollabhain.ie/when-journalists-forget-which-team-they-are-on/

2 http://blogs.dailyrecord.co.uk/jimtraynor/2011/03/are-lloyds-trying-to-sell-rang.html

3 http://www.philmacgiollabhain.ie/rangers-strike-it-lucky-with-their-new-owner/

on Sir David Murray. Now every knight had a champion, or maybe it was the other way round, every champion had a knight. I do not possess the dignity to understand such chivalric matters.

Sir David's current champion is a former regional journalist, Graham Isdale. Mr Isdale has been whispering into the ears of succulent lamb-eating journalists about how good Sir David really was for Rangers. It would seem his only mistake was allowing the Motherwell billionaire to buy Rangers. In this narrative there is no mention of employee benefit trusts, dual contracts or any other potential problems. So the story goes all is well in the kingdom of Sir David Murray.

Now it is strange Mr Isdale finds time to be Sir David's champion as he is executive director of corporate affairs at Glasgow Housing Association (GHA), an organisation that looks after much of Glasgow's former council housing stock. When Mr Isdale was appointed it was thought strange that a man who had boasted to the *Herald* about his American luxury holiday home and who lives in a substantial sandstone pile in one of the most sought after suburbs of the city would be one of the executive team running a charity that looks after housing and services for some of the poorest people in Glasgow. In between deal-ing with dampness, anti-social neighbours, dog fouling and evictions Mr Isdale finds time to whisper sweet nothings to the press about Sir David. Perhaps Mr Isdale can persuade the GHA board to up the rents of their 45,000 tenants by £5 a week to help the Rangers fighting fund.

The guy on the big horse always understood that taxes were for lit-tle people. Although some might think, at this stage, that it would be totally feudal to try to save the Rangers.

A local type of madness

13.03.12

The origin of the word "lunatic" indicates that before psychiatry was established people in Europe thought the moon drove people mad. The belief in the moon's disruptive power on a person's mental wellbeing goes back as far as Aristotle.

Many years ago I trekked across the snow covered Cairngorm plateau under a full moon. No head torches were required as the moonlight and the snow combined to create a situation where I could read the map as if it were daytime. It did not feel like any ordinary night as we approached Beinn Mac Duibh. So I do not discount the potential power of an ghealach and there is some evidence that moonlight can have an unsettling effect on some more sensitive souls.

Some years ago I read a criminological study that found that attempted murders spiked in the full moon, but not murders. The reasoning was that murders, by their nature, involve premeditation and planning. Whereas attempted murder was a spur of the moment, irrational impulse.

It is ironic that the first part of the moon that man ever set foot on was called the "sea of tranquillity" given the disruptive effect that this heavenly body can have on the oceans here on earth. As humans are mainly made up of water then it stands to reason that our own inner tides can also be turned by the same gravitational force.

Now on Planet *Fitba*, we are witnessing another outbreak of our own localised version of lunacy. One of the most common catalysts for an outbreak is usually an "exclusive" in a Scottish tabloid. It breaks the news, the wonderful news, rather like the chap in the sci-fi film 2012. The hack gushes that "something is going to happen . . .", he pauses and shudders in anticipation and then continues: "something WONDERFUL!" There then follows several paragraphs in which various ludicrously optimistic scenarios for the future of Rangers Football Club are outlined.

The next stage of the illness is usually measured by the extent to which it spreads to others. The first signs of a serious contagion are the comments below the initial item of "journalism", and if the fantasy is believed then the delusion can take hold. At this point, there is little that can be done to prevent mass psychosis gripping thousands of already vulnerable people. The disease is particularly virulent if it becomes airborne. Although the initial infection can start with a tabloid "exclusive" it can become a major outbreak if the nonsense is then passed off as fact on a radio phone-in. Within a few hours large sections of the city of Glasgow can be infected.

Symptoms include being deliriously hopeful, then a vengeful over confidence kicks in and the sufferer believes that scores can be settled. At this stage the infected person can become violent so they are best avoided. In the worst of cases the infected person has an evidence-resistant strain of the disease. At this point any intervention is largely futile and no amount of rational discourse will reverse the condition. The fever has taken hold and it must be allowed to run its course. Professional advice is that normal people have little to fear from infection although it is advisable to avoid those who think that they "ARE the people". Unlike an ghealach they are not the brightest and sadly some never recover and remain in their deluded state. Despite this many can be cared for in the community. The worst thing that these people can do is to keep taking the tabloids.

The old response from the Victorian era of using the "Big House" is now seen as backward and oppressive although some still want it to remain open. While our ancient ancestors knew that wolves were particularly susceptible to being disturbed by moonlight it would appear that these days moonbeams mainly afflict the bears.

The usefulness of C4

20.03.12

In my youth the term "C4" meant something that made a big bang. These days it means Channel 4, specifically their flagship news programme.

Regular readers here will know that I am of the opinion that when it comes to Planet *Fitba* journalism in Scotland has been inert for as long as I can remember. The impulse to uncover and publish about the soccer establishment in Glasgow was defused a long time ago. This cosy arrangement gave everyone a quiet life. There was an understanding that there wasn't anything that was going to go off unexpectedly. That is why the Dallas email story broke the rules and the Mark Daly documentary was highly atypical.

The allegations made by Hugh Adam that undisclosed payments to players at Rangers were the norm at the club from the 1990s begged for a serious news organisation to get involved. Despite the impressive façade at Edmiston Drive and Hampden I haven't been convinced since the Dallas email story that the foundations were secure. For the last two years I have waited to see what another tremor would do to the superstructure of Planet *Fitba*. Tonight at 19.00 hrs we might see the impact of a well-placed charge on C4.

A charge of cheating . . .

The price of succulent lamb

24.03.12

These are difficult days for Scottish fitba churnalists. Like the club that many of them love more than their professional integrity, they are being assailed from all sides. First it was a Fenian in Donegal who told the world about their pal "Hughie" and that email about the Pope. Then there was the Whyte Knight who would save the Rangers. How did that "billionaire" and "wealth off the radar" narrative work out for ya lads?

If all of this wasn't enough now the millions of viewers of Channel 4 are being told of the rotten borough that is Planet *Fitba*.[1] The Glasgow hacks should be highly embarrassed by Alex Thomson's analysis of them. The Channel 4 award-winning war correspondent is stating quite clearly that there is something qualitatively different about Scottish sports journalists from ALL the other places he has worked.

A very minor tip of the hat must go to Graham Spiers in at least putting his hands up to the Faustian pact that he entered into when he dined at Murray's table. Thomson's ongoing investigation into Scottish football is a damning indictment of the lobby that operates around Rangers. That system could only continue to function if there was no outside scrutiny by journalists who didn't take the lamb. Anyone within the consumer base who questioned the narrative was slammed as "paranoid" or some kind of crank.

My own experience of being targeted by the Glasgow hacks is that when they can't ignore me then they tend to play the man and not the ball. Conformity to the agreed narrative sees mediocrity awarded and so the churnalism about Rangers continues. Regular readers here will know that I think that the press pack in Glasgow to be not fit for purpose. Now the man from Channel 4 has found the same.

Does that make him a "chancer" as well?

---

1 http://blogs.channel4.com/alex-thomsons-view/
  succulent-lamb-menu-questions/1010

Scotland's other shame

31.03.12

Yesterday was a good point to take stock of the state of the Fourth Estate in Scotland.

A guy based in London who couldn't find his way from Sauchiehall Street to Argyle Street without using Google maps laid out the reality of Rangersgate for the whole of the UK on Channel 4 last night.[1] In the short period since Alex Thomson has started investigating Scotland's establishment club he has revealed that he has been physically threatened by one Glasgow-based journalist.

On the day the two men who attacked Neil Lennon were convicted, the Celtic manager put out a Tweet that was more of a plea than an outburst: "There seems to be no balance in the Scottish media when it comes to us." (2:23 PM – 30 March 2012 Neil Lennon @OfficialNeil).

His assertion, in my opinion, is simply unanswerable. Although he was referring to the club he could have been talking just about his own situation. Unlike his old gaffer, Martin O'Neill, Celtic's current manager doesn't speak for an eternity in ornate phrases. Lennon's way of talking fits perfectly into the world of 140 characters.

As a player he experienced the *Daily Record*'s "Thugs and thieves" escapade. The sustained racist and sectarian abuse he endured rarely made it past a sub editor on a major title in those days. On one of the rare occasions that his manager, Martin O'Neill, decided to do some straight talking about the subject he made sure it was in the presence of foreign journalists. At a pre-match press conference for a European game he made references to the racist and sectarian abuse that his captain had to endure on a regular basis in Scotland.

As we say in Ireland, O'Neill was "waiting in the long grass" when he lobbed in that grenade about the treatment Lennon regularly received in domestic matches. Neil, in my opinion, was badly let down by his employers during his time as a player. The club should have made this racist abuse a major issue for both the SPL and the SFA, but they didn't. I believe that this "back of the bus" acceptance by Celtic was partly down to the non-reaction of large sections of the media in Scotland towards the victimisation of Lennon and Aiden McGeady.

---

1 http://www.channel4.com/news/
   revealed-the-payments-that-may-lead-to-rangers-downfall

The same media who shrugged at the sustained racist abuse of Celtic's Irish players also looked the other way when Rangersgate was handed to them on a plate two years ago. The day after the *News of the World* splash in May 2010 the Scottish hacks knew about the jaw-dropping arithmetic of the "big tax case" and that should have seen a flurry of activity on sports desks across the country. Instead they fell into line. Now the term "succulent lamb" is known across the UK media village as a term of disdain for Scotland's other shame.

I allow myself a small smile of satisfaction.

Answering questions

01.04.12

Over the last two nights I have had the pleasure of meeting a few of the people who regularly visit this site. I took part in question and answer events at two Celtic supporters' clubs in the west of Scotland. The other panellist on the first night was veteran broadcaster Archie Macpherson. He answered the questions on football with precision and aplomb.

I still regard his biography of Jock Stein not just to be the best one on the big man, but the benchmark for anyone wanting to write such a book about any sporting personality. As we sat in the car on our way to Irvine I was able to more or less quote word for word a lovely passage of prose that Archie had written about that day in May in Lisbon 1967. I made it quite clear to the veteran broadcaster that I was a fan of his work.

The crowd at Irvine on the first of the two events were friendly and engaged, some of them were connected to me via the site and social media, others had just heard of this internet thingy. They were all in agreement that the mainstream media (MSM) had failed lamentably on "Rangersgate" and weren't fit for purpose.

This type of journalism is, by its nature, an isolating experience. I was writing about a soccer situation while being in another country. I can walk out of the house and if I don't want to I don't have to have a single conversation about Celtic, Rangers or Employee Benefit Trusts with my Donegal neighbours. It is simultaneously affirming and disconcerting to be approached by a person who had a mild complaint that I had recently gone two days without posting and that he "needed" to read something on this site every day! No pressure then . . .

The second night was more like home turf for me. A Catholic social club in Coatbridge where my mother's side used to go for their Saturday night when we were all much younger. This is the second time within a month that I was back in Scotland's "little Ireland", where I had attended secondary school.[1] Someone in the authorities thought that it would be a really, really bad idea to build a Catholic secondary school in Baillieston so we were shuttled every day to Coatbridge. My first Celtic supporting experience as an "independent" teenager was on the bus that left from Phil Cole's pub. Like I said, when we were all a lot younger.

Joining Archie and myself on the panel was a genuine character and easily the star of the show, ex-Celtic goalkeeper John Fallon. As quick-witted as he used to be getting off his line he is the living breathing archive of a huge amount of vignettes from the Jock Stein era. I was hearing these for the first time, but I know that I wouldn't be complaining if I had heard them again and again. There appears to be something about the male brain that enables you to remember nicknames, but not the proper one on the birth certificate. At the end of the night an organiser of the event thanked me for making the journey from Ireland and for all the craic. I looked at his face, registered it for a millisecond and 40 years had vanished.

"You went to St Ambrose, didn't you?"

He nodded.

"And your name is 'Gnome', isn't it?"

Never forget a face or a nickname. I still have no idea what his real name is, but he's a lovely fella. His folks are from Kerrykeel and he proudly defined himself as a "Donegal man". A meet up next time he is in the county is a stick on.

These two nights confirmed to me why the MSM are becoming increasingly irrelevant in Planet *Fitba*. The audience at both venues were in complete agreement that they could not rely on the old media for the truth. Archie said that Celtic supporters would miss the rivalry if Rangers went out of business. I didn't disagree with the emotional intelligence that framed that proposition. However, I stated that, for the common good and the general wellbeing of the nation, Scotland would be the healthier if Rangers were eradicated.

This is the first time I have taken part in this type of event. I thoroughly enjoyed the experience. They want me back for more and I'll be happy to oblige. That said, the bag is packed and I'm thinking of the Derryveaghs.

---

1   http://www.philmacgiollabhain.ie/a-family-gathering/#more-2306

The importance of having time on your side

02.04.12

I may have made an interesting scientific discovery. The space–time continuum on Planet *Fitba* might be in a wee bit of a fankle!

I have noticed that scenarios that are discussed on here are at first obediently dismissed by the churnalists then, after an appropriate passage of time, the same proposition is earnestly discussed by them as a real possibility. Baffling.

So it is with the liquidation of Rangers. Over the last couple of days the churnalists have been relaying the words of Paul Clark of Duff and Phelps. The co-administrator of Rangers has spelled it out as clearly as he can at this point about the possibility of Rangers being liquidated. "The preferred option remains a CVA and it remains an option for all of the bidders and we still think it's achievable and we're still recommending that as the preferred course of action to the bidders. We must accept, though, that we have in Rangers a financially-stricken institution and there is an amount of toxicity in there as a result of what's gone on." He continued: "So all of the options have to remain open and it may be that some of the bidders decide that they would rather start afresh. We cannot rule out the winning bid could prefer a different structure that meant the sale of the business to a new company and, in that eventuality it is certainly possible that Rangers would be liquidated."

I love this guy. You dream about someone who would produce such lines. "Financially stricken . . . there is an amount of toxicity in there . . ." In one sentence he cuts to the chase on the balance sheet and sums up the supporters! Don't expect the churnalists to make hay with these quotes. They're under orders after all. Then Super Ally was wheeled out to reassure the bears that a NewCo (i.e. liquidation) wouldn't really be that bad. Andrew Smith in *Scotland on Sunday* reported McCoist as saying: "Even if we come back as a NewCo, Rangers will never die. I don't go along with the idea that 140 years of history would be wiped out."

This should have been an opportunity for Smith to get stuck in and hammer home the point that liquidation is EXACTLY the end of their history.[1] I've met Smith, he's a nice fella and ain't the worst in that Blatt, but letting McCoist away with that statement is turning your back on an open goal. Anyone wanting to use the search function on here will

---

1 http://www.philmacgiollabhain.ie/the-end-of-history/

find that the liquidation of Dignity FC has been well discussed on this site. I would suggest that the prospective bidders are interested in the ASSETS of Club 1872, but not in the company. The NewCo will have to cope with three years of no European revenue. Even if they are shoe-horned back into the SPL in a shameful backdoor deal then the owners of the NewCo will have to run them on a vastly reduced budget.

I've done my bit as I have used this site to advertise for a stupid bil-lionaire to step forward. Only such a person can save 1872 FC and, at this late hour, the churnalists might want to finally come clean on this. Of course they would have to seek permission first.

I'm still struggling to explain to myself why a guy in Donegal can have this all laid out and uploaded, it's dissed by the Glasgow hacks, but then it happens more or less like I said. The same churnalists then earnestly discuss among themselves how they were on this from the start. When I jump over to Glasgow and bump into them they don't have an answer for me. Then I pack my little bag and it is back to the future in Donegal.

It isn't easy being a Tim Traveller.

The man from Auntie

03.04.12

This has not been a good day for the succulent lambs of the mainstream media in Scotland. Conference calls are a handy modern communica-tion tool and it would appear that Duff and Phelps have been using them to get out the . . . err . . . news to the media. I am told that there was one such call today. After it was over the hacks got a Twittering. Chris McLaughlin of the BBC announced the amazing news that Craig Whyte was giving his shares over to the "Blue Knights" consortium headed up by Paul Murray. "@BBCchrismclaug 2:13 PM: BBC under-stands Craig Whyte has agreed to transfer his shares to Blue Knights consortium. #Rangers" This is the same Paul Murray that Whyte had sacked from the Rangers board. So it was a hell of a story. If true . . .

Some pesky Fenian seems to have alerted Alex Thomson of *Channel 4 News*. The award-winning journalist, equipped with a state-of-the-art communication device (mobile phone), called Craig Whyte. The war correspondent tweeted this at 2:28 PM: "Craig Whyte tells me any notion he's selling his shares to PM is 'absolute nonsense.'"

I am reliably informed (no, seriously) that Chris McLaughlin has Craig Whyte's number. All it would have taken from the guy at the Beeb would have been a call to the owner of Rangers to check this story out. Are these the same journalists that have been sneering at bloggers during Rangersgate? They have admonished citizen journalists like Paul Brennan of Celtic Quick News about the pressing need to check facts and to be aware of legal constraints. Moreover, the implication is that journalists in organisations like the BBC are held to a higher standard than mere amateurs with websites. Oh dear . . . For the record I can confirm that, at time of writing, Craig Whyte is still the legal owner of Rangers Football Club.

I checked . . .

A PhD in failure

05.04.12

Ah the poor laptop loyal. How the mediocre have fallen. They now have to endure the scrutiny of an award-winning journalist in a, yes you guessed it, award-winning news organisation.[1] (The online article carries a link to a piece by Alex Thomson of *Channel 4 News*: "Rangers: how come nobody saw this coming?" published on 5 April 2012.)

The mainstream media (MSM) have been trounced in the Rangersgate story by bloggers and citizen journalists. Here is my first piece on the impending Rangers financial crisis. Note the date.[2] (The online article carries a link to the piece "The fall of the house of Murray", published on 11 January 2009.)

The MSM scoffed in 2009 that Rangers were in any kind of money trouble. That is because they were told by . . . err . . . Rangers that everything was OK. That was good enough for them.

In November 2010 the world was told that Craig Whyte was a "billionaire" and that he loved Rangers.[3] Alex mentioned in his blog that there was fertile ground for a PhD in media studies on the failure of the laptop loyal. I recently suggested the very same idea to a friend of mine who is a professor of journalism in a leading UK university. He agreed with me and plans to discuss this with appropriate postgraduate students.

[1] http://blogs.channel4.com/alex-thomsons-view/rangers-coming/1088

[2] http://www.philmacgiollabhain.ie/the-fall-of-the-house-of-murray/

[3] http://www.philmacgiollabhain.ie/when-journalists-forget-which-team-they-are-on/

Terms like "laptop loyal" and "succulent lamb" are about to enter the lexicon of academe. It is a form of fame that chaps like Keith Jackson perhaps didn't count on.

What's the point, caller?

06.04.12

What is the point of radio phone-ins?

Last night on Clyde 1 *Superscoreboard* the three guys in the studio – Jim Delahunt, Mark Guidi and Graham Spiers – took a call from a man about a CVA (Company Voluntary Arrangement) to get Rangers out of administration. There then followed an embarrassing tangle where, with great certitude, the three journalists contradicted the caller who had it bang on about the CVA and what percentage of debt a creditor had to have in order to block it. It produced the following tweet from the hack pack's self-styled intellectual: "@GrahamSpiers: Apologies for Spiers-induced HMRC faff on Clyde tonight. Of course Ibrox CVA could be blocked if tax bill is over 25% of debt. #toomuchgolf."

For any journalist working on this story for more than a year to be unaware of the basic mechanics of a CVA is unforgivable. The entire point of calling into a radio show is that the guys in the studio are meant to be more knowledgeable than the callers. Seriously, what is the point of phoning in?

I have, in the past, called in to provide them with key facts on the Rangers financial situation.[1] Just like the lads on Clyde I am not a business journalist. However, I go and ask people who are. I take notes and I check facts. If I am puzzled by any of their answers I go back and seek clarification. This is basic stuff for anyone with a press card.

If you need any more evidence of the point I am making then here is the link where you can analyse the lack of analysis and build up your knowledgebase on their lack of knowledge.[2] (The online article carries a link to a podcast of the Clyde 1 *Superscoreboard*, 5 April 2012 episode.) There is definitely a media studies PhD on their lack of . . . err . . . studiousness.

What is the point caller?

---

1   http://www.youtube.com/watch?v=cynMmAXFBuw
2   http://itunes.apple.com/gb/podcast/superscoreboard/id307483087

Paying the price for the failure of others

13.04.12

Subjecting the powerful to scrutiny is at the heart of journalism. Uncovering information that those in elevated positions would rather remain secret is something that every journalist should aspire to be part of. However, that is journalism at its best. When the Fourth Estate becomes corrupted by largesse and cronyism then THEY become the story.

Regular readers will know my views on Scottish sports journalism. Now that perspective is shared by Alex Thomson, an award-winning war correspondent from *Channel 4 News*. He uses terms like "succulent lamb" and got Graham Spiers to fess up about the extent of the collective failure on the part of the Glasgow hack pack apropos Rangers. By simply doing his job on several journeys north he has attracted the ire of some of the good ol' boys of the Glasgow media village. One hack in particular got particularly exercised and made physical threats to Thomson. I am aware of the details of this, but it is Alex's story to be broken at a time of his choosing. If the objective was to frighten Thomson off then it didn't work.

The idea that someone who has braved the craziness of Haifa Street in Baghdad would cower in fear because of threats made by a sports hack in Glasgow is risible. However, this vignette is a manifestation of a wider reality. It should now be taken as a given that the Glasgow sports desks aren't fit for purpose. I can think of two working sports journalists in Glasgow that I would consider worth the trouble. The rest of them have been behind the curve on the Rangers financial story for two years and some of them privately concede this to be the case. The new media outlets they publicly sneer at are their first port of call when they switch on their machines in the morning. Everything in life has a cost and the price of covering the slow death of Rangers is your good name. I have told this to any journalist who has contacted me and wants in on the act. I tell them to be prepared to be smeared by anonymous posters on football message boards and on social media, especially Twitter. I have endured this since I first took on the Rangers support over the "Famine Song" in 2008.

Yes, dear reader, 2008, and to think some of them still believe that I will give up . . . Ah bless. If I believed half of the lurid fantasies written about myself then I would not want to meet me. The bottom line is that a rotten, racist, corrupt organisation held most Scottish journalists in fear and awe for generations. The reaction to my work in 2008 in the *Irish Post* and in other newspapers, but mainly on this site, was one of shock that a named journalist would take them on. This isn't how it is meant to be, after all. Now Scotland's "establishment club" is about to be liquidated and subsequently this is a terrifying time for the ignorant and illiterate who invest their sense of worth in the continued existence of Rangers.

I know that UEFA are now fully aware of the scale of the malaise in Scottish football. They are watching the domestic association for evidence of swift decisive action if allegations regarding second contracts at Ibrox are proven. Now it is *Channel 4 News* and not some slavering sycophant that the powerful on Planet *Fitba* have to deal with.

This, dear reader, is progress. I am aware of my own contribution to this and I rather like the guy I see in the shaving mirror of a morning. I can exclusively reveal that a few in the Glasgow press pack won't enjoy their own features nearly so much in the coming weeks. They will know that they are looking at failure looking back at them.

Never a pretty sight.

The importance of measuring difference

17.04.12

Context is everything.

One of the reasons that we inhabit Planet *Fitba* is to measure difference. Who has the best team? Which team has the best player? Who will get over the line first? You need two teams for a match.

Martin O'Neill was correct to say that Rangers were the "benchmark" when he took over the Celtic job 12 years ago. He knew his team had to measure up. The league table is, at the end of it, about comparisons. However, when it came to the mainstream media in Glasgow there was very little that the ordinary supporter had to compare the local hacks to.

I would imagine that last night the audience figures for Clyde 1 *Superscoreboard* probably went up, especially after 7.00 p.m., for that very reason. There was, at long last, a comparison on offer. The big guy from *Channel 4 News* was in the studio.

Firstly, fair play to Clyde for having him on as they probably knew
he wasn't going to indulge in the usual mutual back-slapping. The
only thing that was lacking, I thought, was the anchor reminding Alex
Thomson that he was on live radio.

First out of the traps was Hugh Keevins with a white flag at the
ready as he basically announced that this "corporate governance" stuff
was above his pay grade. After last night the term "mainstream football
writer" now has another meaning for me. The main allegation made
by Thomson of succulent lamb laziness on the part of the Glasgow
hack pack when it came to Rangers is unanswerable. Moreover, the
man from Channel 4 was not some caller who could be faded out or
be dismissed as a "fundamentalist" or an "internet bampot" by one of
the resident hacks. As my American cousins would style it, Keevins and
Hannah were "taken to the woodshed" by Tomo. It was the radio equivalent of watching Kirk Broadfoot trying to man mark Henrik Larsson.
What we heard was the difference in perspective between those inside
the tent and those who wish to pull the structure down and show the
people what has been hidden from view.

I'm in the tent wrecking business myself these days . . . To para-
phrase the Clyde 1 *Superscoreboard* rather patronising catchphrase "It's
all about comparisons", and last night the contrast was embarrassing.
Enjoy.[1]

Transcription of conversation between Alex Thomson, Hugh Keevins
and Roger Hannah aired on Clyde 1 *Superscoreboard*, 16 April 2012:

> Hugh Keevins – "Well, Alec has mentioned corporate
> governance, the RBS situation, the government, all very
> well and good but over the weekend we are concerning our-
> selves, Roger, with two Scottish Cup semi-finals, me down at
> Wembley for two English cup semi-finals. I have said before
> on the programme I regard myself as a mainstream football
> writer. Matters of corporate governance, I hand that over to
> Alec and those like him."
>
> Alex Thomson – "Would there not be anybody in Glasgow
> you could hand it over to?"
>
> Hugh Keevins – "Oh yeah, absolutely."
>
> Alex Thomson – "So why didn't they take up the chance
> and do their job?"
>
> Hugh Keevins – "That's not for me to delegate."
>
> Alex Thomson – "It is for you to delegate. You are sitting,

---

1   http://soundcloud.com/jinkylarsson/alex-thomson-on-clyd

Hugh, on what is quite patently a massive story of corporate misgovernance at Rangers. That concerns you, that concerns your daily bread, it concerns the job that you do.

Hugh Keevins – "You're saying sitting on it. I wasn't sitting on it."

Alex Thomson – "Surely it was not in your gift to go to your editor and say look, there are serious questions to be asked of, for instance, David Murray, of, for instance, Craig Whyte. It didn't happen."

Hugh Keevins – "Our newspaper has pursued Craig Whyte from the very outset. We had the Ticketus story, which he denied and threatened action against the newspaper – took action for a day or so – so we are pursuing the matter and have done for months and months."

Roger Hannah – "The matter has been pursued quite vigorously on all sides. Hugh and myself have covered a lot of the football issues. Some of the news desks up here, Gerry, have covered a lot of what Alec's referring to as corporate governance issues. It's a slow and laborious process, it has been for a period of time. It has gathered pace I would say in the last 12 months, since Sir David Murray, for the princely sum of a pound, sold his controlling stake to Craig Whyte and things have begun to unravel at what could I think safely be described as a spectacular rate."

Alex Thomson – "Why was it a slow and laborious process to look on Google for about five minutes and find out who Craig Whyte was, what his record was when he took over the club? Instead of which the story went out as you well know – a billionaire, not true, off the radar wealth, and all the rest of it."

Roger Hannah – "... you will probably know this as well as me, Craig Whyte seems to have paid for his Google history to be deleted."

Alex Thomson – "There's Companies House there. Companies House don't delete records."

Roger Hannah – "Had I been selling Rangers, had I been selling my house, had I been selling my car to Craig Whyte I would probably have done greater due diligence than the people who sold Rangers to him, there's no doubt about that. But as football journalists I think at the time when someone was coming on the scene – Rangers had been for sale for three or four years, Alex, as you know – someone came on the scene, he looked to Sir David Murray, he looked to the majority of the Rangers support, he looked to broader Scottish society in general as a guy who had the wherewithal, David Murray spoke at the time that he has seen a proof of funds, obviously it wasn't clear at the time where the funds had come from, you know, via the Ticketus deal."

Alex Thomson – "I'm not saying for a moment that there's not been good journalism done. I mean John McGarry's done some great stuff recently on this story, for instance. So have the BBC in terms of *Panorama* and so forth. So indeed have the *Sun*. They, I think, were the first paper to actually publish one of these side letters so of course there's first-class journalism but the fact is journalism's been so sycophantic, generally speaking, towards the big two and certainly towards Rangers that you even have your own word for it here. I didn't know what succulent lamb culture was until I came on this story three weeks ago. You say that to anybody involved in football and they all smile knowingly. The fans smile knowingly because everybody knows there's a truth in that. Now you come further forward, I put someone who is very familiar to listeners of this programme, Graham Spiers, and I put him on camera not long ago, to say, and I did an amazing thing – I asked a journalist basically to dump on his own patch to say, look, what is this succulent lamb thing? Now, Graham was the guy who decided to do it. I have not one, not two, but three other journalists, all Glasgow based journalists, who all agreed to do the same thing. You have got four journalists there prepared to go on camera. This isn't me, this isn't Alex Thomson saying this, to say we have got to sort our house out. Our house is not in order."

Craig Whyte and Rangers one year on

04.05.12

One year ago today Craig Whyte bought Rangers Football Club. A good source had given me the tip about four or five days earlier that this was going to happen, but I didn't believe him. I haven't made that mistake since.

The green half of Planet *Fitba* was having great fun about the "fakeover" and few thought that Mr Whyte was actually serious about buying the stricken club. For a couple of weeks I was blindsided. The Rangers chaps crowed about this great result. Those of us who had made much of the "fakeover" had to admit that the club had, in fact, been bought. However, something still didn't add up.

Mr Whyte had been on the scene since the previous November. When he popped up on the radar it was the news that all the Rangers chaps had been praying for.[1] Deliverance was at hand! Unfortunately what the bears didn't realise was that in this drama they were the fat guy on the canoeing trip!

When he had initially been trumpeted as a billionaire in November 2010 I was busy with the Dallas story. Subsequently he didn't really register on my radar. I had spoken with a couple of Scottish journalists in Dublin in February 2011 at an international football tournament in Dublin. We pooled our meagre knowledge about Mr Whyte. Not one of us had unearthed any verifiable evidence of great wealth. However, I got the feeling that they wanted to believe that all of this was true.

A month after he had bought the club for a quid I was satisfied that this was going to be a train wreck. I didn't have all of the details, but I was satisfied that Mr Whyte was no billionaire and no Rangers supporter. I sketched out a possible game plan and, mindful of his litigious nature, cloaked it in satire.[2]

Now the club, in administration, is about to have a new owner. I have no idea who Mr Bill Miller is or what he is about. I don't know what his business background is, nor do I have any clue why he would want to buy that basket case of a football club. One year on it is fair to say that the mainstream media in Scotland got the Craig Whyte story stunningly wrong. It was a case study in the power of PR and how churnalism is becoming the norm, especially in the tabloids.

When I wrote on 7 June that Mr Whyte might not have the best interests of Rangers at heart the mainstream media were still in love with him. Throughout that summer I pursued every tip and every rumour about his business background. In May 2011 I was asked by the BBC to take part in a documentary about the "sectarian" problem

---

1   http://www.dailyrecord.co.uk/football/spl/rangers/2010/11/18/craig-whyte-profile-the-scots-billionaire-on-the-brink-of-taking-over-the-club-he-loves-86908-22722617/

2   http://www.philmacgiollabhain.ie/rangers-strike-it-lucky-with-their-new-owner/

in Scotland.[1] My contribution ended up on the cutting room floor, but I did have useful discussions in the staff canteen at Pacific Quay that there was a story in Craig Whyte. I told a couple of bright young things in the news side of things that a tsunami of excrement was heading towards Edmiston Drive. When I heard that Mark Daly was working on his documentary I allowed myself a smile. I knew this was beyond the pay grade of the sports people. There wasn't any point in trying to get through to them.

Now one year on it is clear that the guys on the sports desks in Glasgow got it stunningly wrong about Mr Whyte. The questions that they didn't ask of the Motherwell-born "billionaire" should now be put to Mr Miller of Tennessee.

Let's see how they do this time . . .

Spinning out of control

09.05.12

I must say that all of this Rangers stuff has my head in a spin.

I am sure I'm not the only one. David Murray, Martin Bain, Alastair Johnson, Craig Whyte, Duff and Phelps . . . a fine band of brothers. But what is the link between them all? Who had the ear of all these champions of truth, honesty and integrity? Who was the doyen of dignity? Who was the spinmeister supreme?

Step forward Media House's very own Ramsay Smith. A dour, some might say stubborn, Aberdonian, the bold Ramsay reflects the worst characteristics of the stereotypical native of the Granite City. It was Ramsay who stood side by side with Craig Whyte on the steps of Ibrox as Craig Whyte faced the baying mobs and committed a form of ritual seppuku.

The bold Ramsay Smith, ashen faced knowing he was in the middle of the biggest PR disaster since, since, since the last one. If Ramsay had been a football player he would have been substituted after that night's performance. It was Ramsay who, last Thursday, gave the gathered press conference a cold "good morning" as he guided the administrators to their moment of glory as they announced their "preferred bidder" Bill Miller. And yesterday, as the roof fell in on the big incubator, surely it wasn't Ramsay who suggested that the spin was to introduce three new

---

1   http://www.bbc.co.uk/news/uk-scotland-13438080

bidders? No, the man who has held senior positions in a handful of newspapers north and south of the border might have left that to the administrators.

Even in a world Pinocchio would have been embarrassed with, the misinformation and spin offered up to the Scottish press from all parties has been embarrassing. A stunning piece by the BBC's insightful business and economy editor Douglas Fraser yesterday is well worth a read.[1] He gives both barrels to Duff and Phelps with the stunning punch line: "They're looking ever more like Laurel and Hardy."

Well, if they are Laurel and Hardy where does that leave Ramsay Smith? If they had wanted laughs and jokes they could have employed Elaine C. Smith.

Liquidation Day

12.06.12

So it was all a Fenian's fantasy? The idea that the mighty Rangers would suffer the humiliation of liquidation was obviously just the ramblings of deluded bloggers in undignified places like Donegal. Yeah?

Today should put the officially sanctioned narrative of Rangers to bed for all time. HMRC will move to have the club liquidated. Their guys will carry out the liquidation. It will be a corporate execution on a digital scaffold to be viewed by all on Planet *Fitba*. Their humiliation will be total.

"Piercing the corporate veil" is a term that we will all become very familiar with in the weeks and months ahead. My thoughts are drawn to a certain knight of the realm whose father served 18 months in prison in the early 1960s for "fraudulent conversation", a trifling matter over some race horses and outstanding taxes.

The mainstream media are programmed to beg for scraps from the Rangers table.

Even when that piece of furniture has been sold in the corporate equivalent of a warrant sale they will still simper at the same place like one of Ivan Pavlov's laboratory-trained mutts. My published interest in Rangers' financial troubles goes back three years.[2] The bank taking effective control of the club was a major step towards oblivion for Rangers.

---

1   www.bbc.co.uk/news/uk-scotland-17999964

2   http://www.philmacgiollabhain.ie/the-fall-of-the-house-of-murray/

Once I had been given the tip about the existence of the "big tax case" in early 2010 it was game on. I started to attract the attention of people who wanted me to stop. In June 2011 journalists in Glasgow were briefed by PR chaps suggesting that my idea that Mr Whyte had used future season ticket money was a monstrous libel. Yeah, sure.

Then there were several attempts to take this site offline last year. Arranging to have the sheriff officer blokes snapped outside Ibrox seemed to be the last straw for some.[1] The Fenian in Donegal had to be silenced. In one instance some "stakeholders" at the Ibrox club complained to the web hosting company that this blog was "damaging Rangers as a going concern" because I was spreading lies. The web hosting company blinked. So I moved to another server. Then there was a DOS attack. We upgraded the bandwidth package at great expense.

The allegation that this site was having a negative impact on the financial health of the business was correct. I was informed that the new regime was having real difficulty raising a credit line because of the negative headlines. I was pleased when I heard this because that was my intention. If the objective of the off the record briefings against me was to reduce the number of page views to this site then it was a total failure! Moreover, if they thought that being called a "chancer" with a "comedy blog" would stop me then that also failed.

It is the mainstream media who are being laughed at as this saga unfolds. I just kept at it and my weapon of choice was the truth.

Today I'm smiling.

Links

http://www.philmacgiollabhain.ie/what-is-your-point-caller/   28.12.10
http://www.philmacgiollabhain.ie/clyde-1-super-scoreboard/   27.01.11
http://www.philmacgiollabhain.ie/
    rangers-tax-case-questions-that-deserve-an-answer/   12.03.11
http://www.philmacgiollabhain.ie/
    the-failures-of-lobby-journalism/   15.03.11
http://www.philmacgiollabhain.ie/
    how-the-rangers-tax-case-went-mainstream/   01.04.11
http://www.philmacgiollabhain.ie/paul-baxendale-walker/   05.04.11
http://www.philmacgiollabhain.
    ie/a-question-of-life-or-death-for-rangers/   10.04.11

---

1 http://www.philmacgiollabhain.ie/photographs-you-were-not-meant-to-see/

http://www.philmacgiollabhain.ie/asking-important-questions/   06.05.11
http://www.philmacgiollabhain.ie/
    breaking-the-gordon-smith-story/   18.06.11
http://www.philmacgiollabhain.ie/telling-the-truth-about-rangers/   07.07.11
http://www.philmacgiollabhain.ie/it-shouldnt-be-allowed-shining-a-light-on-
    the-financial-situation-at-rangers/   15.08.11
http://www.philmacgiollabhain.ie/how-to-defeat-churnalism/   25.08.11
http://www.philmacgiollabhain.ie/the-first-rough-draft-of-history/   09.09.11
http://www.philmacgiollabhain.ie/my-questions-for-craig-whyte/   13.09.11
http://www.philmacgiollabhain.ie/and-in-the-blue-corner/   28.09.11
http://www.philmacgiollabhain.ie/job-done/   18.10.11
http://www.philmacgiollabhain.ie/the-new-bbc/   23.10.11
http://www.philmacgiollabhain.ie/nikica-jelavic/   22.11.11
http://www.philmacgiollabhain.ie/rangers-and-stv/   28.12.11
http://www.philmacgiollabhain.ie/
    the-importance-of-precision-in-journalism/   05.01.12
http://www.philmacgiollabhain.ie/ignoring-the-story/   24.01.12
http://www.philmacgiollabhain.ie/the-daily-record-catches-up/   31.01.12
http://www.philmacgiollabhain.ie/
    when-journalists-forget-which-team-they-are-on/   04.02.12
http://www.philmacgiollabhain.ie/
    the-future-of-journalism-is-bright/   08.02.12
http://www.philmacgiollabhain.ie/
    too-cowardly-to-report-too-bigoted-to-believe/   18.02.12
http://www.philmacgiollabhain.ie/
    two-very-different-conversations/   20.02.12
http://www.philmacgiollabhain.ie/on-the-record/   01.03.12
http://www.philmacgiollabhain.ie/all-right-on-the-knight/   12.03.12
http://www.philmacgiollabhain.ie/a-local-type-of-madness/   13.03.12
http://www.philmacgiollabhain.ie/the-usefulness-of-c4/   20.03.12
http://www.philmacgiollabhain.ie/the-price-of-succulent-lamb/   24.03.12
http://www.philmacgiollabhain.ie/scotlands-other-shame/   31.03.12
http://www.philmacgiollabhain.ie/answering-questions/   01.04.12
http://www.philmacgiollabhain.ie/
    the-importance-of-having-time-on-your-side/   02.04.12
http://www.philmacgiollabhain.ie/the-man-from-auntie/   03.04.12
http://www.philmacgiollabhain.ie/a-phd-in-failure/   05.04.12
http://www.philmacgiollabhain.ie/whats-the-point-caller/   06.04.12
http://www.philmacgiollabhain.ie/
    paying-the-price-for-the-failure-of-others/   13.04.12

http://www.philmacgiollabhain.ie/
    the-importance-of-measuring-difference/   17.04.12
http://www.philmacgiollabhain.ie/
    craig-whyte-and-rangers-one-year-on/   04.05.12
http://www.philmacgiollabhain.ie/spinning-out-of-control/   09.05.12
http://www.philmacgiollabhain.ie/liquidation-day/   12.06.12

Part III: Fans Section

Introduction

The fans are the lifeblood of any football club. The club that played at Ibrox had huge amounts of the stuff, more than any other in Scotland. Estimates vary on the size of the support that travelled to Manchester, but it is believed between 130,000 and 200,000 people were in the city in May 2008 to cheer on Rangers. It was the club's first European final since 1972.

Piccadilly Gardens, in the centre of Manchester, housed a lunatic asylum until 1849. On the night of 14 May 2008, madness returned to the site following Rangers' defeat at the hands of FC Zenit St Petersburg in the UEFA Cup final. When Rangers reached the UEFA Cup final in 2008, their opponents were a Russian outfit, as in 1972. The omens were good.

Zenit St Petersburg – managed by ex-Rangers manager, Dick Advocaat – triumphed 2–0 in a one-sided affair. The fans inside the City of Manchester Stadium were well behaved. However, many of the Rangers fans outside went on a rampage of violence and criminal damage. What was not in doubt in the aftermath of that night of mayhem was the size of support that the Ibrox club could attract. Despite that undeniable fact in 2008, the same supporters were largely posted missing in 2012.

In April 2012, a mere 7,000 of them walked to an empty Hampden Park for a rally where they were addressed by ex-player Sandy Jardine. That isn't even the size of the deceased club's SPL away support. It remains baffling that, when faced with extinction, so much of the Rangers following stayed away.

If a clairvoyant had sketched out this scenario before me on the day of the UEFA Cup final in 2008, I would have predicted many tens of thousands at that march in April 2012. I would have expected a reaction at least on a par with the "Celts for Change" movement, set up by Matt McGlone and Brendan Sweeney in the early 1990s when Celtic were in danger of going out of business.

Part of the inertia can be explained by an important difference in the culture and mores of both sets of supporters. Celtic fans are natural rebels. They have no problem with seeing themselves outside power structures. Within the Rangers subculture there were several pathogens that prevented them from mobilising to save their club. A Herrenvolk hubris convinced many of them that "the Rangers will never die". The idea of their club sliding beneath the waves was just too big for them to take in. This wasn't denial; it was a lack of imagination.

A key component of the Ibrox subculture is an acceptance of authority. Sociologists have long studied the "deferential working class". The north-east of Ireland and the west of Scotland developed a specific subculture of proletarian support for the bourgeoisie, around an imagined set of common interests. The Broederbond of the British Empire had, along with freemasonry, an important role in shaping the Ibrox subculture.

The Orange Order – with their bowler hats, aping the attire of the shipyard foreman – epitomised a specific worldview, permeated by an acceptance of the status quo and a wish to benefit from not rocking the boat that was being riveted.

Although I was writing about Rangers on a daily basis, there were some aspects of their belief system that I simply didn't get. For example, the fixation over whether or not a Rangers manager wore a tie and looked like "a Rangers man" seemed, to an outsider, utterly irrelevant. However, that which is cultural is not amenable to reason. The club tie and brown brogues seemed to say something profound to the Rangers support.

Perhaps it was about not letting the side down because the other lot were looking; the Britisher on the veranda. The natives could be scruffy, but, by God, not us! There are followers of the Ibrox club who are wholly committed to tackling racism and support a tolerant multicultural society. They are Rangers supporters because they were born into a family who supported the club. That is how most people have an affection for a particular football club. It isn't chosen; it is inherited.

What I was writing about was the very worst elements of the Rangers support. However, Scottish society was undergoing profound change as it entered the new millennium. Scotland was now a country with its own legislature and many wanted to take the next step to full statehood. What kind of Scotland people wanted became a topic of debate. Within that conversation it became increasingly clear that the Ibrox song sheet had to get a twenty-first-century civilised makeover.

As the crazier, more vocal elements in the support resisted the change, less and less was heard from the vast majority of decent Rangers fans. As the first decade of the millennium progressed, the bigots at Rangers were called out firstly by the passing of the Criminal Justice (Scotland) Act 2003, and then by UEFA banning the "Billy Boys" song in 2006. The Rangers fans, allowed to act with impunity by the domestic football authorities, were blindsided when UEFA took action against the singing of the "Billy Boys", the song commemorating Billy Fullerton of Bridgeton.

Fullerton was a gang leader in the 1920s who headed a group of razor-wielding street fighters. A member of Oswald Mosley's British Union of Fascists, he founded a chapter of the Ku Klux Klan in the East End of Glasgow in the 1930s.

During the general strike of 1926, Fullerton and his members aided the civil powers when Britain was paralysed by the biggest trade union dispute in its history. Fullerton was awarded a medal for his services to strikebreaking. The Billy Boys attacked shop stewards and terrorised activists. Many of Fullerton's men received certificates of commendation from the Secretary of State for Scotland. For many of them it was their prized possession. In those days "SPL" stood for Scottish Protestant League.

The SPL wasn't a competition where decisions always went Rangers' way, but a political party that did well at the polls. In the 1930s, anti-Catholic parties, including the SPL in Glasgow and Protestant Action in Edinburgh, took up to a third of the votes in local council elections.

This was the era of John White in the Church of Scotland. Born in Kilwinning and inducted into the ministry in Shettleston in the East End of Glasgow, he developed a xenophobic hatred of Irish people. When White was the convener of the Church and Nation Committee, it produced the infamous 1923 report on "The Menace of the Irish Race to our Scottish Nationality".

White wanted an end to Irish immigration into the country. He advocated the forced deportation of the "southern Irish race" in order to create a "racially pure" Scotland. He considered the Irish to be more prone than native Scots to drunkenness, crime and financial incontinence. This was the Scotland in which Billy Fullerton and his gang lived. Reading the views of the Reverend White must have been an affirming experience for them.

In 2002, convener of the Church and Nation Committee, the Reverend Alan MacDonald, told the Kirk's General Assembly his views on the 1923 report: "I am ashamed when I read how badly we got it wrong. We cannot ignore what has been wrong in the past, but we also have to face up to the ugly side of Scotland today."

The 1920s hosted the first generation of Rangers supporters to *know* they were watching a team unpolluted by the Fenian Untermensch. Billy Fullerton and his chaps encapsulated those core elements of the Rangers subculture that have endured for over a century. The key components are: pride in the Empire, monarchism, religious fervour (if not always church attendance), hostility to Irish Republicanism and, to a lesser extent, Scottish separatism. However, a hatred of Catholics, particularly Irish Catholics, is at the core of this imported Ulster worldview.

Ibrox stadium became a sort of Loftus Versfeld to Protestant supremacy. The Rangers faithful knew they would never have to cheer on a "Fenian" in light blue. Ten years ago, when this subculture started to be seriously challenged, there was a backlash. Graham Spiers, in particular, wrote consistently in the *Herald* about the appalling bigotry of the Ibrox crowd. The away support was even worse.

Whereas the 1990s had been glory days for the Ibrox faithful, the first decade of the millennium proved altogether more perplexing. Celtic were no longer broke. The new stadium at Parkhead was bigger than Ibrox and the arch-rivals of Rangers could boast a bigger crowd and more season ticket-holders. Celtic could now match up to them on the field.

In early 2009 I had started to write about the worsening Rangers financial situation, including information that the club's parent company, Murray International Holdings (MIH), was heading for a default on two major loans. This led to a very hands-on approach by the bank at the Ibrox club. I had become a source of high-grade news about Rangers' financial situation. These weren't succulent lamb-fuelled fairy stories. This was the real deal and it wasn't good news.

Although not directly connected to Rangers, my central involvement in breaking and developing the Dallasgate story in 2010 – which led to the dismissal of the SFA's head of refereeing development over an offensive email about the Pope – confirmed my bad guy status in the eyes of the blue half of Glasgow.

By early 2011, the followers of Scotland's establishment club were being regaled with stories of Mr Craig Whyte's fabulous wealth. There was also the steady diet of "don't worry" articles about the big tax case. I took a different view on both matters. I couldn't find any independent verification of great personal or corporate wealth on behalf of Mr

Whyte. Moreover, I could find no evidence that he was a real "bear" or an emotionally committed Rangers supporter. That left me with the working theory that he was not of great personal wealth and he saw an opportunity to make money out of the club. This, I thought, was going to be interesting.

Of course, he was helped in this project by a compliant media. Fans were reassured that his wealth was "off the radar". The good times were here again!

Although I had been in journalism for years in Ireland, I was relatively unknown in Scotland. In 2008, I was interviewed on the *Real Radio Football Phone-In* after my involvement on the Irish side of the "Famine Song" controversy. The case that I presented – that the song was racist and, ipso facto, illegal – was unanswerable. The personal invective directed towards me from the Rangers end of the Glasgow internet continued. It was as if I had turned on a tap in 2008 when I had written about the "Famine Song". There was rarely any attempt to refute the analysis I was proffering, rather just a lashing out.

An early strategy seemed to be to simply state that I wasn't a journalist and my work could be disregarded. Throughout this period I had the unbending support of my colleagues in the NUJ and for that I will always be grateful. The union has a steadfast commitment to promoting journalism that tackles racism head on. My work ticked all of those boxes.

Looking back, I sometimes wonder if there was any thought-out objective to the smears and threats I endured from the Rangers crazies. My home address was posted on a Rangers message board. Then on the same site the modalities of my extinction were playfully discussed. I took screen grabs and presented them to the authorities here in Ireland. The police in Donegal were excellent. They took a formal statement and sent it through the various channels until it finally reached Scotland. I never did hear of the lads in Strathclyde taking any action.

If those responsible thought I was going to go away then this book is evidence enough that they miscalculated. The policy from day one was not to respond. It remains my stance. I doubt I could have changed their minds about anything. They knew what they knew, even if there was no proof of it. This was a hermetically sealed belief system that proved to be evidence resistant. This aversion to facts would become more and more apparent in the last days of Rangers.

The crazier end of the Rangers online community saw themselves as victims of a pernicious Kulturkampf, whereby Protestant Scotland would be turned into Mayo circa 1950. The reality was more pro-saic and more shameful. It was simply that the religious and ethnic hatreds that had been part of the Rangers experience for generations were, finally, no longer acceptable in modern Scotland. What was being asked of the Ibrox support in 2006 would have been unthinkable in the 1970s.

The Rangers owner, Sir David Murray, had experienced this changing world when he had been interviewed for a *Panorama* documentary in 2005. He recoiled in his seat as a real journalist from London went after him about the match day experience at Ibrox, which appeared to involve lots of "wading in Fenian blood". This was not how Murray liked his journalists; the hacks in Scotland were grateful and obedient. The *Panorama* guy was a harbinger of Alex Thomson of *Channel 4 News*. Murray countered with ushering in "British" songs for Ibrox. The statement made much of Rangers being a British football club; it was a coded reference to the Fenian blood waders.

This was also the decade of the internet, and this became a method whereby, as Graham Spiers styled them, "the poorly educated and left behind" were able to convince each other that they were correct and only they saw the true way. The Rangers support, as they were assailed by the mores of modern Scotland, started to resemble a cult, but one without a charismatic leader. That was the only thing that was missing. They craved an alpha male who would speak to them and for them. It was only post-liquidation that John "Bomber" Brown stepped forward.

The response of the assembled throng to his oratory at the front door of Ibrox stadium on 27 June 2012 validated my harshest assessments of what the Rangers support had become in the twenty-first century.

Graham Spiers' excellent journalism on the Rangers bigotry problem had made him a bête noire among the Ibrox hardliners, especially when he had referred to the "white underclass" that had attached itself to Rangers. Clearly, what defined this group wasn't their love of Rangers, but a hatred of Irish Catholics. The football club at Edmiston Drive was the vehicle for this socially acceptable racism – a subculture created around hate and intolerance.

If that wasn't bad enough, this Fenian had started to call them out on the racism of the "Famine Song". The likes of me were meant to sit quietly at the back of the bus and accept whatever was thrown at us. That role was not to my liking.

When I managed to break the big tax case into the mainstream in May 2010 I had established my credentials as a well-known nuisance for the Ibrox tribe. Now the bears had another reason to dislike me. If any of them had parked their bigotry they would have seen I was doing them a huge favour. The red tops, by peddling the feel-good fairy stories were, in fact, inadvertently creating the situation where the club would die.

These days, supporters of the deceased club are the target of jibes and taunts from the fans of just about every other club in Scotland. The agreed narrative is that Rangers cheated the country of tax monies to gain an unfair advantage on the playing field. The Rangers fans now thrash around for a focus for their anger. However, there are so many potential baddies in this melodrama that the Ibrox klan doesn't know where to start. There are the two previous owners of the club, Sir David Murray and Craig Whyte, and now there is Charles Green.

Green's company, Sevco, purchased the assets of the dead club and had the stated intention of trading as Rangers in the future. He has no historical or emotional connection to Ibrox and it is feared that he may not have much money. Moreover, some Rangers fans fear that his true intention may be more to do with valuable real estate as opposed to sporting glory. However, so far there isn't any evidence to substantiate this widely held concern among large swathes of the Ibrox support.

This isn't how it is meant to be for the Ibrox faithful. Their sense of cultural superiority over the rest of the tribes in Scottish football is difficult to convey to anyone outside of Scotland. Even the term "establishment club" doesn't do it justice. The fans are imbued with a certainty that they are, by birthright, number one in Scotland. The connections between the Ibrox club and those in ruling positions at the SFA stretch back a long time. This privileged status was transmitted down to the fans over generations.

This is the only explanation for the silence of the SFA over the decades when Rangers operated an employment policy that was openly discriminatory and sectarian. The Rangers subculture was created at the Zenith of Empire and just as that global polity was beginning to be challenged from within and without. The Ibrox club brought in their ban on signing Catholics in the years immediately before the Great War. This was also the time of the Irish Home Rule crisis. Glasgow's shipyards, with their strong connection to Belfast, provided Clydeside with a "Labour aristocracy" of Ulstermen. They brought with them the Orange Order and a pathological hatred of Fenianism, the ideology it had been set up to oppose. Thus, Rangers became another expression of that politico-religious identity: the integrity of the United Kingdom, loyalty to the Crown and a belief in the Reformed Faith.

The exclusion of Catholics was, at the time, a simple and effective way of making sure no "disloyal" types would wear the light blue jersey. The signing ban came in around 1911, a decade after Irish Catholics achieved occupational parity in New York. The same religious ethnic group would achieve that sociological milestone in Glasgow in 2001.

It was that generation of modern Glaswegians – of Irish ethnicity and reared in the Catholic tradition – born into an era of employment equality who would not tolerate the attitudes of hostility and racism. To use the Deep South analogy: they would not, unlike their parents, be prepared to sit at the back of the bus.

When the market in football talent became global, the ban on Catholics made no sense. Players from southern Europe and the Americas were now available. The Ibrox "No Catholics" policy was actually a simple way of excluding players of Irish ethnicity. Anti-Irish racism was what defined the Rangers worldview for much of the last century.

In the Ibrox worldview, I'm a Fenian. I was reared in the Catholic tradition. I have one Irish-born parent and a mother called Bridget, whose four grandparents hailed from various parts of rural Ireland.

To state that the bigotry problem at Ibrox is about anti-Catholicism is to befriend nonsense. It was always about anti-Irish racism. Subsequently, someone like me ticked all of their boxes. I had made choices all of my adult life that had asserted an Irish identity. I applied for Irish citizenship when I was an adult.

From 2008 onwards I was getting in their face. I was a Fenian from central casting. I was everything they didn't like. I was also a Fenian who wasn't meant to exist in their racist worldview – university-educated, an accredited journalist and an NUJ member. I had access to the media; I was able to converse with MEPs, UEFA and the Irish government about the antics of the Ibrox klan. As well as campaigning against their racist chanting and the fact that the club they loved seemed incapable of signing a first team player from the Irish Republic, I was also doing them a service. I was, for a while, one of the few sources of information about the extent of the financial mess at Ibrox. There was only one problem. They wouldn't believe a Fenian.

The sports desks were on message and not about to challenge the official narrative that everything was fine. There was a reticence to go after this story by the sports desks in Glasgow and this was a huge factor in the fans not having the information they needed about the state of the club. By the time Craig Whyte took over and the season ticket money rolled in it was already too late for Rangers. A series of events were now in train that would lead to the liquidation of the 140-year-old club.

Even when they were warned by a BBC documentary in October 2011 about Craig Whyte's business background, the Rangers fans chose deference over deliberation. They did not analyse what Mark Daly's investigative reporting had revealed. Instead, as with this writer, they played the man and not the ball. The BBC man's religious background was discussed. After the Daly documentary, Whyte continued to get the benefit of the doubt from the vast bulk of the Ibrox faithful.

At this juncture it is fair to point out the qualitative difference between Celtic supporters presented with the bad news about their club in 1993 and what was revealed to their city rivals from 2009 onwards. The Celtic fans mobilised. In the Parkhead firmament the names Matt McGlone and Brendan Sweeney are well known and fondly remembered. Their Celts for Change movement captured the moment. It proved decisive.

The fans boycott forced the bank to act and Fergus McCann moved in and wrote cheques that didn't bounce. The man dubbed "the Bunnet" saved Celtic. McCann could have liquidated the club and bought the assets, but he wanted to preserve the history of a special club. Celtic – broke and hours from going out of business in March 1994 – were the first team in Britain to lift the European Cup, in 1967.

As Archie Macpherson said, that achievement made Celtic a special club and, ipso facto, one worth saving. Because of these subtle, but crucial differences in the Rangers subculture, there was no 'Gers for Change movement and, ultimately, no blue Bunnet.

What Rangers needed as debts piled up was a Fergus McCann figure – someone with money who was willing to spend it and a business plan to put the club on a paying basis. Rangers had been saveable, even when the big tax bill was known to be a real possibility. It would have taken honesty and humility from those in leadership positions at Ibrox. A fire sale of the best players and an acceptance of second fiddle to their city rivals for several years would have been the price of paying the bill from the EBT decade. However, a 'Gers for Change-type fans' rebellion just didn't sit well with a group of people reared on deference. People who venerate the word "loyal" rarely rebel against those in power. The positive self-image of the Ibrox chap is of a reliable and hardy state functionary.

The only large public assembly of Rangers supporters during the period of administration came on 28 April 2012 when 7,000 fans marched to Hampden. It was a Saturday and the people who actually run the Scottish game weren't there. When I saw the YouTube footage it seemed somehow poignant that these people didn't realise that the boat had sailed on the tide of history. Their club was doomed and they were beached.

The belief system that had sustained generations of Rangers supporters before them was burnt out, a husk. The Ibrox worldview no longer made sense of a modern Scotland that could produce people like Dame Elish Frances Angiolini, the late Paul McBride QC and a pesky Fenian in Donegal with a press card who wouldn't give them a moment's respite.

From the point of the club going into administration on 14 February until the Company Voluntary Arrangement (CVA) was formally rejected on 14 June 2012 by HMRC, the fans slowly realised just how powerless they were. They were helpless onlookers, but it wasn't always so. There was a time when they could have acted, and to good effect.

When I was writing about the Rangers support after the club went into administration, I was taken back to my social work training. I had been trained in bereavement counselling and the model of Dr Elizabeth Kubler Ross emerged from my long-term memory. Her five stages of grief remain extant in the literature and clinical practice to this day. DABDA: Denial. Anger. Bargaining. Depression. Acceptance.

The culture of the fans and the stance of the mainstream media assisted in keeping huge amounts of the Ibrox faithful in the initial denial stage for a critically long period of time. The belief that nothing had really happened meant that large-scale, meaningful mobilisation didn't materialise. The Rangers Fans Fighting Fund (RFFF) organised a sponsored walk around Ibrox on Sunday, 20 May 2012. The duration was one mile and 872 yards – to symbolise the year the club was founded, 1872. The Rangers Fans Fighting Fund raised several hundred thousand pounds, but by the time the money was brought in it was like bailing the *Titanic* with a bucket. Given the crowd in Manchester in May 2008, it was an alarmingly weak response to a deadly threat. In the end it wasn't enough. Too little, too late.

While they weren't mobilising, the subject matter on the Rangers message boards continued with the obsession around Celtic manager Neil Lennon, priests, paedophilia and . . . me. Increasingly, they sounded like the good ol' boys in Alabama hankering after the days when the world was more to their liking. The old days of structural discrimination against Catholics, especially those of Irish ethnicity, is thankfully a thing of the past. There is nothing unique in that story. Immigrant groups in many countries experience a difficult generation or two. In the case of the Glasgow Irish it was more than a couple of generations, only achieving occupational parity a century after their cousins in New York.

Like the African American walk to equality in the Deep South there are, no doubt, a few old Klansmen who still tell some younger followers that things used to be better. There were days when the blacks knew their place. Similarly, I have no doubt that there are still people in multiracial democratic South Africa who secretly venerate images of Eugène Ney Terre'Blanche as a sort of Afrikaans Che Guevara. The Volkstaat isn't coming back but bigots, once deposed, are pained by equality.

The inability to organise a mass mobilisation of people around an aim tens of thousands agreed with – to save Rangers FC – in a peaceful city within a democratic state in the age of social media is, quite frankly, astounding. At best, the various fans organisations, working together, could not put 10% of the Manchester crowd on the streets. Their best effort was less than Rangers would take as a travelling support to Pittodrie.

Yet no one in the mainstream media pointed this out. Perhaps people in positions of power in Scotland breathed a little sigh of relief that the Ibrox club was allowed to die quietly without too much fuss. Stewart Regan's comments about "social unrest" caused something of a stir. Although highly inappropriate for someone in his position it, perhaps, revealed a lingering concern about the potential of the Manchester mob on home turf.

Over the years I have been writing on the subject of the finances of the Ibrox club, I have been contacted by many Rangers fans through my site or across various social media platforms. A composite message (with expletives deleted) would read as follows: "You've got it wrong. The authorities will never let the Rangers go out of business. We Are The People!"

There was a simple failure to entertain the possibility that something untoward could happen to their football club. What I was suggesting was such an appalling vista that the Copeland Road end suddenly became full of Lord Dennings! The emotionally driven belief in the permanency of Rangers fed the inertia of the fans. This Herrenvolk hubris was not just a key factor in their failure to mobilise; it rather defined their presentation to the world.

Their city rivals, by way of contrast, exuded a put-down chippiness of always being at the back of the bus. Celtic was the club of Irish Catholic immigrants, an ethnic group which had suffered a level of social exclusion unique to the global Irish diaspora in the twentieth century.

Across the Anglophone world the Irish Catholic did less well in Glasgow and the West of Scotland than anywhere else – something that has engaged historians and sociologists. This is, perhaps, why the Lisbon triumph of 1967 inflicted such a deep psychic wound on the self-esteem of the Rangers tribe.

Another aspect of this perfect storm was the role of the media in Glasgow. Although their contribution to the death of Rangers is covered at length elsewhere in this book, it is appropriate to note their role in misinforming the supporters of the Ibrox club. The red tops had a need to keep the good news coming for those in the blue half of Glasgow. It was circulation driven. The people in leadership positions in Glasgow newspapers knew that a steady diet of doom and gloom about Ibrox would hit sales. This led to the fans not being made fully aware of the nature of the crisis at their club.

When there was some negative copy about Rangers there tended to be an angry backlash from Rangers supporters. This became a feedback loop. It was signal and response for titles that were close to the edge apropos circulation figures. Basically, this allowed the people at the top of the marble staircase to escape from serious journalistic scrutiny.

Alex Thomson of *Channel 4 News* came on to the Glasgow football beat by happenstance in 2012. The Geordie of Scots Presbyterian stock could not be dismissed as a Fenian and his journalistic credentials were impeccable. The award-winning war correspondent, no stranger to trouble spots, had a new experience; he was threatened by a journalist in Glasgow for running with the Rangers story. The term "fans with typewriters" took on a whole new meaning.

Thomson reported the incident to Strathclyde police and included other journalists who had been on the receiving end of threats in the complaint, including this writer. At time of writing, neither I nor the guy from Channel 4 has received any indication that an investigation is ongoing. We're not holding our breath.

When threats were clearly not working, Thomson had to be dismissed by the Rangers fans, including members of that persuasion within Glasgow journalism. The narrative developed that Thomson had been duped. The poor fool. During his work on the Rangers saga he was whisked away by ITN to work on the Syrian civil war. His work covering the massacres there is award-winning material yet we were asked to believe that this veteran journalist had been taken in by some Machiavellian Celtic supporters. The very notion was risible.

On the other side of the city, many Celtic fans could not believe what was unfolding in front of their eyes. I had more direct contact with Celtic supporters online and I became a sort of cyber counsellor, especially on the home beat, Celticminded.com. Fretful Hoops fans would just want to know that the most awful things were about to happen to *them*.

All I did for the Celtic fans was exactly the same as I did for the Rangers fans – I laid out the facts. Many of them harboured a nagging doubt that somehow the establishment would, at the eleventh hour, save the establishment club. What they couldn't grasp was that Rangers represented an earlier incarnation of the establishment. They had been the football club that symbolised a class alliance along ethno-religious lines on Clydeside. The native bourgeoisie and the skilled shipbuilding workers met in lodges and followed the same football team. The emotional contract was strong and everyone bought into it. There would be no Fenians on the park for the Rangers and God would be in his heaven.

As the CVA vote approached I attended a question and answer session at a social club in Lanarkshire. Once more, the same question came at me, driven by worry and a lifetime at the back of the bus. My answer was the same; I was in broken record mode: "The CVA will be rejected. HMRC won't wear it. There is evidence enough for a case to be made that evasion occured. Rangers will die and no one will save them. There won't be anyone coming in at the last minute with a masonic defibrillator. It's over, they're gonna die."

The crowd applauded; it was what they wanted to hear. It happened to be the truth, as I saw it, or I would not have said it. I wasn't out on a limb; I was utterly convinced that there was zero chance of HMRC going for a CVA. There was no caped crusader to save Rangers on the day.

The British state, like many in the developed world, had turned the banking crisis of 2008 into a fiscal disaster. HMRC were going after every available penny. For the Rangers fans it had to be a Fenian conspiracy – it is how they see the world. The reality was more nuanced, more prosaic. However, what they had proved over the years of my journalism was that they held a highly evidence-resistant belief system.

The banking collapse of 2008 had finally turned off the tap of cheap credit that had sustained Sir David Murray's business empire, of which Rangers Football Club was part. The shareholders' meeting on 14 June 2012 was merely the final chapter. As stunned supporters were caught in the vox pop they looked ashen. One of them likened it to a death in the family. Another stated that 140 years of history was over.

The following day the tabloids, to be fair to them, didn't hold back. It was the imagery of death that was used. The *Sun* showed a coffin with a Rangers crest being lowered into the grave. Despite all of this, almost a month later the followers of the Ibrox club remained in steadfast denial that anything really bad had happened. They told themselves that only a holding company was gone when, in fact, FIFA, UEFA and even the SFA knew they were now dealing with a new club.

Of course, Rangers' 140-year history is not "lost", but it has been concluded. The Charles Green consortium bought the assets of Rangers which were then put into Sevco Scotland Ltd.

The administrators Duff and Phelps then renamed Rangers and the club established in 1872 is now called "Rangers Football Club 2012 PLC (IA)".

This club, the original Rangers FC, now has no assets and £5.5million in a bank account awaiting the liquidators, BDO.

Sevco Scotland Limited bought the intellectual property rights from "Old Co" and now they trade as "The Rangers Football Club Limited (TRFC Ltd).

The Ibrox fans smart from taunts from other clubs about being "Sevco" fans.

No matter how strongly they riposte it is undeniable that,in the eyes of FIFA, liquidation is the end of a football club.

The fans, still smarting from the Craig Whyte humiliation, finally got smart. They were suspicious of the Sevco consortium, headed up by Charles Green. The coach and ex-player, John "Bomber" Brown, emerged at the head of another consortium. His rallying cry to the faithful and their response to him confirmed my bleakest analysis of what this element of the Rangers support had become. Filmed on a mobile phone and uploaded to YouTube, Mr Brown would test all the skills of a PR specialist to put a positive spin on his "oratory".

Yet still the fans believed. What congregated outside Ibrox stadium to listen to "Bomber" was a rather tragic gathering. These people have been consistently lied to. They were told everything was fine with their football club when it was trading while insolvent. When information was published in 2010 about the big tax case it was dismissed and, once more, they believed.

I am writing this during the close season and it is always something of a phoney war for football clubs and their supporters. However, all of the pre-season friendlies that Rangers had entered into at the end of season 2011–2012 have been cancelled by the other teams, fearful that Sevco would not be able to fulfill the fixtures. The only tangible sign that all is not well at Ibrox is the fact that the majority of the first team squad have decided not to "TUPE" over to Sevco. Under the "Transfer of Undertakings (Protection of Employment) Regulations 2006", all of the employees of the liquidated company could move to Sevco. However, they also had the right to walk away. This is what most of the star players in the first team squad decided to do. This was probably the first visible sign to Rangers fans who were still in denial that something massive was happening at their club.

One Rangers fan was quoted as saying that if the team played football on the streets, he would support from the pavement. This speaks of a deep emotional need to belong. Affiliation needs is the academic term, but it is an essential part of being human. Many people misinformed the Rangers fans about the state of their club. I wasn't one of them.

They saw my journalism as damaging Rangers. If that is true then my weapon was the truth and that should be the only thing in the armoury of a journalist. The guy who would buy a season ticket for his spot on the pavement manifests an admirable loyalty, but in the cold light of liquidation the support that invaded Manchester in such huge numbers was eerily passive as the club was led to the gallows. The vast majority of the support that took the road to Manchester merely looked on as the club was put to death.

The day after the UEFA Cup final in 2008 there was an awful mess to clean up and plenty of recriminations about what went wrong. As with many of the misdemeanours in the past, the Rangers fans sought to blame an external entity. It was never their fault; the screen had gone dead; the police – just like in Spain on many occasions – were "heavy handed". The bears were blameless.

The financial and organisational wreckage left in the aftermath of the death of Rangers is still to be fully audited. The collateral damage on the national game is epochal. Unlike 2008, this time the Rangers fans did not play a major role in the carnage. Their passivity and inertia in 2012 is something that no one could have imagined the day after the battle of Piccadilly. The unwillingness of Rangers supporters to act in substantial numbers at a time of terminal crisis for their club will be one of the enduring mysteries of British sport for a long time to come.

Why did Rangers supporters stand by and allow their club to bleed out?

The unbearable truth

17.03.11

Denial is the default setting in humans when they are faced with very bad news. Rangers supporters are human. The club's mid-term accounts are still unpublished. It is a requirement of the SFA that they are published by 31 March.

Last year Rangers published them in mid-February, with time to spare. I am sure that it would have been the same in 2009 and before. Accountants are notorious for working to rigorous schedules. It is one of the things that define them as an occupational group. Why, then, have the accounts not been published?

Several onside Scottish journalists were briefed last week that they would be published this Monday, 14 March. Still, they are unpublished.

It would appear that the collective response from Rangers fans is something akin to: "If one of them says there's a problem at the Rangers then there isnae!" This, of course, prevents the fans from asking pertinent questions of the people in charge of the club.

So, if your heart is at Ibrox and you think that your club is in rude financial health, that there is about to be a takeover by Mr Whyte, that the bank isn't controlling the club, that there is no tax case looming which will put "The Rangers" into administration and that there isn't a dispute going on at boardroom level that is delaying these mid-term accounts, then my work is done.

All I have wielded is the truth. It has been enough.

Our gallant allies in Europe

17.04.11

Once more the task has fallen to UEFA to deal with the discriminatory chanting that seems to be the norm among a section of the Rangers support.[1] The reaction of the mainstream media in Scotland has been to investigate the method by which the Ibrox club had been

---

1   http://www.scotzine.com/2011/04/
    uefa-charge-rangers-for-a-second-time-over-sectarian-singing/

"shopped" to those interfering continentals.[1] The implication is that Glasgow tribalism is at the root of this case and that somehow UEFA has been "got at".

The stark reality is that there is prima facie evidence from numerous European games involving the Ibrox club. Their fans have indulged in discriminatory chanting in many of the club's matches in Europe this season. Rangers were warned in November by UEFA and the club passed the import of that on to their fans. Still the chanting continued.

After the away match against Sporting Lisbon, FARE (Football Against Racism in Europe) was tasked by UEFA to attend two Rangers v. PSV Eindhoven games to provide an expert opinion on whether or not there was discriminatory chanting from the Rangers supporters. As usual, they didn't disappoint.

The Rangers support was intent on looking for a culprit, but didn't use a mirror. Many thought that FARE had acted in a hostile manner towards "the Rangers".[2] Paranoia is an evidence-resistant condition. The people to blame for the charges being laid at the door of Rangers are the club's own supporters.

One wonders what UEFA would have thought of the Scottish football authorities and the Scottish government had they sat in Hampden Park during the Scottish Communities League Cup final between Celtic and Rangers on 20 March. A river of bile flowed from the blue half of the national stadium. There was hardly a football song to be heard from them. Instead, it was Fenian bastards and Fenian blood all the way. Despite this, there were few arrests and a statement of commendation, not condemnation, from the Scottish Justice Secretary and the police afterwards.

This is a public stance at variance with the facts on the ground that one normally associates with North Korea. The leaders of the Irish community wrote to the Justice Secretary, Kenny MacAskill, and to SFA Chief Executive, Stewart Regan. These communications can be viewed on this site, but have not been deemed newsworthy by the mainstream media in Scotland.

Can you imagine if tens of thousands of football supporters at Hampden had been chanting bile and invective about the Prophet Mohammed? Would there have been the same statements about the fans playing their part in a great occasion? Any written communication

---

1 http://scotlandonsunday.scotsman.com/news/
   Sectarian-row-chief-married-to.6753118.jp

2 http://www.farenet.org/default.asp?intPageID=7

from the Islamic community to the authorities would have been splashed all over the front pages of the main titles in Scotland.

In a sense, the good old boys on the Scottish sports desks do have a point. The UEFA guys don't get it. They simply do not understand why this anti-Catholic, anti-Irish venom is tolerated in Scotland. Moreover, they have no idea of the status of Rangers as the establishment club. Indeed, to attempt to explain the underlying social dynamic of modern Scotland – complete with its Punch cartoon view of the Catholic Irish – to an urbane, polyglot UEFA administrator is a major task.

However, the good people of UEFA have got their heads around the basics of the RFC songbook. Instead of songs about the peerless Jim Baxter, the brilliant Paul Gascoigne or great victories on the field of play, there is a constant output of hatred for Popes, priests and the Irish. Remember, dear reader, this is 2011. Whatever the decision reached by the UEFA disciplinary body in two weeks, one thing is certain: justice will be done and will be seen to be done.

UEFA's response to the club about the origins of this disciplinary case makes that much very clear. The bottom line is that discriminatory chanting will not be tolerated by supporters of any club playing in UEFA controlled competitions, even "the Rangers".[1] The comparison between the attitude of Europe's ruling soccer body and the domestic authorities in Scotland could not be starker.

Why it's too late for 'Gers for Change!

04.09.11

Originally published on Scotzine

During the Dallas email story last November I met up with Matt McGlone. These days he's the editor/proprietor of the highly successful Alternative View, but back in the days before "The Bunnet" landed in Scotland, Matt was a streetwise revolutionary. As we chatted in the foyer of a Glasgow hotel with my laptop hooked to the wi-fi, it seemed another age, another world to those nights at the City Halls and the Celts for Change rallies.

One thing that struck me when recalling those times was how well informed the Celtic supporters were about the perilous financial

---

1   http://www.scotzine.com/2011/04/
    uefa-hit-back-at-rangers-over-deliberate-and-targeted-campaign-comments/

situation of the club. No matter how much the old board tried to put a brave face on the situation, the media would reveal the truth. That's the media's job, of course.

The old Celtic board tried to say that the club would move to a new stadium in Cambuslang and everything would be wonderful. The mainstream media gutted that story, explaining why the figures didn't add up and that the site itself was a toxic disaster area that would take millions to clean up, even if the authorities were to allow it to be excavated.

Before any group of people mobilise for a common purpose they must have information. That is why a free, unimpeded press is a central pillar of any functioning democratic society. Celtic supporters in the 1990s were well informed by the traditional media.

Today, in 2011, Rangers supporters are not well informed. Since I started writing on Rangers' problems with HMRC back in April 2010, the main response from Rangers supporters has been one of disbelief. This can't be true. Well, it is.

Rangers are currently in the tribunal process for an assessment that, if it crystallises (i.e. Rangers lose) would become a bill for some £60m and change. The most recent issue, over a £2.8m tax bill (the "wee tax bill"), has seen sheriff officers visit Ibrox and, last week, have the RFC bank account legally impeded to secure those funds.

I arranged for a freelance snapper to be there to capture the moment and I tipped off another colleague who is a regular freelancer with the *Sun*. Even with these pictures on my site the day before the *Daily Record* and the *Sun*, Rangers fans were on their message boards saying things like: "Two bemused men who had just left Ibrox after trying to book a function room!" When one has that level of denial then it is easy to spin to them that everything is OK. They want to believe the spin.

It is now the opinion of several key insiders that Rangers FC will go into negative cash flow without a credit line to tide them over. Martin Bain sought to arrest Rangers bank account this summer. His application for "a warrant for the diligence on the dependence" was refused. His legal team expressed their client's fear that the company would not exist. This is the club's ex-chief executive. What does he know that Rangers fans don't?

When the Bunnet landed in Glasgow, I didn't have long to wait to know everything I had to know – good and not so well – about Fergus McCann's business history. What do Rangers supporters know about Craig Whyte's financial status? I would contend that they know very little indeed. In the internet age, is it really plausible that someone taking over such a high-profile company could escape scrutiny from the main-stream media?

It is, sadly, too late for 'Gers for Change. In the age of social media it would have been so much easier to organise and mobilise the club's huge fan base. Imagine the 2008 crowd at Manchester marching as one. The time for that has gone. Rangers supporters are now helpless spectators, just as they are when they file into Ibrox and things aren't going well on the park. They can shout and boo, but they cannot, of course, score a goal.

The own goal from the Rangers support was to believe the spin being put out by the old regime and now the new. They have been let down badly by sports journalists in Scotland. In time to come they might ask, "Why didn't we know this at the time?"

The thing is, from the *News of the World* last summer and through social media, they were being told. Partly, perhaps, that the main source of this information was a journalist called Phil Mac Giolla Bháin in Donegal. They chose not to believe this bad news because of the ethnic-ity of the journalist and his location.

It is truly a tragedy that people can be so limited because of the toxic belief system into which they have been socialised. It isn't their fault. Scotland's biggest club stands at the door marked "administration" and my trade did next to nothing to highlight the danger. It is too late, and if people of the light blue persuasion don't believe this man in Donegal then they should go and ask Martin Bain, because they shouldn't expect a Scottish sports journalist to do it for them.

The time for their Matt McGlone to step forward has passed. Like most things in life it's all about timing. All Rangers supporters can do now is watch and wait. The time for action has gone.

The end of history

05.02.12

A sense of history and continuity is vital to all football fans every-where. The date of establishment is almost always on the club's crest. Rangers Football Club was founded in 1872. If the company that was set up when Queen Victoria was on the imperial throne is liqui-dated, then it will be no more. The historical thread of tradition will be broken.

There will, in time, perhaps be a Rangers, but it won't be the Rangers. It won't be the same club because Rangers (1872) will be dead. Another club called Rangers, or some variant of that name, may be set up.

The supporters are the lifeblood of any football club. To attract the previous clientele, the new company will have to look at what created such a loyal customer base for the club established in 1872. What was the unique selling proposition that created the huge following? Was it the sectarian employment policy for most of the twentieth century? Was it the swaggering Herrenvolk hubris and imperialistic jingoism? Was it the inexplicable failure to find one player from the Republic of Ireland good enough for their first team in the last fifty years?

Rangers have been a nexus for the most toxic aspects of a north British sub-Victorian worldview that should go into the landfill of history. Every time Rangers play, it allows an opportunity for the mob to authorise and validate the birth defect of modern Scotland – anti-Irish racism and anti-Catholic hatred.

In the age of Holyrood and a growing Scottish awareness, is there truly any room for the belief system that nurtures this fascist underclass? If there is a new club born can it be different from the old one? Can the supporters sing songs about the club's players? When, for example, have you ever heard the crowd at Ibrox sing a song about the majestic Jim Baxter?

The question that I have when considering the post-liquidation scenario is this: Can the new Rangers be normal?

There may be doubts about where money for the NewCo will be sourced from. However, I believe the pressing issue is whether or not the new club can get new fans because the current supporters do not deserve anything other than the misery and angst they are now enduring.

The good news for decent football fans in Scotland is that their emotional condition is about to get much worse. As for Rangers? Soon they just might be history.

When the truth makes you a target

13.02.12

When people are asked to think about high-risk occupations, they often don't give a thought to journalism. Soldier might be the top one, but of course, combat troops often have a journalist along for company.[1]

Last year I attended a one-day conference in Belfast around the issue of safety for journalists. The event was sponsored by the Northern Ireland NUJ branches and the Sunday World. The conference was held, in part, to mark the tenth anniversary of the murder of journalist Martin O'Hagan by Loyalist gunmen in Portadown. Martin was a constant thorn in the side of Loyalism as he exposed it for what it was – a criminal enterprise first and last.

A minute's silence was held to honour his memory. A decade on, his killers have still not been brought to justice.

There were many veteran journalists at the conference, and these reporters had spent decades covering the Northern conflict. They all agreed that professional training was seriously lacking in addressing the issue of coping with trauma and health and safety issues. It was agreed in the plenary that the NUJ had a pivotal role to play in pushing the training establishments to teaching coping strategies to student journalists.

I am aware that in recent years threats have been made to several journalists in Scotland. The anonymity of the internet allows actionable bile to spew forth, and the main offenders are the quintessentially British people who trashed Manchester in 2008.[2]

Although I questioned the rationale of the SNP's new legislation governing behaviour at football matches, I do agree with the sections covering the policing of the internet.[3] I am glad to report that the NUJ is leading from the front in protecting its members in Scotland. A free press is a sine qua non of democracy, and it is correct that the Scottish government is lobbied on these matters.[4]

I know of a recent threat to a journalist based in Glasgow which emanated from the dignified end of the city. The guy has a young family and he was extremely shaken by the experience. His "crime" was to report the truth and do his job. Once more, the NUJ at workplace and national level were not found wanting. Thankfully, Strathclyde's finest are all over this one.

---

1   http://www.journalism.co.uk/news/record-number-
    of-journalists-killed-on-dangerous-assignments-/s2/
    a547267/

2   http://www.philmacgiollabhain.ie/goerring%E2%80%99s-eleven/#more-561

3   http://www.philmacgiollabhain.ie/a-bad-law/

4   http://dl.dropbox.com/u/32661772/The%20Journalist%20Paul%20Holleran%20
    approaching%20Salmond.pdf

As the death of Rangers approaches, I suspect that there will be more of this hateful nonsense. Just as when the light blues are playing in Europe, I know which side I'm on. I support the police.

Waiting for a new saviour

17.02.12

One of the most striking things about the last week on Planet *Fitba* has been the response of Rangers supporters. Even now there does not seem to be any organised movement of fans to implement an agreed agenda for change. Why should this be so?

Back in my undergraduate days at York, we spent many intense seminars on the pressing subject of the "deferential working class". We wanted to know how to fix it. "False consciousness" was the diagnosis of these proletarians who accepted their lowly status within class society. Looking back, much of the optimism about changing this was all highly risible. However, with a charismatic professor like Laurie Taylor, anything seemed plausible.

The problems of a deferential working class re-emerged from my long-term memory when considering the inaction of Rangers supporters to the current crisis. There has been no equivalent of Celts for Change among the Ibrox faithful, and now it is too late.

What will happen, will happen.[1] Quite simply, they are not the stuff you make rebellions with. They worship power and strong leaders. This is a subculture of the happy underling. Neither Empire nor Auschwitz could function without such biddable types. Social scientists like Milgram and Zimbardo have tried to discover the origins of this blind obedience and worship of authority.

In the Rangers support, we have an excellent example of what Hitler's propaganda guru Goebbels understood could be done with a compliant crowd where the little man could be transformed from "a little worm into part of a large dragon". In their deference to Mr Whyte, the Ibrox crowd was the perfect subculture to buy into their own collective oblivion. The assembled throng at Ibrox on Saturday would much rather wade up to their knees in Fenian blood than collectively organise against their own ruling class. Instead of exerting their collective might against existing power structures, some of them would prefer to prowl the streets in search of the next Mark Scott.

---

1 http://www.scotzine.com/2011/09/why-its-too-late-for-gers-for-change/

Even as they turn against Craig Whyte, they pray for another feudal overlord to worship.

My idealistic colleagues were correct to concern themselves with this social problem in the civilised environs of York University sociology department. The gathering at Ibrox tomorrow will once more confirm that we are no clearer to finding a cure. Until then, the rest of us on Planet *Fitba* would be better off without them.

A carnival of reaction

25.02.12

It couldn't get any worse, could it?

A club built on dignity brought to its knees by maladministration, lies and deceit. But surely the good name honed in Manchester, Barcelona, Newcastle and Pamplona couldn't sink any deeper into the gutter, could it? The inane utterings of Rangers security boss, David Martin, should have made many associated with Rangers squirm. He said of alleged sectarian chanting at the recent Rangers v. Kilmarnock game: "Last Saturday's match was one of high emotion following an extremely difficult week for the club . . . The club held a number of meetings and conversations with the football authorities, police and administrators prior to the match and everyone agreed that the priority on Saturday was to ensure there was no disorder around the match due to the highly-charged atmosphere that was anticipated."

So, are we to take it from Mr Martin that there was an agreement with the police that sectarian and racist singing was to be allowed because of the "highly emotional" atmosphere? According to independent reports, almost half of those attending the match were taking part in the singing of illegal songs, yet there was only one arrest. For those interested, that emotional fellow will not face charges.

But get set for more from the highly emotional hordes. Powerful groups of Rangers supporters associations are passing around the blue bowler to see if they can raise enough cash to take the SFA and the SPL to court. The crime in the bloodshot eyes of the Rangers loyal is that both the SFA and the SPL should have seen through the Motherwell billionaire and blocked his takeover of Rangers.

And they say comedy is dead?

Under pressure they reveal their soul

27.02.12

It is an axiom in many professional organisations that extreme pressure reveals the true person. This is why the people who construct training courses build stressful situations into them. I have had the logic of this approach proven to me many times over the decades.

The military and the emergency services are looking for stable extroverts. They need good team players, and that is why they put recruits under controlled pressure during basic training, so that the personality of the trainee can be assessed.

I believe what is true for an individual is also valid for groups of people.

Over the last two weeks, the supporters of Rangers Football Club have been brought face-to-face with an extreme pressure situation. At Ibrox, during the first match after going into administration, they sang about being up to their knees in Fenian blood. Yesterday, in Inverness, they felt moved to chant about paedophilia as if it were a suitable subject for sporting rivalry. What appears to be in short supply among the Rangers choir are any songs about their own football club. There are remarkably few tunes or chants in their repertoire recalling great players or past victories. They appear to prefer Fenian Bastards to Fearless Baxter.

Is this actually a football club? Moreover, is it any wonder that so many on Planet *Fitba* pinch themselves at the tantalising prospect of a world without Rangers? Following administration and the possibility of the club being liquidated, the Rangers support have revealed their inner self. Their collective soul is one of distilled hatred for Scotland's Irish community and for people of the Catholic faith.

This is who they are. Please let this football club die . . .

How to assemble a lynch mob in one easy session

26.04.12

The threats to the safety of the "SFA three" prove why their identities should not have been revealed. Given that Rangers are about three weeks from liquidation, the assertion that the decision had "killed" the club is risible. Rangers cannot come out of administration because there are no credible bids on the table. Stuck in that insolvency event, they are about to run out of cash. Therefore the idea that the transfer ban was the coup de grâce is nonsense.

The demand from Ally McCoist to be told the identities of the panel members is also puzzling. The club has a letter from the SFA with their names on it. Andrew Dickson, the head of football administration, went to the hearing and sat across a table from them. I was aware of their identities yesterday morning as my description of them will clearly attest. However, I would never have named them.

By yesterday afternoon, the names of the three men were on Rangers supporters' message boards and on Facebook. The police are now involved and perhaps this will be a first outing for the internet provisions of the new controversial legislation.

Yesterday I was speaking with one of the three-man panel who had recently sat in judgment of Neil Lennon. That was a private conversation and must remain so. However, we did speculate what the furore would have been if the current scenario had been instigated by Neil Francis Lennon and not the cheeky chappie. Quite.

The mob of misrule

01.05.12

There are several cultural differences between both of the big tribes on Planet *Fitba*.

When I listened to Neil Doncaster last night explaining the imminent admission of an Ibrox NewCo into the SPL, I thought of one of those differences. I believe that it is important for the blue tribe to believe that people are frightened of them. This is the conqueror's respect. Hence they hate to be mocked and laughed at.

On Sunday, those who the Rangers people believe to be their ethnic inferiors collapsed in hilarity at the state of the Ibrox club as the light blues fell to pieces on the pitch. It is the essential difference between Seville in 2003 and Manchester 2008. Mirth versus malice.

Over the past month I have spoken to several journalists in Glasgow who are simply frightened of becoming a target of The People.[1] (The online article carries a link to a piece in The Drum in which Hugh

---

1   http://www.thedrum.co.uk/news/2012/04/30/
    sportswriter-hugh-keevins-claims-intimidation-after-criticising-rangers-fc-manager

Keevins reveals he has been subject to intimidation for criticising Rangers manager Ally McCoist.) I haven't spoken with Mr Keevins about this, but I am not surprised at what he reveals.

There isn't anyone within the Scottish media village who doesn't think that Rangers are done for. Everyone in the know accepts that the Ibrox club established in 1872 will be liquidated soon and that isn't up for debate. What is at issue now is what happens to any NewCo. The senior decision-takers and those who write about the game in Scotland appear to be, in part, influenced by how the Rangers mob will perceive them. The "Hampden 3" have already experienced a little of that venom.[1]

The only person to put cash on the table in believable amounts is Mr Bill Miller of the USA. His strategy is clearly the NewCo route. When Rangers die in liquidation there will be an angry mob looking for vengeance. Given that Mr Miller is from the fine state of Tennessee then that should give him enough scope to understand what he is about to become embroiled in.

The klan that marched to Hampden at the weekend still has some evolving to do.

Ibrox apocalypse

04.06.12

I recently likened the current Rangers debacle to a movie script. I said that the director had decided to speed up the action.[2] As often with throwaway remarks, you can stumble upon something useful. There is definitely a film in the situation that has unfolded for the Ibrox club since February.

Regular readers here will know that I was not taken aback by Rangers going into administration. Some of the twists in the plot have been unexpected, but the basic course of HMS Dignity has not altered. When I made the movie quip I was writing for a Spanish publication, therefore I threw in a reference to Pedro Almodóvar. However, given this is a Caledonian epic, it would have to be directed by Mel Gibson.

You may, dear reader, think that I am giving the job to the Aussie because of his brave-hearted assault on Scottish history. If you have made that assumption then you are wrong. Rather, I was thinking of

1 http://www.philmacgiollabhain.ie/how-to-assemble-a-lynch-mob-in-one-easy-lesson/

2 http://www.vavel.com/en/uk-football/scottish-premier-league/glasgow-rangers/166421-rangers-the-movie.html

his examination of the circumstances that caused the Mayan civilisation to be liquidated. His dark masterpiece, Apocalypto, is what gets him the gig.

For the uninitiated, Gibson's 2006 movie is highly recommended and works wonderfully well on various levels. There are themes that work for everyone, from the erudite movie connoisseur to the Rangers supporter. As in Braveheart, people have blue paint daubed on their skin, but the reason for this adornment in Apocalypto is much more germane to the current situation at Ibrox.

Lucky winners in the lottery of Mayan life are daubed in the Rangers home colours before having their heart ripped out for public spectacle. Some denizens of Ibrox might be able to empathise with that situation. This macabre ritual is part of Mayan sun worship. They think this barbarity will appease their deities, the poor dears. Standing at the top of steep steps, the holy man gibbers nonsense and the confused, fearful, adoring crowd lap it up. They are desperate to believe and out of their minds with worry. They are simultaneously vulnerable and vicious.

If Mel wants to remake this epic in Scotland I think I know of a great location in Mount Florida. However, we would have to shoot that scene when the building was empty, but I think that's been done before. Sorted.

Fooling the mob in order to control them has an important place in human history. Agriculture created settled living and this in turn produced large cities. In these great conurbations, the mob emerged for the first time. As civilisation developed it was not only livestock that had to be herded. A central part of the Rangers saga now is how to control and harness the rabble that wrecked Manchester. The Ibrox mob needs to continue to believe and, crucially, to stump up.

Their season ticket cash is vital for cash flow and when the CVA fails and the venture goes into the NewCo phase, the lucky things will be offered a share issue opportunity.

At the very beginning of Apocalypto, a quote is put up on the screen from philosopher Will Durant: "A great civilisation is not conquered from without until it has destroyed itself from within." It is a less than gentle hint from Gibson that what we are about to watch is self-inflicted. At the end of the movie, the Spanish turn up with all types of assorted goodies, like steel swords, Bibles and, most killing of all, germs. To borrow a term from social anthropology, from then on in the Mayans are well fucked.

We should not mourn their demise, for this was no land of saints and scholars. This Mesoamerican polity attacked their hunter-gatherer neighbours, abducted them and murdered them in human sacrifice rituals. The great cities are built using a method of construction that poisons the land. When the crops inevitably fail, the superstitious clowns decide that they aren't offering up enough of their ecologically-forest-dwelling neighbours to a sociopathic deity that doesn't exist. The good guys in the movie finally escape their clutches and withdraw to the forest which gave birth to them.

In 2012, the last in the Mayan calendar, we see another "civilisation" coming to an end.[1] The Rangers subculture are not Mesoamericans, but they think that they represent a higher social order in this part of the world. They don't.

I don't see what is attractive about being the trailer trash of a dead empire. When the Spanish turned up on the Yucatan peninsula at the start of the sixteenth century, they were one of the four major powers that built three-masted sailing ships. The English were in that European quartet.

Now it is reasonable to discuss a twentieth century where Britain effectively doesn't have blue water navy of any size or import. The bigoted shipyards on the Clyde and Lagan that did much to nurture the Rangers subculture a century ago are tiny industrial theme parks where once there was a rain forest of cranes. The process is called history. The Mayan's demise was constructed by their own actions and, crucially, through their own hubris.

The green half of Glasgow will enjoy a popcorn summer for entirely those reasons. One of the most delicious things about all of this is that these apocalyptic events were created within Ibrox over many years. It was not the victims of the Rangers belief system who plotted and orchestrated this dramatic downfall. The custodians of Scotland's establishment club, in order to appease the craziness of the mob, undertook a course of action that has led to this. This collapse is a wonderful spectacle and should be captured on film for future generations to enjoy. For the good guys in Glasgow, this will be a time to search out a new beginning. One without Rangers.

Links

http://www.philmacgiollabhain.ie/the-sash-cloud/   14.07.10
http://www.philmacgiollabhain.ie/uefa-match-delegates/   24.02.11
http://www.philmacgiollabhain.ie/neil-lennon/   04.03.11

1   http://www.philmacgiollabhain.ie/a-mayan-moment-for-rangers-in-2012/

http://www.philmacgiollabhain.ie/958/ A Wise Appointment   15.03.11
http://www.philmacgiollabhain.ie/the-unbearable-truth/   17.03.11
http://www.philmacgiollabhain.ie/
    trade-union-equality-officer-is-famine-song-defender/   15.04.11
http://www.philmacgiollabhain.ie/our-gallant-allies-in-europe/   17.04.11
http://www.philmacgiollabhain.ie/
    live-bombs-sent-to-lennonmcbride-and-msp/   19.04.11
http://www.philmacgiollabhain.ie/aicsc-statement-on-neil-lennon/   21.04.11
http://www.philmacgiollabhain.ie/the-teachable-moment/   23.04.11
http://www.philmacgiollabhain.ie/helping-rangers/   03.05.11
http://www.philmacgiollabhain.ie/
    attack-on-neil-lennon-at-tynecastle/   11.05.11
http://www.philmacgiollabhain.ie/the-obdurate-order/   04.06.11
http://www.philmacgiollabhain.ie/the-other-neil-lennon/   20.07.11
http://www.scotzine.com/2011/09/
    why-its-too-late-for-gers-for-change/   14.09.11
http://www.philmacgiollabhain.ie/for-the-record/   18.09.11
http://www.philmacgiollabhain.ie/safety-in-the-workplace/   02.10.11
http://www.philmacgiollabhain.ie/sing-a-rebel-song/   19.11.11
http://www.philmacgiollabhain.ie/anthony-stokes/   29.11.11
http://www.philmacgiollabhain.ie/an-illicit-ethnicity/   13.12.11
http://www.philmacgiollabhain.ie/a-bad-law/   20.12.11
http://www.philmacgiollabhain.ie/
    how-to-be-a-racist-in-scotland-and-get-away-with-it/   10.01.12
http://www.philmacgiollabhain.ie/the-view-from-strasbourg/   20.01.12
http://www.philmacgiollabhain.ie/the-end-of-history/   05.02.12
http://www.philmacgiollabhain.ie/
    when-the-truth-makes-you-a-target/   13.02.12
http://www.philmacgiollabhain.ie/waiting-for-a-new-saviour/   17.02.12
http://www.philmacgiollabhain.ie/a-carnival-of-reaction/   25.02.12
http://www.philmacgiollabhain.ie/
    under-pressure-they-reveal-their-soul/   27.02.12
http://www.philmacgiollabhain.ie/
    the-freedom-to-vent-is-part-of-the-game/   23.03.12
http://www.philmacgiollabhain.ie/neil-lennon-at-ibrox/   26.03.12
http://www.philmacgiollabhain.ie/the-neil-lennon-problem/   27.03.12
http://www.philmacgiollabhain.ie/the-price-of-silence/   30.03.12
http://www.philmacgiollabhain.ie/anger-management/   18.04.12
http://www.vavel.com/en/uk-football/scottish-premier-league/148488-neil-
    lennon-s-life-in-scotland.html   21.04.12

http://www.philmacgiollabhain.ie/how-to-assemble-a-lynch-mob-in-one-easy-
    lesson/ 26.04.12
http://www.philmacgiollabhain.ie/a-culture-of-hatred/   27.04.12
http://www.philmacgiollabhain.ie/the-mob-of-misrule/   01.05.12
http://www.philmacgiollabhain.ie/ibrox-apocalypse/   04.06.12

Part IV: SFA Section

Introduction

When Stewart Regan launched *Scotland United: A 2020 Vision* in January 2011, he clearly did not envisage the tsunami of trouble that was heading his way, but he should have. You don't need perfect eyesight to see how cruelly ironic the opening words of this impressive document are when looking back over the past eighteen months: "Traditions and heritage are the foundations of our game. Yet they can also be a barrier to progress." These words could have been written with Rangers Football Club in mind, but not in the way that Regan imagined.

In January 2011, the iceberg was already on its way towards Scottish football. At that point, Craig Whyte and his diligent team were in the data room at Ibrox examining the club's finances in minute detail. The first-tier tax tribunal in Edinburgh was about to resume to hear the last of the evidence in the big tax case.

The EBT case, in the public realm since early 2010, had made the club unsellable to anyone but Craig Whyte. His catastrophic period of ownership would force the club into administration, and ultimately liquidation, when HMRC refused to accept a Company Voluntary Arrangement.

Despite Regan's claim to have a 2020 vision for Scottish football, he would never have imagined a vista with a NewCo Rangers in Division Three of the Scottish Football League (SFL). Faced with that unfolding situation, he would try everything in his power to prevent it. It looked a done deal on 7 May; Rangers NewCo would be parachuted into the Scottish Premier League (SPL). The numbers seemed to be stacking up in favour of a "yes" vote.

At this point the American truck tycoon, Bill Miller, had been given a "period of exclusivity" by the administrators, Duff and Phelps. Miller's people were clear that they'd been given assurances from the people who run the Scottish game that a NewCo Rangers under his ownership would play in the SPL. There is no reason to doubt that the American's advisers were well briefed by senior members of the SFA and the SPL about where the NewCo Rangers would play.

When he was challenged about the morality of the NewCo route, SPL chief executive Neil Doncaster spoke blithely about this being a perfectly normal way of "shedding debt" for football clubs. That was the plan. However, the decision was avoided and postponed by the football authorities, which seemed paralysed by hesitation. That was a critical mistake for those who wanted the Ibrox cash cow in the SPL.

While the authorities stuttered, a *No To NewCo* fan-led campaign was gaining ground across social media. It swept across SPL fans' message boards like a brushfire. Club chairmen were under pressure from those who had held season tickets for decades. The message was simple: "Put them back into the SPL and I'll never be back!" The weight of opinion from the fans was not in question. Despite the warnings of "Armageddon" from those in charge of the game in Scotland, the supporters didn't want a Rangers NewCo in the SPL. In the end, the fans won.

Jock Stein had long ago spoken of the centrality of supporters to the national game. June 2012 was the moment that fans became aware of their power. Throughout this debacle there was a clear need for the steadying influence of the constitutional monarch of Scottish fitba, the president of the SFA. Of course, in that position remains Campbell Ogilvie and as the club secretary of one First Division club reminded me as I was writing this chapter: "Campbell is cup-tied on this one!" It was a point brilliantly made by a guy who deserves the title "SFA insider".

Suspicion lingered that those in charge of the game had an agenda to push a NewCo Rangers back into the SPL as if nothing had happened and it would be business as usual. This was largely confirmed when Alex Thomson of *Channel 4 News* published an email from Stewart Regan on his blog on 15 July. One would have thought that, given his experience with the Dallas affair, Regan would have been more careful about what he committed to sending in an email.

The leaked email, dated 23 June 2012, read:

"Dear all,

Many thanks for your contribution and support over the last two weeks in trying to deliver a programme of change that will move Scottish football forward whilst addressing the need to deal with the Rangers matter with integrity and in line with our own values as an organisation.

I was hugely encouraged with where we got to last night on a long and tiring phone call and I thank all of you for your efforts to move this issue forward.

I thought it would be helpful if I summarised where I think we are:

1. The Rangers Football Club will be relegated to the 1st Division of the SFL with immediate effect and will be replaced in the SPL by Dundee FC.

2. The television rights for Rangers FC matches in the SFL will be purchased by the SPL for the sum of £1m as a one-off fee for the season 2012/2013.

3. The two leagues will merge into a single league body – The Scottish Professional Football League – effective season 2013/14 – with a working party set up immediately involving representatives from the SPL, SFL and (if required) the Scottish FA to plan the integration of the two bodies – people, rules, rebranding, commercial considerations and so on.

4. A new Board of Directors will be appointed to govern the single league. The makeup of this Board will consist of an Independent Chairman, CEO, 3 representatives from the Premier League, 2 representatives from the Championship/Leagues 1 & 2 and 2 Independent Non-Executive Directors.

5. Play-offs will be introduced immediately with the first matches taking place at the end of the coming season 2012/2013.

6. Enhanced parachute payments will be implemented from the end of the season 2012/2013 to soften the landing for club(s) relegated from the Premier League.

7. A revised all-through distribution model will be put in place to provide: a) An all-through distribution model for clubs 1–22 and a minimum guarantee for 20 clubs in Leagues 1 & 2, equivalent to what they would earn under the current settlement agreement.

8. A Pyramid System will be put in place which [will] open up the bottom of League 2 effective from the end of season 2013/2014 with the first opportunity for promoted clubs to enter the league being 2014/15 thus allowing for licensing to take place.

9. Consolidation below the Third Division to take place to create a Lowland & Highland League structure effective 2014/15 with appropriate play-offs and promotion/relegation to be put in place. Clubs to be briefed that the previous season 2013/2014 will involve the opportunity to enter play-offs for the first time.

In terms of actions/timings I think the following needs to happen in this coming week:

A) A joint statement today from all 3 bodies confirming that productive discussions have taken place on a new blueprint for Scottish football. Consultation will continue over the next two weeks with a view to clubs getting together week commencing 2nd July to try and agree the way forward. (D Broadfoot to provide this and circulate to DL/ND for approval)

B) Rod P/Jim B to finalise the all-through financial model by Wednesday this week latest.

C) Neil/David to finalise the detail on Governance, Commercials and Play-Offs (ideally Monday/Tuesday) and incorporate these, plus the financials in B) above into a legally binding Heads of Terms 'draft' for presentation to each league body w/c 2nd July.

D) DL to organise SFL Board Meeting w/c 25th June to gain buy-in to the plan and also arrange an all club meeting w/c 2nd July

E) ND to gain support from SPL Clubs 28th June

F) SFL Clubs Meeting to be planned for 3rd July

G) SPL Club Meeting to be planned for 4th July

H) Scottish FA Board to sign off on the final plan post 4th July. Subject to approval all bodies (including NewCo) to sign legal documentation.

I) Agree joint communication strategy

J) In parallel to A–D above, could Rod Petrie please brief Charles Green confidentially on the discussions from a Scottish FA perspective so that there are 'no surprises' and there is a general acceptance of the plan plus all of the other conditions discussed e.g. transfer embargo, fines, repayment of football debt, waiving rights to legal challenge, acceptance of relegation and so on.

K) Andrew to ensure our check list of disclosures relating

to NewCo and Fit & Proper Person criteria are delivered by 2nd July. The Board will need these plus the
Heads of Terms above in order to complete this plan.

The Scottish FA Board have agreed to provide a one-off
restructuring budget of £1m on condition the above plan is
delivered.

I hope this covers everything.

Speak soon . . . now off to the airport!

Regards

Stewart"

Regan failed in his plans to have NewCo Rangers shoehorned back
into the SPL and his failure was brought about by the very values that
his glossy document claimed to espouse. Page eight of *Scotland United:
A 2020 Vision* starts with a quote from Henry Ford: "If you always do
what you've always done, you'll always get what you've always got." It
was an interesting choice. The father of the ubiquitous Model T ran his
factories like work camps; he did not recognise trade unions and had
scant regard for his customers. It was his way or the highway. In twentieth century American business lore, he is the great dictator. It continued: "The Scottish FA takes its values seriously. Without values, the
vision will be blurred and the goals unfulfilled. Values are more than a
set of words: they represent a mirror for the organisation as a whole, its
staff members and volunteers to ensure the highest standards of professionalism are achieved and maintained. The Scottish FA's values should
be reflected in all that we do, both internally and externally."

When I showed this document to the chairman of an SFL club who'd
had dealings with Regan over the Rangers situation, he laughed like a
drain. Looking at *Scotland United* now, I am reminded of the late Paul
McBride QC and his quip about a "lost Monty Python script". In his
pomp, the flamboyant lawyer tore the SFA to shreds. McBride is dearly
missed in Scotland and one can only wonder what he would have made
of the most recent shenanigans at Hampden. It is not an overstatement
to say that the collapse of Rangers has created the biggest crisis in the
governance of Scottish football. The realities of the establishment club
being condemned to liquidation in June 2012 made nonsense of all the
fine words in the *Scotland United* document.

Messrs Regan and Doncaster must truly curse their luck that they
ever decided to come north to this strange country of which they knew
little. Planet *Fitba* probably seemed like a pleasant enough backwater
for two high fliers like Doncaster and Regan to burnish their CVs. One

SFL chairman told me of the first time he met Regan: "He spoke a lot about 'corporate restructuring'. It could have been about any blue-chip company. He never once mentioned the clubs or the supporters. It was all about 'branding' and 'customer base'. I knew he hadn't a clue about Scottish football."

Regan took over as SFA chief executive from Gordon Smith in July 2010.

With a background at Yorkshire County Cricket following a stint in the brewing industry, Regan was not prepared for what was about to drop on him in his new role. On 6 November 2010, I broke the *Dallasgate* story. On the day of His Holiness Pope Benedict XVI's state visit to Britain, the SFA's head of referee development, Hugh Dallas, forwarded an offensive email about the Pontiff. The resultant scandal led to Dallas being sacked from his post by the SFA.

My own assessment of Regan was that he had handled a difficult situation as well as anyone in his position could have. He was faced with allegations that there was a "canteen culture" inside the SFA of anti-Catholic bigotry and anti-Irish racism. Moreover, referees went on strike during the Dallas scandal and foreign replacements had to be brought in to cover games. The match officials said that they wanted respect and were sick of having to endure abuse and accusations of partiality.

My take was that Regan had been hampered by bad advice from both his communications department and his in-house human resources specialist. However, ultimately it was his call, and I thought he had shown courage and determination. When he launched the *Scotland United* document, he may have thought that his troubles were behind him.

Something that should not have been possible under Regan's brave new world on Planet *Fitba* was any question mark over the granting of a UEFA licence to a Scottish club that was "owing to a taxation authority", and when that question mark became apparent, Regan's SFA came under the spotlight.

Many of Regan's problems throughout this saga involved two key components: social media and people he clearly had not thought were of any significance – the fans. A small group of fans set up a website, with the objective of getting a petition signed by as many as possible raising the question of Rangers' UEFA licence and sent it to Stewart Regan. It was not long before Ask the SFA was the talk of the fitba internet. The site provided the following information on what they considered the problem to be: "The small tax bill (£2.8m) was, perhaps significantly in obfuscation terms, first officially recognised in Rangers' delayed accounts for 2010, published on 1 April 2011, as if that put the liability after a key 31 March date under UEFA licensing requirements. In fact, the liability was uncovered as part of the new Rangers owner Craig Whyte's due diligence that began long before 31 March, but presentation is all."

The website sent a petition to Stewart Regan at the SFA, stating: "I would like to draw your attention to the Scottish Football Association rules and regulations, in particular article 8.2.20 of the Finance Criteria. Can you confirm that Rangers Football Club met the criteria, set out by UEFA and the Scottish Football Association to enable them to rightfully obtain a licence from the Scottish Football Association for season 2011/2012?"

Over 2,000 people signed the petition. It was sent to Mr Regan in January 2012 and Ask the SFA has yet to receive a reply from the self-proclaimed advocate of transparency at the Scottish Football Association.

Another issue that remains unresolved at time of writing is the dual contracts issue; the allegation that, in order to make the EBT system work, Rangers operated a two-contract system but only lodged one contract with the SFA and the SPL. This would have meant that some players were improperly registered and, ipso facto, ineligible to play. Given the number of players involved in the EBT scheme and the length of service of some of them – e.g. Stefan Klos, who played 208 times for the Ibrox club – as many as 700 Rangers matches could have involved invalidly registered players.

A probe into alleged dual contracts was instigated by the SPL in March 2012 and a Glasgow law firm, Harper McLeod, was instructed to investigate the claims. SFA rules state that all payments made to players in respect of their earnings from football must be declared on one contract. Clubs falling foul of those rules could face sanctions from the league. The SPL investigation covers the period stretching back to the league's inception in 1998. However, ex-Rangers director, Hugh Adam, claimed that "off-contract" payments had been the norm at Ibrox before 1998, and it was his accusations which led the SPL to set up its investigation.

If the inquiry finds against the Ibrox club, history books will have to be amended and all league titles and cups won during the time would be taken away – under FIFA rules, fielding an ineligible player means that the guilty team forfeits the game 3–0. One analogy used was of cheating athletes like Ben Johnson, who had an Olympic gold medal taken from him. However, with the failure of the CVA in June, Rangers headed towards liquidation and the investigation was put on hold.

With Charles Green and his consortium in pole position to buy the assets of Rangers and move them into a NewCo structure, the investigation was parked as the authorities stumbled around the issue of who should be held accountable. The dual contracts investigation led to a face-off between Sevco and the folks on the sixth floor at Hampden Park in the last week of July, as the new club's membership of the SFA hung in the balance. The debate between Charles Green and the football authorities stuck on the point of Rangers' history. Sevco Scotland Limited was happy to leave Rangers' debts in the past, but wanted all of the club's 140 years of history. When HMRC refused to accept the CVA in June, an entirely new chapter of the Rangers saga unfolded, and it would bring those who govern the game and those who pay at the gate into direct conflict.

I called it "the Scottish Spring"; it was an uprising of sorts, organised through social media by people who were meant to do as they were told. While Rangers supporters had, for the most part, been extraordinarily passive, supporters of other SPL clubs mobilised on the fitba internet. The fans suspected that the SFA and the SPL had concocted a plan to keep the Ibrox franchise in the SPL no matter what crimes against football and common decency Rangers had committed. They were not mistaken.

One leading football lawyer told me: "What transpired was beyond the most paranoid ramblings of a member of the Green Brigade!" English and based in his home country, he regularly acts for clubs like Arsenal and Manchester United. The Court of Arbitration in Sport is his professional habitat. When he first contacted me he said that he was "professionally offended" by what was being proposed in Scotland by the people in charge of the national game apropos the Rangers fiasco.

I put the following question to him to him in an email on 27 July: "Given the values espoused in the *Scotland United* document and the current FIFA regulations, how, in your legal opinion, has Stewart Regan handled the RFC situation since 14 February?"

He replied on 30 July and his answer is worth reproducing here in its entirety: "In short, my view is that the Regan administration's handling of the Rangers crisis has been disastrous, shambolic and without any apparent understanding of the role of a sports regulator. It has pushed the self-regulation model of sports governance to its very limits. In isolation this is bad enough, but occurs in an apparent pattern of lurching from one poorly managed regulatory crisis to another (referees, the Neil Lennon situation etc.).

"The SPL and SFL cannot really be criticised for seeking to act narrowly in the interests of their members. They are essentially trade associations and owe no wider duties than to their members. Doncaster and Longmuir might be criticised for how effectively (or not) they are doing this, but the principle behind their actions is fine.

"The SFA, however, are supposed to have wider responsibilities. Fundamental to these is acting as custodians and protectors of the national game. Regulations are very important to this – sport has to have rules. Ultimately this is about delivering to the public something on the field of play that they can believe in and enjoy. The 100m is the Olympic flagship event, but if one competitor got to start at 80m in all his races or was exempt from anti-doping rules it would not be much of a spectacle and the fans wouldn't watch it.

"Sports governing bodies are often criticised for being ineffective in enforcing regulations, sometimes unfairly. In football, for example, there are many well-meaning regulations aimed at controlling the behaviour of football agents. However, these are routinely ignored in practice.

"However, it is completely different once the wrongdoing is discovered, as in the Rangers case. In theory it should be simple – if a rule has been broken they should be punished according to what the rules say. It should therefore have been simple for the SFA to say our rules say x, so if found guilty Rangers will be punished and we will work with clubs within the framework of our rules to deal with any fall out. If that had been the statement on day one (and it had been stuck to) we would not have had the absurd situation where a new category of SFA membership had to be invented (with no obvious basis in the rules) two days before kick-off to accommodate NewCo playing a match. This would have been better for all concerned.

"If the SFA had behaved in this manner, it could arguably have been seen as acting in the manner set out in its *Scotland United* strategy document. The first value set out in that document is 'trust', with the statement: 'We are open, honest and trusted to do the right thing, in a manner that reflects the highest standards of integrity.' Also included is 'professionalism', stating: 'We act in a businesslike, responsive and correct manner.' The SFA sets as one of its aims in this document that it be 'respected and trusted to lead'.

"There is little doubt that Regan and his team have failed to meet these standards to the extent that the *Scotland United* document now looks more like satire. The SFA has tried to engineer secret deals to get NewCo into the SPL and then First Division. Regan has predicted the 'slow, lingering death' of Scottish football if the rules are followed. The SFA has secretly considered 'blocking' NewCo entering into the SPL and then the chief executive has been stated to have lied to the public by the SFL clubs. The matter of NewCo's membership has not been resolved even days before the start of the season. There have been a number of legal and regulatory blunders.

"From a regulatory perspective, the rules appear to have been an inconvenience rather than something which are enforced without 'fear or favour' as Regan put it. The SFA have been either largely ignorant of their own regulations, and those of FIFA etc. or have chosen to disregard them to help Sevco. If this had succeeded, it would have been very difficult to believe in the SFA as a credible and independent regulator, which would have long-term consequence for the game. The fans that drove their clubs to vote against NewCo could credibly be seen as having saved the SFA (and the wider game) from itself.

"This doesn't even include the failures regarding tests for owners (which don't seem to have been learned from and instead self-declarations in a slightly different form continue), the inability to discover that an entity that it regulates has stopped paying taxes and the basic management failures to make contingency plans for the entirely predictable (at some point because of the big tax case even if Craig Whyte had never appeared) insolvency of Old Rangers."

It goes without saying that you would not read such an analysis of the people who run Scottish football in the mainstream media. A significant element in this entire saga was the failure of the Fourth Estate in Scotland, especially sports journalists, to hold the powerful to account for their actions and inactions.

The men that run the national game in Scotland did their utmost to enable NewCo to parachute seamlessly into the SPL. Doncaster and Regan had their corporate ducks in a row, but they did not factor in the fans. It was the classic mistake of people who see supporters as customers and clubs as brands. In an outburst of consumer sovereignty, the fans of SPL clubs let the guys in the boardroom know that it was not acceptable to allow reformed Rangers back into the SPL.

Neil Doncaster is, in effect, the head of a trade association. His bottom line is just that, the bottom line. However, the amorality of it all was breathtaking. The term "sporting integrity" was almost sneered at by the people on the sixth floor at Hampden. This was two belief systems talking past each other, one based on the love of a sport and the other built around marketing opportunities. However, Doncaster's motivations weren't personal, it was just business.

Stewart Regan, on the other hand, is FIFA's point man in Scotland and he should have seen the bigger picture apropos the necessity to apply the rules without fear or favour. Integrity, not TV deals, should have guided his moral compass during this saga. As the chief executive of a domestic association, he is there to make sure that the laws that govern the professional game worldwide are adhered to.

When Rangers went into administration, the plans were put in place for the awful eventuality of the club going under completely. Given the size of the club's liabilities, anyone who was interested in taking over from Craig Whyte was always going to go down the NewCo route and buy the assets in a liquidation sale. That meant that the SFA would have to deal with a scenario that no one at Hampden ever thought they would have to face. So started an awkward dance where rules were bent out of shape from day one or, if need be, the regulations were simply ignored.

I reported in November 2011 that Celtic had given the nod via back channels for a new Rangers to come straight into the SPL as a NewCo. The response from Celtic fans was instant. The green half of Glasgow left the suits in Kerrydale Street in no doubt that a cosy Old Firm deal was not on. The club did not issue a formal denial of the story on Celtic's official website, which would have been normal practice, but they did get an employee of the club to say on Facebook that fans should take no heed of these outlandish claims. The proof would come when push came to liquidation.

Throughout the fraught weeks after the liquidation process began in mid-June, Celtic remained enigmatically silent. Once the decision was made by the SPL clubs not to allow the NewCo into the top flight, Celtic issued a fairly anodyne statement welcoming the move. Given the settled view of their fans, they really could do no other.

My view is that people in leadership positions within Celtic were entirely comfortable with a NewCo Rangers in the SPL. As there would have to be sanctions that would hamstring the Ibrox outfit, for Celtic this would be win–win. They would still have the lucrative Glasgow derby matches but would be odds-on to lift the title. Of course, it is not straying into the territory of the conspiracy theorist to suggest that this is the scenario that also pleased Neil Doncaster and Stewart Regan. Prior to this disaster, the SPL economic model was based around the Glasgow derby matches and the tussle between the big two for the title.

Like so much of this story, it is about people in positions of power being out of touch with the grassroots. In a previous age the ordinary folk did not have access to the game-changing tools of social media.

James Cameron, a web designer and Celtic supporter, decided to become active against what he saw as a basic injustice: "As soon as the old Rangers went into administration on 14 February 2012, I had a gut feeling that the authorities in this country would treat that club in a totally different way to any other club. I knew that all Scottish fans had to get out of the starting blocks early to make sure the NewCo were not parachuted into the SPL.

"On 15 February I set up the No to NewCo Twitter account and Facebook page, along with a Wordpress blog. I used the power of Twitter to get the message out and within one week the account had over 5,000 followers from not only Celtic fans, but fans of other SPL clubs.

"I also felt it was important that we got fans from the SFL involved, so by the end of March I had scrounged some free web space from a friend and set up a new site built on Wordpress but with a forum built in. The idea was to have a space on the web to allow fans to come together and plan protest campaigns. Some people stepped up to the plate and contributed blogs to the site.

"At the same time, I designed No to NewCo banners and badges for people to add to their websites and social media platforms.

"I advertised on the forum and social network platforms for people who had experience in organising and coordinating non-violent protests. Unfortunately, no one put themselves forward except the wonderful Trish Brown, who agreed to be the treasurer. However, it was clear we would not get enough people to organise a committee to oversee any planned process.

"Personally, I had a lot going on in my private life so I decided I did not have the time or energy to push on myself with trying to organise a campaign so I closed the site at the end of April/beginning of May.

"However, I know social media and I knew that by mid-April No to NewCo was all over the internet and really, apart from supporting the cause by mentioning No to NewCo on Twitter etc., my job in getting the issue into the public domain was done.

"That we had opposition up and running from the start of the

Rangers OldCo's demise was enough for me and I'm delighted that I played a part in getting the movement off the ground.

"At the end of the day No to NewCo won the day because we got the message out early and fans from all over the country backed the cause and not only took it forward but beat the corrupt system that was hell-bent on dropping the NewCo into the SPL. The fact that the NewCo ended up in its proper division is a testament to the power of social media and football fans who want an honest and transparent game, regardless of what the money men wanted."

The SPL clubs, heavily pressurised by supporters' groups and lifelong fans who said they wouldn't be back if the NewCo deal went through, were panicked. They knew what they had to do, but feared the consequences. The SPL clubs had been ready to admit NewCo into the top flight of Scottish football in early May. However, the men who run Scotland's top clubs were taken aback by the strength of feeling among their own fans against this move. The final decision was postponed by the SPL clubs throughout May.

By the end of June it was clear that the tipping point had been reached. One by one the SPL clubs issued statements on their official websites informing fans they would be voting "no" to NewCo. The only statement to come out of Celtic was from chief executive Peter Lawwell on 10 May: "Our guiding principle is that we will do what is in the best interests of Celtic Football Club and our supporters, consistent with upholding the interests and reputation of Scottish football."

Many other SPL clubs just said they would vote no.

Charles Green's Sevco Scotland Limited bought the assets of Rangers Football Club from Duff and Phelps for £5.5m. Because this was, in effect, a new club they had to apply for transfer of Rangers' SPL share to the NewCo. During their presentation to the SPL, there were several own goals by Sevco. The first was the shoddily produced in-your-face "We are Rangers!" brochure given to the SPL clubs.

A senior person at an SPL club who was inside the room told me that Ally McCoist's presentation was warm and genuine and went down well. However, the same source described Sevco Chairman Malcolm Murray's presentation as "a disgrace".

At the same time as SPL representatives were hearing that the new club would abide by the transfer embargo, someone's Blackberry wobbled with news that ex-Hearts player Ian Black was preparing to move to NewCo Rangers. This news was whispered among some of the delegates and the mood only became colder towards the Sevco *arrivistes*.

On the evening after the SPL clubs had voted by ten to one to refuse NewCo's application to join them, Stewart Regan stated that "social unrest" could be caused if Rangers were not in the top flight. He later clarified the statement by saying that he was talking about a scenario where there was no Rangers at all.

Although Regan attracted opprobrium for this "social unrest" gaffe, it wasn't without context. In March an SFA judicial panel, headed by Gary Allan QC, considered charges of "bringing the game into disrepute" against the Rangers owner Craig Whyte and the club itself. They were deliberating upon evidence compiled by a panel chaired by Lord Nimmo Smith. Their findings were given to the SFA compliance officer who then presented the case against Rangers and Whyte to the three-man judicial panel. The independent panel found the Ibrox club guilty of breaching six regulations and imposed a twelve-month ban on signing players, accompanied by fines totalling £160,000. Craig Whyte was found guilty of breaching three SFA rules, fined £200,000 and expelled for life from holding office in Scottish football. These monetary penalties imposed upon Rangers and Whyte were the statutory maximum under the rules. Whyte's response was to tell the world that the SFA's punishment was of no consequence to him whatsoever.

The tribunal also placed a one-year registration embargo on the club. This meant that they would not be allowed to register players over seventeen years of age. The panel concluded that the offences were only slightly less serious than match fixing. Ally McCoist went on Rangers TV after the judgement was delivered and demanded to know the identities of the three men on the panel. McCoist said that the men could have killed the club and driven the final nail into Rangers' coffin.

In the ensuing media storm the SFA published the reasoning of the tribunal. It was not long before the names of Gary Allan QC, Eric Drysdale, director at Raith Rovers and former British Forces Broadcasting football commentator, Alastair Murning, were across the Rangers internet. The three members of the original panel suddenly found themselves on the receiving end of threats and the police became involved.

Drysdale's club, Raith Rovers, was targeted in a planned arson attack. Kirkcaldy police contacted the club and said that "money had changed hands" and that two known criminals were involved. The Rovers put on extra security and the plan was foiled. It was a clear indication that there was a lunatic fringe among the Rangers support that was willing to act in a criminal manner against anyone they saw as an enemy of their club.

In demanding to know the identities of the three men, Ally McCoist was being, at best, disingenuous. The club was informed in writing of the identities of the panel before the tribunal took place and Rangers' club secretary Andrew Dickson was in the room with the men during the hearing. It was part of a new system that had an agreement that names would be kept out of the public realm. Breaking with the protocol of identity protection, the appellate tribunal was named in advance – Lord Carloway chaired, alongside him on the panel sat Spartans chairman Craig Graham and former Partick Thistle chairman Allan Cowan.

The appellate tribunal upheld the original decision, prompting Rangers' administrators Duff and Phelps to make a game-changing move. They took the decision of the SFA's in-house judicial system to an appeal at the Court of Session – the highest civil court in Scotland. This broke FIFA rules, which state that football disputes should be dealt with through the relevant domestic association's own procedures.

Lord Glennie found in favour of Duff and Phelps and the Court of Session ruling sent the ball back in the direction of the SFA's appellate tribunal. The judge ruled that the transfer embargo was a sanction that was not available to the original tribunal and should not have been upheld by the appellate tribunal. Shortly afterwards, Lord Carloway resigned from the SFA's judicial list. A source close to his lordship confided in me that the eminent judge considered that he had been "exposed to amateurism". Moreover, he was appalled that the SFA was "backtracking on its own procedures".

Meanwhile, the language used by both Regan and Doncaster about the consequences of an SPL without Rangers could not have been more florid. While social unrest may have had some historical merit, more desperate suggestions, such as "Armageddon" and "slow lingering death", were stated as assertions. Despite these apocalyptic warnings, Sevco Scotland did not get the required votes to be allowed into the SPL.

On 4 July, Charles Green's NewCo failed to secure the majority of eight to four needed to allow their entry into the SPL. This was a huge victory for fan power and a manifestation of the efficacy of social media as a method of organising lots of people very quickly at little or no cost.

With NewCo out of the SPL, the question about what to do with Charles Green's new club passed to the SFL. The day before the SPL voted to reject Sevco into the SPL there was an information day held at Hampden to inform the SFL clubs about the importance of having NewCo Rangers in SFL Division One. This was Plan B for Regan and

Doncaster and people from the "diddy clubs" had to be clear about what was expected of them.

This meeting took place on 3 July, by which time it was clear that the SPL clubs – pressurised by their own fans – had largely declared that they would vote "no" to NewCo. At that meeting, a contemporaneous minute of most of the proceedings was taken on an iPad by the finance director of one of the clubs.

This minute, which was leaked to me, is reproduced as Appendix II in this book.

It is clear that the atmosphere in the meeting of the representatives of the SFL clubs was one of extreme pressure. It was spelled out that they, in effect, held the future financial health of Scottish football in their hands. They were told that voting Rangers NewCo into SFL Division Three was unthinkable. The tenor of the meeting was no different to what was in the mainstream media, which was full of dire warnings from Stewart Regan about the terminal decline of Scottish football without Rangers in the top flight. Yet, the rules were quite clear: this was a new club and had to start in Division Three of the SFL.

The people in charge of the game at Hampden wanted NewCo in the SPL, but failing that, it quickly became apparent that the next option was to fit the reborn Ibrox outfit into SFL Division One. The No to NewCo rebellion then spread to the SFL clubs. To everyone outside Hampden it looked like preferential treatment for one club because of the size of the fan base. As the campaign mounted, even the Ibrox klan realised that they would be forever tainted if there was some sweetheart deal. To make matters worse – which under the circumstances was quite an achievement – Stewart Regan himself stated that NewCo Rangers would go into Division One and would ideally be promoted into the SPL the next year.

Here was the head of the domestic football association stating a preference for a particular team to win a division before a ball had been kicked in anger. Within that situation, any debate on questionable penalty decisions or iffy offside calls were utterly irrelevant when the head guy at the SFA had stated as a wish that Rangers NewCo should win the First Division for the good of the game. It was breath-taking arrogance akin to a proconsul – a glimpse of an arrogant imperial mindset.

While the internet was proving a new problem for those in charge of Scottish football, harassed at every turn by knowledgeable bloggers, it was Turnbull Hutton, chairman of Raith Rovers, who presented a much more venerable threat. A man of gruff integrity who isn't frightened to speak his mind and confront authority, he knew that stepping up might well bear a personal cost. He, of course, was fully aware of the arson threat against Starks Park over Eric Drysdale's involvement in the SFA judicial panel. Despite this, he spoke on camera about the SFL clubs being "bullied" and said that the game in Scotland was "corrupt"; the SFL clubs realised they were expected by Regan and Doncaster to do as they were told and vote NewCo into SFL Division One.

Whereas the SPL chairmen were panicked by a fans' revolt they did not expect, the SFL men seemed much more in tune with their fan base from the get go. This, almost certainly, is in part due to the small numbers involved and the community nature of the SFL clubs, especially in Divisions Two and Three.

When decision day arrived on Friday 13 July, twenty-nine of the thirty SFL clubs accepted NewCo Rangers as an associate member of the SFL, while twenty-five clubs voted in favour of placing the NewCo team into the bottom tier. It is believed that the club which did not want the Ibrox outfit at all was Clyde. SFL chief executive David Longmuir said: "The member clubs of the Scottish Football League have today voted to willingly accept The Rangers Football Club as an associate member of the Scottish Football League."

A source who attended the meeting informed me that Charles Green and Ally McCoist attended and addressed those present: "Ally did his cheeky-chappie routine and he was fine. Charles Green said it was our decision, totally in our hands and that he respected that. He then said that it was a done deal that they would be playing in Division One so it didn't really matter which way we voted! He then walked out. The mood in the room changed. A few clubs that were wavering for Division One then voted for Division Three."

It was clear that many of the SFL chairmen were incensed at Regan's behaviour towards them. East Fife chairman Sid Columbine said: "Regan's attempt to have Rangers parachuted into the First Division is a disgrace. The SFL clubs made it clear that we weren't interested in any backhanded deals. Rangers were voted into the Third Division because it was the right thing to do. Everyone wants to go forward now with their heads held high – including Rangers. I don't think that could've happened had there been any other decision. It's up to the SFA to decide Stewart Regan's future but he has been guilty of poor leadership."

With the SFL decision made it was then down to the SFA to decide if NewCo would be granted membership of the association. Without this, the club wouldn't be eligible to play professional football matches at all. At the eleventh hour a "conditional membership" was granted to Sevco to allow the new club to play its first competitive match, in the Ramsdens Challenge Cup, on 29 July 2012.

One SFL chairman remarked to me: "This is the elastic rulebook! There is no conditional membership. They're making this up as they go along."

My leading football lawyer source said: "It is pretty embarrassing for a regulator to be reduced to begging a club to accept a sanction. Consider if the Westminster parliament was reduced to doing the same with Barclays over the LIBOR rate fixing."

It seems that although this was a new club, the old establishment arrogance of Rangers had also migrated over under TUPE (Transfer of Undertakings (Protection of Employment) Regulations 2006) to Sevco Scotland Limited.

Since the iceberg struck Scottish football on 14 June, the people entrusted to steer the ship have been making rules on the hoof. They knew what they wanted to achieve – the Ibrox "brand" in the top flight – and they didn't much care what they had to do to achieve that. The SFA rulebook was collateral damage to a strategy driven by marketing.

Regan and Doncaster spoke a different language to the SFL chairmen. The representatives of "diddy clubs" cared about the integrity of the game and the reputation of their football teams. For them, it was about sport and integrity, not about branding and revenue. There were two simultaneous conversations going on using two different languages. Regan and Doncaster spoke business: Turnbull Hutton and John Alexander talked of sport and community.

CEOs of large organisations are highly rewarded because they have to have vision and an ability to see the bigger picture and the road ahead for those to whom they provide leadership. Leaders who do not have these qualities stumble from crisis to crisis and are never in control of events. Although he could not have foreseen Craig Whyte's colourful reign of error at Rangers, Stewart Regan did know about the big tax case. Indeed, the chairman of the Ibrox club, Alastair Johnston, admitted at a press conference in April 2011 that the club potentially faced a bill from the taxman that it simply could not pay. Therefore, when Rangers went into administration in February 2012 – even though it wasn't as a result of the big tax case being delivered – those in leadership positions in Scottish football should have been prepared.

The fans, firstly in the SPL, then across the thirty clubs of the SFL

made their views very clear. From Peterhead to Stranraer, ordinary people bridled with outrage that an amoral sweetheart deal was being instigated without their approval. The people who run the game just didn't
see the basic injustice of a football club stiffing hundreds of creditors for
upwards of £100m and continuing as normal in the domestic top flight.

Moreover, the idea of "moral hazard" did not seem to have entered
into either Stewart Regan or Neil Doncaster's reasoning. They made
dire warnings about the implications for the Sky TV deal if there was
an SPL without Rangers in the top flight. The lexicon of the Book of
Revelation was freely used to discuss the future finances of the game.

As I write this, the satellite television company has just announced
that viewers will see thirty live matches per season, plus a wealth of
highlights. A new agreement between Sky Sports and the SPL will
guarantee the continued coverage of Scottish league football for at least
another five years.

It would appear that the Armageddon prophesied by the people on
the sixth floor at Hampden has been postponed, at least for a while. If
Scottish football is largely united in July 2012, it is not how Stewart
Regan and his marketing people envisaged it when they launched their
glossy document eighteen months ago.

Notes

http://www1.skysports.com/football/news/11781/7953178/
    Scottish-football-on-Sky

http://www.scottishfootballleague.com/news/article/press-statement-67/

http://local.stv.tv/glasgow/112782-rangers-crisis-sfa-to-offer-temporary-mem-
    bership-ahead-of-season-opener/

http://www.scribd.com/doc/93212354/SFA-Rangers-Note-of-Reasons

http://www.dailyrecord.co.uk/2012/07/18/revealed-football-chiefs-
    secret-plan-to-strip-rangers-of-nine-trophies-over-ebt-tax-
    dodge-86908-23909684/

http://www.scottishfa.co.uk/resources/documents/SFAPublications/
    ScottishFApublications2011-12/Scottish%20FA%20Handbook.pdf

http://sport.stv.tv/football/clubs/rangers/111861-newco-rangers-agree-
    player-signing-ban-u-turn-to-get-scottish-fa-membership/?utm_
    source=twitterfeed&utm_medium=twitter

http://www.askthesfa.co.uk/index2.html

http://henryclarson.wordpress.com/2012/07/24/
    its-time-to-take-the-gloves-off-with-the-sfa/

http://www.guardian.co.uk/football/2012/may/07/
    rangers-scottish-premier-league
http://blogs.channel4.com/alex-thomsons-view/rangers-leaked-email/2305
http://www.scotsman.com/sport/football/top-football-stories/mcbride-
    dismisses-sfa-s-legal-threat-as-missing-page-of-a-monty-python-
    sketch-1-1587232
http://www.dailymail.co.uk/sport/football/article-2109018/Rangers-accused-
    misleading-SFA-secret-deals.html?ITO=1490
http://www.bbc.co.uk/sport/0/football/18459762
http://www.facebook.com/pages/
    Say-No-to-Rangers-New-Co/329849957058267
http://www.telegraph.co.uk/sport/football/teams/raners/9376852/Rangers-in-
    crisis-Stewart-Regan-warns-of-social-unrest-if-Ibrox-fans-have-no-club-to-
    support-next-season.htgml
http://www.bbc.co.uk/sport/0/football/18719894
http://www.telegraph.co.uk/sport/football/teams/rangers/9095958/SFA-has-
    appoint-Lord-William-Nimmo-Smith-to-chair-Rangers-inquiry.html
http://www.scribd.com/doc/93212354/SFA-Rangers-Note-of-Reasons
http://www.telegraph.co.uk/sport/football/teams/rangers/9226911/Trio-who-
    ruled-on-Rangers-named...-and-threatened.html
http://www.telegraph.co.uk/sport/football/teams/rangers/9260391/Rangers-
    given-SFA-appeal-date-as-panel-members-are-named.html
http://scotslawthoughts.wordpress.com/2012/07/13/
    why-even-with-yes-vote-sfl-board-cant-but-will-put-sevco-into-sfl1/
http://www.breakingnews.ie/sport/rangers-to-play-in-division-3-next-sea-
    son-559006.html
http://www.dailyrecord.co.uk/news/scottish-news/2012/07/15/sfa-
    chief-stewart-regan-faced-vote-of-no-confidence-until-ally-blocked-
    move-86908-23908714/
http://www.scottishfootballleague.com/news/article/press-statement-67/

SFA to move against Paul McBride QC

13.04.11

EXCLUSIVE

The SFA has decided to report Paul McBride QC to the Faculty of Advocates after his comments yesterday about the association's disciplinary committee. A senior SFA source told me that officials in the association were "furious" with the QC's performance on TV when he commented upon the fact that Rangers players Madjid Bougherra and El Hadji Diouf would escape bans for their behaviour in the Scottish Cup tie at Celtic Park last month. The QC blasted the SFA: "The SFA are tonight officially the laughing stock of world football," he told *BBC Scotland*. "And they have been shown to be not merely dysfunctional and not merely dishonest but biased."

This is a developing story.

Questions about Rangers in Europe

25.10.11

Rangers' European campaign for season 2011/2012 didn't go well. Defeated by Malmö in the Champions League and then by Maribor in the Europa League, it was a financial disaster as well as an on-field disappointment. Should they, however, have been playing in these competitions at all?

UEFA's rules are quite clear: a domestic association cannot approve a club to participate in European competitions if it is "owing to a tax authority". It was this stipulation which, in part, led to the English FA refusing to award a licence to Portsmouth FC in 2010, despite the fact that the club had qualified for European competition on sporting merit.[1]

In any event, in order for a club to obtain a UEFA club licence for the 2010/11 season they need to show that as of December 2009 they had no outstanding money owed to the tax authorities or football clubs. This is manifestly not the case for Portsmouth FC. The English FA refused to nominate a member club because it did not meet the criteria to acquire the UEFA club licence required to compete within UEFA competition.

And so to the SFA criteria – the finance criteria within the SFA Articles state, at 8.2.20, that:

"A licence will be refused:

    a)   If the information in respect of payables overdue towards employees and social/tax authorities is not submitted to the licensor

    b)   If the club submits information that does not meet the minimum disclosure requirements

---

1   http://www.thefa.com/TheFA/NewsAndFeatures/2010/FAStatement_280410

    c)   If the club has payables overdue at 31 March towards employ-
ees and social/tax authorities which arose before 31 December
preceding the season to be licensed."

However, there are exceptions to what is above, notably in relation
to part c). These, in laypersons' terms, are that the respective club has
either paid the bill in full, been able to show that the claim of a creditor
is without foundation or had written agreement from the creditor, in
this instance HMRC, to extend the deadline for payment. The additional exception is that the individual club instigates an appeal against
the claim.

It is, of course, through such a process that Rangers are currently
travelling in relation to what is now commonly referred to as the "big
tax case", and it is such an appeal that has allowed Rangers FC to compete in Europe before this season.

Earlier this year, at the beginning of April, Rangers FC released
interim accounts. These were made available for public consumption,
and within these accounts, for the six months to 31 December 2010,
there is reference to the tax bill of £2.8m, the sum based on a core
amount and interest. This is, of course, the tax bill that had sheriff officers enter Ibrox last August.

I knew that HMRC had instructed a firm of sheriff officers about this
unpaid tax bill on 2 June. This piece from the *Daily Mail* in April suggests that the bill was known about well before the SFA deadline of 31
March 2011.[1] (The online piece carries a link to an article in the *Daily
Mail* headlined *Cashflow blow: Record deal still haunting Rangers as tax
bill could hit transfer fund*, published on 3 April 2011.)

I have had correspondence with both UEFA and the SFA over the
matter for some time now. UEFA provided answers on general rules
and regulations, but would not comment on the specific case of Rangers
FC. It is perhaps useful to share these exchanges to give a fuller picture
of the state of play.

I put questions to UEFA last month about their regulations apropos
the granting of UEFA licences.

    "1)   On what date(s) did national associations nominate their rep-
resentatives to compete in UEFA club competition for season
2011/2012?

    2)   When national associations nominate clubs, does UEFA
accept that the respective clubs are criteria-compliant apropos

---

1   http://www.dailymail.co.uk/sport/football/article-1372818/Rangers-Ally-McCoists-
transfer-dealings-hampered.html

the club licence?

3) If a club, which has qualified to play in UEFA competition, is 'owing to a social/tax authority' on and after 30 June, does this jeopardise its entitlement to a UEFA club licence?"

This is the correspondence that ensued.

"Monday 12 September 2011

Dear Mr Mac Giolla Bháin,

The deadline for registering clubs for the current UEFA club competition season was 1 June 2011. As deemed in the UEFA club competition regulations, all clubs competing in UEFA competitions are required to have obtained a licence by a competent authority.

Please see further information in the UEFA club licensing and FFP regulations attached, especially p. 32 for the responsibilities of the licensor and the licensee.

On your final question, the relevant part of Article 66 can be found below:

Article 66 – No overdue payables towards employees and/ or social/tax authorities.

1) The licensee must prove that as at 30 June of the year in which the UEFA club competitions commence it has no overdue payables (as specified in Annex VIII) towards its employees and/or social/tax authorities (as defined in paragraphs 2 and 3 of Article 50) that arose prior to 30 June.

2) By the deadline and in the form communicated by the UEFA administration, the licensee must prepare and submit a declaration confirming the absence or existence of overdue payables towards employees and social/ tax authorities.

3) The following information must be given, as a minimum, in respect of each overdue payable towards employees, together with explanatory comment:
   a) Name of the employee;
   b) Position/function of the employee;
   c) Start date;
   d) Termination date (if applicable); and
   e) Balance overdue as at 30 June, including the due date for each overdue element.

4) The following information must be given, as a minimum,

in respect of each overdue payable towards social/tax authorities, together with explanatory comment:
a) Name of the creditor;
b) Balance overdue as at 30 June, including the due date for each overdue element.

5) The declaration must be approved by management and this must be evidenced by way of a brief statement and signature on behalf of the executive body of the licensee.

6) If the licensee is in breach of indicator 4 as defined in Article 62(3), then it must also prove that, as at the following 30 September, it has no overdue payables (as specified in Annex VIII) towards employees and/or social/tax authorities that arose prior to 30 September. Paragraphs 2 to 5 above apply accordingly.

Hopefully this helps.

Best regards,

UEFA Media Relations"

I then sent a specific question about the SFA and their interaction with UEFA regarding these licences.

"15 September 2011 15:23

Thank you for your recent answers. Here are my supplementary questions:

On what date did the Scottish Football Association nominate clubs to play in UEFA competitions for the season 2011/2012? Did the Scottish FA confirm that all nominated clubs satisfied both their criteria and the criteria of UEFA in relation to receiving a UEFA club licence for the season 2011/2012? Was UEFA made aware, by either the Scottish FA or the club in question, that one of the nominated clubs had, on or around 2 June 2011, received a tax bill from Her Majesty's Revenue and Customs, the 'tax authority' in Britain and, therefore, Scotland in a footballing context, for approximately £2.8m? Was UEFA made aware, by the Scottish Football Association or the club or both, that one of the aforesaid nominated clubs had experienced an 'event of significant economic importance' as specified in Article 67 – Monitoring Requirements of the UEFA Club Licensing and Financial Fair Play Regulations Edition 2010? Would a club 'owing to a tax authority' on 30 June and not having paid said bill, nor made plans or arrangements with the respective tax authority to pay said bill, or without having instigated an appeal regarding said bill, be entitled to a UEFA club licence?"

I received this reply from UEFA on 16 September:

"Dear Mr Mac Giolla Bháin,

UEFA does not comment on specific cases, as it is the responsibility of the respective national association to issue the licences. UEFA is in regular contact with the Scottish FA and we can confirm that the SFA issued all licences for the 2011–12 season in accordance with the regulations."

I replied:

"Thank you for the response, dated 16 September, regarding club licensing. Can the following be answered? Is the general recourse of UEFA to open an investigation if there is evidence that a club has either lied or withheld information in order to receive a club licence to participate in UEFA competition? And was this the procedure which led to the three-year ban for Gyori ETO FC from Hungary?

Regards,

Phil Mac Giolla Bháin"

A UEFA spokesman wrote:

"Dear Mr Mac Giolla Bháin,

UEFA does not comment on specific cases, as it is the responsibility of the respective national association to issue the licenses. UEFA is in regular contact with the Scottish FA and we can confirm that the SFA issued all licences for the 2011–12 seasons in accordance with the regulations.

Best regards,

UEFA Media Relations"

With UEFA repeatedly referencing the domestic authority, I then contacted the SFA with the following questions on 3 October:

"There has been widespread coverage, acknowledged by Rangers FC publicly, that a bill for approximately £2.8m is owed to HMRC by the club. Can you please inform me of the date Rangers FC informed the SFA of this £2.8m tax bill?"

This question was posed apropos part a) of the SFA Finance Criteria 8.2.20, which states that a licence will be refused "if the information in respect of payables overdue towards employees and social/tax authorities is not submitted to the licensor".

An SFA spokesman responded ten days later: "We are not in a position to discuss individual cases."

Subsequently, I returned to the SFA with a more straightforward line of questioning: "Is the SFA confident that Rangers FC satisfied the criteria around finance in order to be eligible to play in UEFA competition in 2011/2012? Why did the SFA nominate Rangers FC to represent Scotland in UEFA competition when the club had received a tax bill for approximately £2.8m?"

This was more than a week ago. The SFA has not got back to me with an answer.

Questions that should be answered

01.12.11

Regular readers here will know that I have raised the question of whether or not the SFA should have approved Rangers to play in UEFA competitions this season because they may have been "owing to a tax authority".

So far, despite my persistent questioning, I haven't received an answer that puts the issue to bed. Here are copies of a correspondence between SFA chief executive Stewart Regan and a concerned Celtic supporter.[1] (The online piece carries a link to www.celticunderground.net.) This excellent website lays out the issues for the SFA.[2] (The online piece carries a link to Ask the SFA.)

Recently, I was contacted by a Celtic shareholder who is concerned about the possibility that Rangers may have been granted the opportunity to play in the Champions League in place of Celtic. This would, of course, cause a serious loss of revenue to the Parkhead club. His settled view, from the correspondence he has had with a senior figure at the club, is that he has been fobbed off and his questions have been dodged. He continues to press Celtic for straight answers. In the absence of satisfactory answers, he believes that his club is giving the SFA and, ipso facto, Rangers a pass on this very important issue. The SFA has refused to answer my questions on this pertinent issue. I merely received a "we don't answer questions on the finances of individual clubs" reply from the SFA.

---

1 http://www.celticunderground.net/index.php?option=com_
   content&view=article&id=787:did-the-sfa-deny-celtic-a-place-in-the-champions-
   league&catid=47:season-2011-2012&Itemid=83
2 http://www.askthesfa.co.uk/

Perhaps they would find it more difficult to give a similar response to the club which has potentially been denied participation in the lucrative Champions League competition because of this honest mistake. It would appear that the people who call the shots at Kerrydale Street don't want to ask tough questions of the SFA these days. Why should that be?

There may be no case to answer, but until the issue is put to bed by a clear, unequivocal on-the-record statement by the SFA then the doubts will remain. I am surprised that the SFA hasn't dealt with this issue before now. What will also linger is the suspicion that people in leadership positions at Celtic do not want to pursue this one with the SFA.

Unanswered questions

02.12.11

There are two key questions to ask when you want to get to the bottom of any story: Who knew what? When did they know it?

What did the SFA know about Rangers' tax issues when they granted the club a licence to play in the Champions League this season? Today in the *Daily Record* you would be none the wiser. The piece by Keith Jackson looks at whether or not Rangers will meet the UEFA licensing criteria for NEXT season. This piece has us looking forward to next season, not looking back to the start of this one. The fact that the Ibrox club would currently fall foul of UEFA regulations for not having an audited set of accounts is actually beside the point. The question is: were Rangers eligible to play this year?

Regarding their eligibility to play in European competitions this season, Jackson quoted "an SFA insider". The source said: "When Rangers submitted their application for this season they were up-front about a number of financial issues they were dealing with. They were in dispute with the taxman but this was declared and, as it was a legitimate dispute, it was allowed and they still satisfied the criteria."[1]

Were they "up-front" that they were already owing to a taxing authority and, ipso facto, in breach of UEFA rules? The only thing in dispute at the start of the year was the penalty for late payment. The £2.8m tax bill itself was not in dispute. The SFA has yet to state, unequivocally and on-the-record, that it was satisfied that Rangers FC were "not

---

1 http://www.dailyrecord.co.uk/football/spl/rangers/2011/12/02/rangers-face-euro-ban-unless-accounts-are-signed-off-by-independent-auditor-86908-23604254/

overdue any payables to a tax authority on 31 March 2011". Did the SFA ask that question of Rangers? They should have. If they did and Rangers told them that all was in order then the SFA has done its job appropriately. The position at the SFA which looks after club licensing is a post that is partly funded by UEFA. This is a specialised position and the employee is not allocated any other duties. Clearly, the SFA must accept the bona fides of member clubs.

Yesterday I outlined the questions surrounding this story.[1] As it stands I'm agnostic on this story. Rangers could kill this story stone dead if they issued an unequivocal statement on the club's website. They would only have to state that, as of 31 March 2011, all of their tax affairs were in order and they were not owing to any UK tax authority. One can understand why they have not done so heretofore. However, now that this story is in the mainstream they should do so now. At the end of it all these questions remain. Questions which are still unanswered.

Petition sent to the SFA about Rangers and their UEFA licence

05.01.12

The SFA chief executive received a petition today, holding 1,197 signatures, regarding the decision to award Rangers FC a licence to compete in UEFA competition this season.

"Petition

To Stewart Regan, Chief Executive of the Scottish Football Association:

There is much speculation that Rangers Football Club wrongfully obtained a licence to participate in European competition as they had outstanding debts to the tax authority.

I would like to draw your attention to the Scottish Football Association rules and regulations, in particular article 8.2.20 of the Finance Criteria.

Can you confirm that Rangers Football Club met the criteria, set out by UEFA and the Scottish Football Association

---

1   http://www.philmacgiollabhain.ie/questions-that-should-be-answered/

to enable them to rightfully obtain a licence from the Scottish
Football Association for season 2011/2012?
      Yours,"[1]

Regular readers here will know that I believe there are questions on
this issue which remain unanswered.[2] Should this petition grow in size,
these questions will be increasingly difficult to ignore.

The second contract. Fact or rumour?

24.01.12

Did some Rangers players have two contracts? Darrell King, an experienced journalist with the *Herald* and *Evening Times*, seems to think they
did and said so on live radio.[3] From what I can gather, the story centres
on the possibility that Rangers players had a PAYE contract that stated
how much they were being paid and the amount of PAYE and NI they
would have deducted at source. So far, so ordinary. However, there is an
allegation that there was a second contract which informed the player
how much would be lodged in the employee benefit trust (EBT) for
him. These monies would then be "lent" to the player from the trust. If
these second contracts exist, they effectively constitute suicide notes for
Rangers in the big tax case.

If the story is true then it has possible consequences for the football
authorities. A player's contract has four parts and they are identical in
content. One part goes to the SFA, one goes to the appropriate league
(SPL, SFL etc.), one is retained by the club, and the player, of course,
has his part. Therefore, players' contracts being lodged with the SFA is
non-negotiable.

So, who knew what and when did they know it? Any reasonable
person might ask the following:

   (1) Did the second contract exist?
   (2) Were both contracts lodged with the SFA?
   (3) If only one contract was lodged with the SFA, were officials
        aware of the existence of the second contract?

I spoke to someone involved in football administration today about

---

1   http://www.askthesfa.co.uk/

2   http://www.philmacgiollabhain.ie/questions-about-rangers-in-europe/

3   http://audioboo.fm/boos/637325-rangers-players-had-2-contracts-says-king?utm_
    campaign=detailpage&utm_content=retweet&utm_medium=social&utm_
    source=twitter

these putative second contracts for some Rangers players. He said that the SFA accepted paperwork from clubs "on face value" and did not have the resources or the inclination to investigate them. I think that may have to change.

The need to be crystal clear about the UEFA licence story

19.01.12

A colleague of mine from the NUJ, who works in PR, was explaining some of the basic rules of his craft to me: "When you are trying to kill a story you must avoid being tied down on something specific, a fact or a detail that will give it another lease of life for a reporter who is digging."

Stewart Regan of the SFA had a little local difficulty recently when he received a letter with almost 1,200 signatories asking him for some facts about the granting of a UEFA licence to Rangers this season.[1] The SFA chief has tried to put out the flames by tweeting that the bill had not crystallised and that it was perfectly OK to grant a UEFA licence to Rangers.

There are two ways in which a bill from HMRC crystallises:

    (1) The recipient of the assessment agrees with HMRC that they do indeed owe that amount;

    (2) A first-tier tax tribunal finds in HMRC's favour.

There are various ways that the taxpayer can agree with HMRC. I have reason to believe that this bill crystallised over a number of communications between HMRC staff and senior personnel at Rangers FC. It is, of course, the "wee tax bill" of £2.8m which led to sheriff officers being at Ibrox last August that is at dispute here.[2] [3]

The key point in this story is when that tax bill crystallised. If it was before 31 March 2011, the SFA should not have granted Rangers a licence to play in UEFA-controlled competitions for season 2011/2012. If Stewart Regan is certain that the bill crystallised after 31 March 2011 and he knows when it did, all he has to do is publish that date. He could even tweet it. However, that course of action might present him with a problem if my sources at Edmiston Drive – the ones who told

1   http://www.askthesfa.co.uk/

2   http://www.philmacgiollabhain.ie/the-sheriff-is-in-town/

3   http://www.philmacgiollabhain.ie/photographs-you-were-not-meant-to-see/

me that the sheriff's men were on the way – have a different recollection of events.

The date of the crystallisation of the wee tax bill is the key detail. However, that sort of detail is exactly what my PR colleague was warning against if you want a story to go away. I don't know if it will be a leaked document or a pesky email that will break this story, but this reporter hasn't put his spade down.

The utmost good faith?

26.02.12

While the media frenzy swirls around the conduct of Craig Whyte during his time as owner of Rangers, a far more significant story is being missed by the Scottish media. In the furore over Ticketus and the unpaid taxes since last May, the wider significance of the big tax case on the governance of the Scottish game has not been fully analysed.

Let us assume that the first-tier tribunal finds in favour of HMRC and against Rangers. That will mean that Rangers, in the first decade of the millennium, operated an illegal tax evasion scam. During this time, directors of the Ibrox club signed off on accounts stating that everything was OK and submitted annual club licence applications to the SFA to permit their participation in Scottish and European football. Moreover, if we look at who was doing the signing in the boardroom at Edmiston Drive, we find people simultaneously holding key positions on both the SFA and the SPL. For the first half of the "EBT decade", Campbell Ogilvie was a Rangers director and company secretary at the same time he sat as treasurer of the SFA. Martin Bain, the Rangers CEO, was a director on the board of the SPL in 2008. John McClelland, a founding director of the SPL in 1997, sat on the SPL board until he was replaced by Bain in 2008. McClelland was chairman of Rangers from 2002 until 2005 and only recently resigned from the board.

So, here are three men, Rangers directors during the time the Ibrox side was running an employee benefit trust scheme which has exposed the club to a potential bill for unpaid taxes, interest payments and penalties that could top £50m. These three splendid fellows also, during that time, occupied senior positions on the ruling bodies of the game in Scotland. Wearing their SPL and SFA hats, it was incumbent upon them to make sure that all clubs in Scotland abided by the laws of the game. If the current rules were in operation during the "EBT decade" then Bain, McClelland and Ogilvie may have a little explaining to do.

Given what we know about how Rangers are alleged by HMRC to have operated EBTs, consider the following:

SFA Articles as previously advised, plus rule 2.2.1 of the Registration Handbook.

"Rule 2.2.1

Unless lodged in accordance with Procedures Rule 2.13 a Non-Recreational (professional) Contract Player Registration Form will not be valid unless it is accompanied by the contract entered into between the club concerned and the player stating all the terms and conditions in conformity with the Procedures Rule 4."

Also, from SPL Rule D1.2:

"An application for a Player to be registered or to change Status must be made, in the case of Professional Registration, by submitting to the Secretary a fully completed and executed Contract of Service for the Player concerned."

Rule D1.13:

"A Club must, as a condition of Registration and for a Player to be eligible to play in Official Matches, deliver the executed originals of all Contracts of Service and amendments and/or extensions to Contracts of Service and all other agreements providing for payment, other than for reimbursement of expenses actually incurred, between that Club and Player, to the Secretary, within fourteen days of such Contract of Service or other agreement being entered into, amended and/or, as the case may be, extended."

Rule D 9.3:

"No Player may receive any payment of any description from or on behalf of a Club in respect of that Player's participation in Association Football or in an activity connected with Association Football, other than in reimbursement of expenses actually incurred or to be actually incurred in playing or training for that Club, unless such payment is made in accordance with a Contract of Service between that Club and the Player concerned."

A3.1:

"In all matters and transactions relating to the league and company each club shall behave towards each other club and company with the utmost good faith."

If Rangers directors signed off on accounts and knowingly failed to disclose to their director colleagues at the SFA and SPL that Rangers had invalidly registered players while they were holding senior positions on the governing bodies of the game in Scotland, then they will have been in breach of their duty to act in utmost good faith. They will also have breached their fiduciary duties to these governing bodies and their members. Did Rangers, by virtue of their alleged failure to lodge full and complete contracts in the form prescribed by FIFA, field invalidly registered players throughout the last decade? Did these Rangers directors, as formal directors of the SFA and SPL, in failing to disclose potential breaches of player registration rules, conspire to deceive members of these governing bodies?

These questions have to be asked by the Scottish media, unless they are willing to wait until they are mere spectators in a UEFA probe into the governance of the game in Scotland. It will be interesting to see if the sports desks in Glasgow go after this story with the same ferocity as they have been pursuing Craig Whyte since Scotland's establishment club went into administration two weeks ago.

The SFA on a sticky wicket

06.03.12

His time at Yorkshire County Cricket must now seem like another historical epoch to Stewart Regan. He wasn't long in the SFA job when the Dallas email story hit the organisation. In the round, I thought he handled that one well enough. Now he has something to tackle that dwarfs the problems he faced in November 2010 with his head of referee development.

The allegations made by ex-Rangers director Hugh Adam in the *Daily Mail* could not be more serious for the SFA and the governance of the game in Scotland.[1] (The online piece carries a link to an article in the *Daily Mail* headlined *A new twist in Rangers controversy: Club accused of misleading SFA on secret deals*, published on 2 March 2012.)

---

1   http://www.dailymail.co.uk/sport/football/article-2109018/Rangers-accused-
    misleading-SFA-secret-deals.html

In fairness to Regan he immediately responded to this game-changer:
"Independent Inquiry Update, Friday, 2 March 2012.
Stewart Regan, the Scottish FA Chief executive, has today
provided an update on the progress of the independent
inquiry into Rangers FC chaired by The Right Honourable
Lord Nimmo Smith. We are now in the final stages of our
independent inquiry into the situation concerning Rangers
FC. The report by The Right Honourable Lord Nimmo
Smith is expected to be completed next week and will go
to a special board meeting for consideration. It would be
inappropriate to make any further comment at this stage in
relation to the details gleaned from the inquiry, the potential contents of the report or any possible sanctions. We are,
however, aware of the most recent allegations made against
Rangers FC today by a former director of the club. We shall
investigate this matter thoroughly before making any further
comment."

The investigation into Craig Whyte is now something of a sideshow
next to the allegation by an ex-Rangers director that the Ibrox club
broke the rules on player remuneration and registration throughout
the Murray years. Even the mainstream media have copped onto
how serious this could be.[1] Now the SPL has announced a probe
into the two-contract allegations.[2] We will then be able to compare
and contrast the modalities of both investigations as well as what
they unearth.

Mr Regan said that he wanted to put transparency at the heart of the
SFA, and I believe him. Now he has an opportunity to demonstrate his
bona fides that he could not have dreamt of, even during Dallasgate
in 2010. He will know from cricket that sporting integrity is a fragile
thing. It requires public confidence, and that comes from action that
people can have faith in.[3] The playing field must be level in any sport
and any allegation that it is not must be thoroughly examined. Rangers
are not accused of match fixing, but of financial doping on an industrial
scale.

Planet *Fitba* is watching.

---

1   http://www.eveningtimes.co.uk/sport/gers-could-face-a-ban-from-sfa-1.1151165

2   http://www.scotprem.com/content/default.asp?page=s2&newsid=11135&back=h
    ome

3   http://www.dailymail.co.uk/sport/cricket/article-2056073/Pakistan-trio-guilty-
    cricket-match-fixing.html

Game on

14.03.12

In the digital media age, the optics of a situation is everything. So when Campbell Ogilvie did the draw for the semi-finals of the Scottish Cup it sent a message. With the very serious allegations made against him by Hugh Adam, the guy who drives the Scottish Football Association bus should have taken action.[1] He didn't, and because of that, the SFA appears to me to be compromised as an organisation on these serious issues. At this stage, this situation requires action by Scottish sports minister, Shona Robison.[2] Given the nature of these allegations, the Scottish Football Association cannot, in my opinion, investigate itself.[3] The cosy relationship that the SFA has had with the Scottish media no longer provides defence either, as serious journalists based in London are now on the case.

I was called yesterday by an award-winning television reporter who told me that he wanted to get to the bottom of "Rangersgate" and he has the considerable resources of his organisation at his disposal. He shared with me the content of a "conversation" he had just had with an SFA "press officer" and it was, quite frankly, risible. I sent the journalist several detailed emails with links to various pieces and some previously unpublished material of my own, the latter being particularly explosive.

Everything has a cost and the Scottish press pack, by being pals with the football establishment at Hampden and Ibrox, have made themselves largely irrelevant. As I write this, the Scottish tabloids are illuminated by more moonbeams about a wonderful future for Rangers and how a new sugar daddy will soon kiss it better. All of this is as evidence-based as the churnalism that confidently stated that Mr Whyte was a "billionaire" and that he would finance the club from his own wealth.[4] The big boys from London are now digging and they appear to have no problem engaging professionally with a diligent worker in Donegal.

Game on.

---

1   http://www.dailymail.co.uk/sport/football/article-2109018/Rangers-accused-
     misleading-SFA-secret-deals.html

2   http://www.legislation.gov.uk/ukpga/2005/12

3   http://www.dailymail.co.uk/sport/football/article-2109233/Rangers-investigated-
     SFA-Hugh-Adam-claims.html

4   http://www.philmacgiollabhain.ie/when-journalists-forget-which-team-they-are-on/

The right to due process

15.03.12

Imagine, if you will, the following scenario. A story breaks in the media that an organisation has been involved in a financial scandal of the type that puts it in contravention of the local authority's code of conduct. The chairman of the local authority is also in a senior position at the organisation named in the alleged scandal. What would the chief executive officer of that state organisation do? The first thing would be that extended "gardening leave" would be granted to the chairman and, secondly, the CEO would call in central government and hand the mess over to them. This would be an acknowledgment that the organisation would not investigate itself. This course of action would safeguard the rights of the chairman and also protect the local authority from allegations of a cover up.

This is the scenario that Stewart Regan now faces after the allegations from former Rangers director Hugh Adam regarding SFA president Campbell Ogilvie's current position. If Mr Adam's allegations are proven, then what we have is the director of a company that was running a tax scam. Moreover, he has admitted being a beneficiary of that tax scam while being the supposed guardian of the scammed![1]

If Mr Regan does not act now then the potential reputational damage for the SFA cannot be overestimated. This story has attracted the attention of *Channel 4 News* and foreign media organisations. This morning I spoke to two journalists who work for major titles in continental Europe. They wanted to know where this story was going. I don't know, but I am pretty sure that it isn't going away any time soon.

The SFA's press people can expect more difficult questions from foreigners in the weeks ahead. Given that the Hugh Adam allegations go to the heart of the governance of the Scottish game then the SFA cannot investigate itself. The current in-house probe will investigate allegations that name Mr Ogilvie and, as the current president of the SFA, will report to him about, well, him. What opinion will he come to about, err, himself? What action will Mr Ogilvie decide to take against the man he sees in the mirror every morning? This is an impossible

---

1   http://www.dailymail.co.uk/sport/football/article-2109018/Rangers-accused-misleading-SFA-secret-deals.html

position to place him in and it isn't fair. Campbell Ogilvie has the right to due process in all of this and that can only happen if he is asked to take extended leave of absence until an independent, public inquiry into the SFA has concluded its work. That inquiry cannot be set up by the organisation that has its offices at Hampden Park. This is now a task for Shona Robison, once she gets the nod from her boss, Alex Salmond.

Is feidir linn

24.04.12

One of the most difficult obstacles to change is the mindset of those who will benefit from a new dispensation. There are people who, deep down, are comfortable sitting at the back of the bus. There is a form of moral superiority in being oppressed. It makes you one of the good guys.

Over the past few years, I would get plaintive communications from members of the Celtic family. The common denominator was always that I was wasting my time and that things would never change in Scotland. The "things" they referred to was the special place reserved for Rangers FC in the pecking order of Planet *Fitba*. All of them doubted that change would ever come. However, I suspected that some of them didn't want change to arrive as it would take away their moral superiority. To all of these people, I would merely say that these things do take a long time to change. They do. Then, suddenly, visible signs that the tide is turning can appear very quickly.

Last night something happened. The SFA judicial panel simply looked at the facts and checked the rules. There was no special treatment. Suddenly, Rangers was just another member club of the association. This is a scene that the late Jim Farry would not have recognised. He acted with bad intentions to assist Rangers in denying Celtic the services of Jorge Cadette. The Bunnet did for him. Nothing personal you understand, just business.

The decisions made yesterday are, of course, open to appeal. This is largely academic, as Rangers will soon die. The sanctions, I am told, will only transfer to a NewCo if that new club acquires Rangers' SPL share. Liquidation is death, although the journalists who shouted that Craig Whyte was a "billionaire" who loved Rangers are now stating that the big "L" is not the end of Rangers FC. They're wrong. Liquidation IS the end.

In the future, historians will note that as Scotland's establishment club was breathing its last the good folks on Planet *Fitba* stopped being fearful of that marble staircase. When Rangers die, the people who used to follow that club may be offered a new team to support. The new team will land on a level playing field. Things will have changed, changed utterly. For the bears this vista is terrible; for me it is beautiful.

Rangers finally became a UK and then a global story. What was happening was so scandalous that it couldn't be kept in-lodge and under wraps by the succulent bambs. A tip of the hat to Thomo at Channel 4. He didn't need to get involved, but he did, and because of that the quintessentially British club is known as a scandal club throughout Britain. To the members of my own clan who girned about the immovability of the status quo, my response was always "Yes, we can".

This is what history feels like.

Due process

25.04.12

The angry reaction from the Rangers supporters following on from the findings of the SFA judicial panel was predictable. What was interesting was the interview given by Ally McCoist on Rangers TV. He said he wanted to know the identities of the panel, which struck me as strange as all he had to do was ask Andrew Dickson, the head of football administration at Rangers, who attended the hearing. He sat across the table from the three men. The trio comprised a very senior chap from the legal profession, a club official (non-SPL) with a background in banking and a retired journalist. These three were selected from a "taxi rank" of 100 people.

The next three are called for an upcoming case, but they can be deselected if there is a conflict of interest. Therefore, no one connected to an SPL club can be involved in an SPL case. The SFA's compliance officer, Vincent Lunny, presents the evidence – usually a referee's report – to the adjudicating trio. In this case, the three men simply examined the rules and looked at the actions of Craig Whyte and Rangers Football Club. This is exactly the same process that Neil Lennon went through recently.

Rangers, of course, can appeal. This will then go before an appellant tribunal. That will be chaired by a QC or a senior judge. This doesn't come cheap. Rangers are getting due process. They are being treated in the same way as everyone else. The howls of outrage tell you a lot about that club and how things used to be on Planet *Fitba*. This is better. Tip of the hat, Mr Regan.

Help required

26.04.12

Sometimes when you're in a fix you need to call for outside help. I think that the SFA might be there already. What happens to the three people on the appellant tribunal? Will they be named? Will they feel safe?

Let's say that they, without any outside interference, decide on the merits of the case to overturn all or part of the sanctions. Will that decision be seen to be the product of intimidation? I am under no doubt that the "outing" of the original trio has caused some on the SFA's "taxi rank" to think about getting the hell out of Dodge.

Despite all the spinning by the laptop loyal, Ally McCoist was, at best, ill advised on Rangers TV on Tuesday. There will be huge outside pressure now from the Queen's underclass to overturn the original decisions, especially the twelve-month transfer ban. Scottish football's system of justice is now being attacked. Perhaps the moment has arrived to call in the UEFA compliance officer.

I am reliably informed that the governing body in Nyon is watching the situation in Scotland closely. They can, of course, just invite themselves. However, I suspect that the first step will be to politely offer their assistance and support to the SFA. The beleaguered guys at Hampden Park should take it.

A watershed moment

06.05.12

Even as death approaches, it would appear that Scotland's establishment club still has some of the old power. It would appear that the cultural clout of Rangers can still make amoral fools out of the people who run the game. As the club established in 1872 is about to be liquidated, the status of any new company utilising the Ibrox brand has to be addressed. Any new club in Scottish football should apply to the Scottish Football League for admittance to Division Three. The morality of that case is unanswerable if a NewCo is created in these circumstances.

If you were to write a case study of bad behaviour by a football club over a protracted period then it would look rather like Rangers over the last decade or so. Even some of the laptop loyal have conceded this. Instead, what is being planned is for a NewCo to be parachuted into the SPL with minimal penalties, if any.

What we have seen recently, with the intimidation of the "Hampden three", is the nasty side of a sense of entitlement. I would not be surprised if those original sanctions are overturned. If that is the case then it could be argued that intimidation has been successful. If, after more than a decade of cheating, a new club utilising the Rangers brand is allowed into the SPL as if nothing happened, that Herrenvolk swagger of the Ibrox support will be fed steroids. The belief system that felt authorised to trash Manchester and urinate on war memorials in Barcelona will KNOW that it is above the law in Scottish football.

This is a time for the people in charge of the national game to act with good authority. What is needed are people of courage with a serviceable moral compass. John Yorkston has made a stand.[1] Kilmarnock chairman Michael Johnston has already presented his excuses for capitulating: "There is a feeling that member clubs see the commercial benefits of having Rangers in SPL, even if it is a NewCo. Member clubs are mindful of a sporting integrity aspect but the commercial benefits outweigh that."

The supporters of Rangers are outraged that anyone has the temerity to suggest that they should be subject to the same rules as everyone else. They believe they are a special case because they have been just that in the past. Rangers have always enjoyed an elevated status within the corridors of power in Scottish football. They marched in anger to Hampden because they feared that the old order was dying.

We are now at a watershed moment. It remains to be seen if money and the mob will triumph over what is morally correct. People in the rest of Britain are agog at the extent to which Scottish football appears to be a rotten borough. Thanks to the excellent journalism of Alex Thomson of *Channel 4 News*, the quintessentially British football club has been truly revealed to people in England.

---

1 http://www.scotsman.com/sport/football/top-football-stories/rangers-takeover-john-yorkston-calls-on-spl-chairmen-to-relegate-newco-rangers-1-2278177

I am not surprised that there appears to be zero contrition coming out of the blue half of Glasgow. There are no expressions of remorse or embarrassment that their club has behaved "like spivs", as Graham Spiers put it on *Clyde* recently. Instead there is a defiant "we're too big to be punished" attitude from the supporters of the Ibrox club. It would appear that they enjoyed victory on the field of play even when it was achieved through an unfair financial advantage. Apparently cheating isn't undignified in these circumstances.

With the leaders of Scottish football lining up to capitulate to the Ibrox mob, it may require intervention from Switzerland. As with the "Famine Song" choir, it was left to UEFA to act with good authority. The SPL leadership shrugged impotently as the law was broken in a racist karaoke wherever Rangers supporters congregated. Match delegates reported the singing of the "Famine Song", but the people at the top of the SPL refused to act. Now, UEFA appears to be the only guarantor of any sanction on this football delinquent.

The new club will have no European football for three years. If some of the chaps in the SPL hierarchy get their way, it will be the only real penalty imposed on a NewCo using the Rangers brand. I know that important types in Nyon are watching the Rangers situation closely. The Scottish authorities have the opportunity to do the correct thing. In the last week, SPL chief Neil Doncaster sent out soothing messages to the Ibrox mob. Amidst all of this turmoil, I find the silence of Celtic FC rather puzzling.

Planning blight

08.05.12

Over thirty years ago, I was told that a bad plan was better than no plan. That was true then and it is still in the "not wrong" category. It would appear that the people at the SPL top table don't have a plan for an Undead Rangers. That's bad.

When the SPL was set up over a decade ago, no one involved in this sporting cartel thought that they would have to face this scenario one day. The idea that the Ibrox club formed in 1872 would die by liquidation was bizarre. Subsequently, the notion that they would have to admit a new club using the body parts and clothing of the dead club into their league was just crazy. However, that day is almost upon us.

Yesterday was the day to make a decision on what to do about Nosferatu FC, but when the guys from Duff and Phelps asked for an adjournment, they were pushing an open door. SPL chief Neil Doncaster has tried to pass off the NewCo route as a perfectly normal way to "shed debt" and move on. Yet, creditors will be left with next to nothing. The amount of money being offered by the preferred bidder, Bill Miller, for a CVA doesn't pass muster.

Yet, the mainstream media are rather muted in this aspect of the Rangers circus. If this car crash was happening on Kerrydale Street then I would wager that the opinion-formers on Planet *Fitba* would be screaming about the unpaid bills of the ambulance service and small family firms facing insolvency. The media would make the moral case and they would be right to do so. Of course, this is different because it is the Rangers. Sandy Jardine was entirely correct that the Ibrox club is a special case. The SPL guys adopted the rabbit-staring-at-headlights stance yesterday because two cultures, two dispensations, are clashing.

Rangers as the special case is from the days of Jim Farry and, even further back, from when the SFA wanted Celtic to take down the tricolour. As the Irish community gathered around the new football club in the East End of Glasgow, the Rangers became the great white hope of racists in Scotland who wanted to keep the Fenians in their place. Sporting rivalry became a metaphor for the struggles of an immigrant community trying to establish itself within a hostile milieu. The club in the East End was open to all but it was, and remains, a vivid expression of Irishness in Scotland. Celtic, like the community that gave birth to it, was socially excluded from the start. That was the old paradigm.

Now, the people in power in Edinburgh state that the new Scotland will be different, that there will be one nation made up of many cultures. The people who run the national game claim that there is a new dispensation based on fairness and transparency. We are currently in a situation where some of the actors in this drama are in the past and others are in the future. People appear terminally confused by the new order. Paradigm shifts are like this. Social progress is not linear nor is it predetermined. The people who run Scottish football could decide that their sport will remain an artefact of the old Scotland. That was a country where Paddy knew his place, partly by seeing that the club at Edmiston Drive was above the law both on and off the field of play.

Ibrox was Caledonia's Loftus Versfeld, a sporting reminder of a highly unequal society based on ethnicity. The elevated status of the Rangers mirrored the unfairness of a society based on discrimination towards Irish Catholics. There is a sense of outrage among the Ibrox mob – partly authorised by club icons like McCoist and Jardine – that the Rangers are finally being asked to explain themselves. When Sandy Jardine joined Rangers, Scotland was a very different place and so were the power structures of the game. When McCoist was the club's star player, that paradigm was still in place. Under Sir David Murray the club behaved like Lehman Brothers with goalposts.

At Ibrox, those structures were made highly mobile in order to gain any financial advantage. There is a sense of exasperation among those who marched to Hampden that there has to be consequences for their club's actions. The bears rage that HMRC officials in England and UEFA bureaucrats in Switzerland just don't get it. This is the Rangers! These outsiders just don't see why the club is a special case. The other eleven SPL clubs know what has to be done. However, some of them just don't want the backlash from the Ibrox rabble. The hit to their bottom line from an SPL *sans* the Rangers is overstated.

As I have written before, this is a decision between the mob and money versus morality. The most honest thing to do in all of this would be to come clean and say any club operating the Rangers franchise can do what it wants. Rules, like taxes, are for little people after all. If this isn't to be a grace and favour ruling for the establishment club then the moral hazard of this debt amnesty for the Ibrox franchise is quite clear. Will the Tynecastle franchise be the next to NewCo their creditors? Once this has been agreed for one SPL club, the debt abandonment genie will be out of the bottle.

There are no good outcomes for the other eleven SPL clubs in this situation. They are faced with the reality that the Rangers behaved appallingly, and not just under Craig Whyte. Moreover, the imminent liquidation of the club will stiff hundreds of creditors. Now, the prospective owners of a Rangers NewCo expect to waltz back into the SPL as if nothing has happened simply because it is based at Ibrox. That is an even more pressing reason why the guys who met at Hampden yesterday should come up with a plan.

Even one that isn't very good.

Justice served

17.05.12

Hampden has witnessed many dramatic contests: last minute winners, contentious decisions and medieval tackles in the rain. However, 16 May 2012 is the date of one of the most historic results in the auld sang of Scottish fitba. What makes this one stand out even more is that this victory for sport happened inside a room, not out on the turf. There was no crowd looking on, but we should all be cheering. Lord Carloway, Allan Cowan and Craig Graham have done the state some service.[1]

The treatment of the original "Hampden 3" suggested that the Rangers mob might be able to pervert the course of football justice in Scotland. They certainly seemed determined to give it a try! The people in charge at Hampden decided to publish the notes of the original judgement. It was a PR masterstroke for the SFA. That is a sentence I never thought I would write, dear reader.

The response of the appellant tribunal was vital to the moral health of the game in Scotland. These three men – one of them an eminent judge – analysed the original judgement, found it competent and, crucially, they decided that the sanctions were appropriate. This is justice without fear or favour. I understand that this is something that is culturally incomprehensible to the average bear. However, it won't stop at this appeal hearing. There's more to come. Much more.

In the weeks ahead, Rangers Football Club will publicly disintegrate from a myriad of self-inflicted wounds. However, the main cause of death will be hubris.

Campbell Ogilvie's garden

22.05.12

Today I was asked by a foreign journalist to sum up the Rangers crisis in a few words. It seemed an impossible task, especially for someone with anorak status in the whole train wreck. Then the light bulb switched on in my head. I referred him to the Scottish Cup final on Saturday and explained who was giving out the medals.

---

1 http://www.philmacgiollabhain.ie/a-time-for-justice/

Campbell Ogilvie is the embodiment of the problems of corporate governance at the heart of the Rangers crisis.[1] The term "gardening leave" was invented to describe a situation where people have to be removed from their workplace while they are investigated. The president of the SFA is horribly compromised by the allegations made by Hugh Adam.[2] Campbell Ogilvie has the right to due process and for his good name to be safeguarded. However, the positions he held throughout the period referred to by Hugh Adam mean that he cannot escape scrutiny. While that investigation is underway the only acceptable course of action would be for him to step aside. That he has not done so means that the allegation that he has remained in a position to influence events is hard to dismiss.

My continental colleague said that such a scenario could not happen in his country. Sadly, I believe him.

Decision making

22.05.12

Before you make an important decision it is vital to have all the available facts at your disposal. The people at the top of the Scottish Premier League are in possession of some very powerful information. I understand that an interim report compiled by the solicitors Harper McLeod was presented to the SPL leadership yesterday. Mr Neil Doncaster and Mr Iain Blair now know the strength of the evidence gathered to support Hugh Adam's allegations regarding the existence of second contracts for Rangers players. In the interests of clarity and transparency, I would expect that the other SPL clubs be informed of the existence of this interim report and a summary of the findings without further delay. That way they will have all the necessary information to make a decision on the NewCo Rangers.

I am sure Mr Doncaster would agree with me.

---

1   http://www.philmacgiollabhain.ie/the-utmost-good-faith/

2   http://www.dailymail.co.uk/sport/football/article-2109233/Rangers-investigated-SFA-Hugh-Adam-claims.html

Franchise football in Scotland

22.05.12

There is nothing wrong with franchise sport. As long as you know that is what you are paying to watch. If everything goes to plan next season, the SPL will have a new type of club. NewCo Rangers 2012 will be operating the Ibrox franchise. It will not be Rangers, as the club established in 1872 will have passed away before the start of the new season. The SPL leadership intend to parachute the new club back into the league. They will do this despite knowing that the old club committed financial doping on an industrial scale and they used ineligible players for over a decade. With this *coup d'état* against decency achieved, the show will go on as if nothing much has happened.

The followers of Rangers make much of the word "dignity" and, in a sense, claim exclusive ownership over it on Planet *Fitba*. I cannot see what is dignified about cheating to win. Moreover, I do not think that the supporters of any SPL club will support this sleight-of-hand. If the NewCo attracts a following from the deceased club then I expect that they will be informed at every SPL match about the immorality of the situation. In the SPL this new club will be tainted. If Mr Doncaster gets his way, a weakened New Rangers with a depleted squad will be in the SPL next season.

What happens in twelve months if they are relegated? Will Mr Doncaster arrange for the league to be expanded at the last moment to keep this valuable franchise in the top flight? Is there anyone at the top of Scottish football with the faintest idea of the damage they are about to cause to the standing of the national game on the international stage? It would appear that the term "moral hazard" does not have any meaning for the people in leadership positions in Scottish football. Hopefully, that important cautionary concept will be better understood in the powerful corridors at Nyon.

Smart moves for powerful people

23.05.12

"Plausible deniability" is an important concept if you are at the head of an organisation. It allows you to conceal a greater truth while telling no lies. Imagine you are at the top of a major organisation. Ah, go on . . . You can do it! Now, let's say a firm of solicitors has carried out a sampling exercise for you and they uncover a major problem in your operation. In fact, they unearth a major clusterfuck. They submit an interim report and then ask you for authorisation to go through every single piece of paper from way back. Their request is denied. Clever you!

As CEO of the organisation you can say that the full report is not in your possession. That isn't a lie. If the communication is handled between the legal people and the organisation's number two then that is another good move. As the head honcho, you can swear blind that you haven't received anything onto your big shiny desk. Once more, no lie is told. Clever, isn't it?

The only problem arises if there are pesky journalists digging around asking difficult questions, as opposed to docile hacks who wait in line for a press release.

The great escape?

24.05.12

When a bad situation unfolds it is always a good response to claim that you have no knowledge. If you don't know then you aren't really responsible. However, the Sergeant Schultz defence of "I know nothing!" no longer works down at Stalag Hampden. If people at the top of Scottish football are not aware of the scale of the ethical and organisational challenge posed to them by the Rangers scandal then they are working very hard at being ignorant.

The Mark Daly documentary last night laid out the extent of the second contracts debacle at the Ibrox club. Even just including Barry Ferguson and Stefan Klos, the number of games in which these players took to the field may force history to be rewritten and trophies to be re-engraved. The German keeper played 208 games for the Ibrox club between 1999 and 2007. Barry Ferguson, in his second spell at Rangers, played 137 times between 2005 and 2009. If the second contract inquiry finds that these two players were ineligible then all of those matches which the club won are now 3–0 defeats.

Remember, dear reader, I have selected just TWO of the players implicated in the EBT story. TWO. According to the Mark Daly expose, there are another 36 with these side letters. When all of the players are included this is cheating on a massive scale, unparalleled in Scottish football history.

I am confident that Rangers will lose the big tax case. I have not spoken to anyone with knowledge of what went on in that tax tribunal who expects that HMRC will not win. However, apart from the issue of a massive bill that the dying club (in administration) can't pay, there is the breaking of the football regulations. This makes any sweetheart deal for a NewCo operating the Ibrox franchise much more difficult to sell to the rest of Scottish football.

After the Mark Daly documentary, the guys at Hampden have an even tougher task. If, in the interests of clarity and transparency, Mr Doncaster and Mr Regan canvassed the opinion of the supporters of ALL Scottish clubs then I think they would have a clearer picture. They would find that there is a genuine hostility to a NewCo Rangers being allowed back into the SPL, even with sanctions. The idea that they are allowed back in without any domestic sanctions is truly unconscionable. The coverage from the mainstream media has helped insulate the Rangers klan from the morally indefinable position that they have assumed. They see their club as a victim of a bad man (Craig Whyte) and believe Rangers are blameless in the entire mess. The Mark Daly documentary really should put that fairy story to bed once and for all.

If a NewCo Rangers is parachuted back into the SPL with no sanctions then it will be entirely appropriate that the theme tune from *The Great Escape* becomes the new club's anthem! The Ibrox faithful are very fond of their World War II heroes. Such a pity that Hogan is an Irish name . . .

Wars are often started over resources and the side with the best logistics usually wins. Rangers, under David Murray, signed players and paid wages that they could not have afforded if everything had gone through the PAYE system. In doing so, the Ibrox club had a genuine financial advantage over other clubs. The David Murray boast from the year 2000 about fivers and tenners now takes on another meaning. Rangers could afford to spend double what the Parkhead club could because the chaps in Kerrydale Street were paying all due taxes.

It is, of course, just the bad luck of Neil Doncaster and Stewart Regan that they are the guys in charge when all of this poo has collided with the air conditioning. They are blameless in all of this. However, they weren't conscripted to serve and they willingly stepped forward. No doubt when they volunteered neither of them could have seen this mess happening on their watch. However, it has and it needs to be dealt with in a way that saves the national game. There is now a clear choice that both men have to make. They can either save the Ibrox franchise or save Scottish football. At this stage it does seem to be a mutually exclusive proposition. All the facts are there for them to make their deliberations.

On a human level you could forgive these guys at Hampden for starting a tunnel of their own!

On rule 66

30.05.12

It is still difficult to quantify the long-term consequences of the decision made yesterday by Lord Glennie. However, one thing is clear. Duff and Phelps have scored the type of own goal that will have an impact on Scottish football long after they have left the scene. It is perhaps a result of the trauma they have been through since mid-February that this court ruling was seized upon by Rangers supporters as a great victory. It isn't.

What Lord Glennie noted was that the twelve-month transfer embargo was not available to the SFA as a sanction. The explicit punishments stated in the SFA's rule 66 are a maximum £100,000 fine, suspension or expulsion from participation in the game, ejection from the Scottish Cup or termination of membership. The fine has already been imposed but was considered by the original tribunal to be insufficient for the crimes committed by the Ibrox club. Lord Glennie inserted the crucial caveat at the end of his ruling. He told Rangers that they should not expect a lighter punishment when their case is reassessed by the appellant tribunal.

I called a member of the SFA's 100-strong "taxi rank" of judicial panel members. He told me that it was his understanding that the case would go back to Lord Carloway, Allan Cowan and Craig Graham. Lord Glennie did not find in Rangers' favour regarding their guilt. He was not asked to do so.

Therefore, the Ibrox club remains guilty of what the original judicial panel report stated, that in their view "only match fixing in its various forms might be a more serious breach" than the financial irregularities committed by Rangers. The report, mainly authored by chairman Gary Allan QC, revealed that the tribunal had considered suspension of membership of the SFA to be an "appropriately severe punishment", but had, in the final analysis, deemed it "too severe". The appellant tribunal, under Lord Carloway, concurred. Now they have to look again at the sanctions that are written down under rule 66.

There is little wriggle room and Rangers are not off the hook on this one. What could also happen now is action taken by the SFA against the Ibrox club for seeking redress in the civil courts. If the domestic association decides to turn a blind eye to this then FIFA have already issued a strong statement. They want the SFA to act on Rangers for going outside the normal football channels.

Quite simply, if the guys at Hampden don't move on this one then FIFA will want a word with Mr Regan. That this is all unfolding while "the great administrator" Campbell Ogilvie is SFA president is wonderfully ironic.

Rangers: the movie

30.05.12

ORIGINALLY PUBLISHED ON VAVEL

If the Rangers saga was a movie then yesterday the director decided to speed up the action and today it hasn't slowed down. The administrators, Duff and Phelps, finally sent out the CVA to creditors. This is an offer to the companies, individuals and organisations owed money by the Ibrox club. In CVAs there is a percentage offered to settle the debt, say, 10% of the amount owed. Under UK law, creditors owed 75% of the total monies outstanding must agree. The two biggest creditors are HMRC and the company, Ticketus. Either of these could block the CVA.

It is expected that HMRC will not agree to this settlement, which is much worse than the deal offered to them in early 2011. Then, Rangers offered the British tax authorities £10m in settlement of the "big tax case". At that point, HMRC was seeking £24m in unpaid tax, £12m in interest and £15m in penalties. The case is still to be adjudicated upon by three judges.

However, if Rangers lose this case then their total tax liabilities could be in excess of £70m, as the club under Craig Whyte's ownership simply didn't pay ANY tax. If the CVA is voted down then the new prospective owner, Charles Green, has an agreement to buy the assets of the club for £5.5m. For this sum he would get the stadium and the training ground. This would mean that a new company – a "NewCo" – would exist to trade as Rangers. The club itself would be liquidated.

The trick is to get the supporters to attend the stadium next season as if nothing has happened. The issue for those who govern Scottish football has been what to do about a club that has broken many rules and wants to continue on without any punishment. Yesterday, the club's administrators took the Scottish Football Association to court and challenged the transfer embargo imposed on Rangers for "bringing the game into disrepute". This was a result of the club not paying other clubs for players they had purchased, like Lee Wallace of Hearts. The Edinburgh club is still owed £800,000 for the defender.

The judge in Edinburgh, Lord Glennie, found that the SFA tribunal did not have the authority to impose the transfer embargo, which prevents Rangers from registering players over the age of eighteen for the next twelve months. The case will now be looked at again by the SFA's tribunal, and Lord Glennie told Rangers not to expect a more lenient punishment. It is possible that the club could be suspended from membership of the SFA or even be terminated as members of the domestic association in Scotland.

FIFA released a statement expressing their disquiet at this turn of events. It is a major crime in professional football for a club to take the ruling body to the civil courts. FC Sion did this last year and was heavily punished by the Swiss FA on orders of FIFA. The course of action is clear: if the SFA do not act on Rangers then FIFA will act on the SFA. This could mean all Scottish national teams and club teams could be banned from any international competition, including the World Cup and the Champions League.

Today, the Scottish Premier League clubs met to vote in a series of "financial fair play" regulations, but the proposals fell. The SPL chief executive wanted a new rule whereby any club in the league could "phoenix" back in as a NewCo without any vote. However, this was also rejected. The SPL is also carrying out the "second contract inquiry" into Rangers. This probe was sparked after allegations made by a former Rangers director, Hugh Adam, that the club had paid players by way of a second, hidden contract. This is in contravention of the football rules in Scotland and would mean that the players with the second contract would not be properly registered and would, therefore, be ineligible to play. Teams that field an ineligible player forfeit the match 3–0. This is what happened to FC Sion in their two matches against Celtic in the Europa League last year.

These allegations of a policy of second contracts at Rangers over more than a decade have also been made in a recent BBC documentary by investigative reporter Mark Daly. If proven, titles and trophies could be taken from the Ibrox club. When I read back through this article it is clear that the plot has more unforeseen developments than could be envisaged by Pedro Almodóvar. The most poignant theme is that Rangers – often called "Scotland's establishment club" – is now threatening all of Scottish football by opening the door to FIFA action.

It is fair to say that the long love affair between Rangers and the Scottish Football Association may be at an end. There are broken embraces on the steps of Hampden.

A game-changing gaffe

01.06.12

The scale of the Court of Session own goal scored by Duff and Phelps is only starting to emerge. I had to check again that it was only two days ago that I wrote the following.[1] (The online piece carries a link to On Rule 66.) Since then I have canvassed opinion from Aberdeen to Zurich on the likely fallout from this crime against a football authority. I am now as convinced as I can be that Rangers will be temporarily suspended from membership of the Scottish Football Association. Had one even considered this two weeks ago it would have been risible. It now seems a racing certainty.

Someone very close to the action advised me today that "the sanction will have to go north from where it is now". My source explained that the fine would remain in place, but that merely suspending Rangers from the Scottish Cup would not be sufficient. I detected a genuine exasperation and, after a while, real anger at what Rangers had inflicted on Scottish football by going to court. People within several provincial clubs, who had previously been well disposed towards the Rangers situation, more or less threw their hands in the air after this one.

I hope that the chant of "no one likes us, we don't care" wasn't an idle boast. FIFA are, I was informed, "comfortable that the situation is back inside football". However, the world governing body wishes to be appraised of events more or less as they happen in Glasgow.

---

1 http://www.philmacgiollabhain.ie/on-rule-66/

Lord Carloway and his colleagues now have very few options to choose from. They will, once more, review the sanction imposed on Rangers, this time with the knowledge that rule 66 trumps article 95.

The original judicial panel, headed by Gary Allan QC, created a sanction that kept the show on the road, but acknowledged the seriousness of what had happened at Ibrox under Craig Whyte. Now that option is not open to them.

The question that I can't answer is why this was done by Duff and Phelps in the first place. A well-placed insider offered the following analysis: "Look, they've been getting lambasted by the Rangers support since February, suddenly they had a move that bought them fifteen minutes of love and they took it." That is the opinion of someone who is well placed to conjecture. I simply don't know.

My guy was also contemptuous of the Duff and Phelps defence that they weren't aware of the FIFA ramifications of going to law. What I was also reminded of was that it was likely that the Ibrox club would now face fresh charges for going to court. In fact, FIFA may well insist on this.

At the start of this little drama, Ally McCoist demanded to know the identities of the original "Hampden 3", claiming that these men "could have killed this football club". I believe the Rangers manager spoke too soon on this one. His club will die, but the final blow will not have been struck by the unmasked judicial trio, but by two chaps much closer to home.

Dealing with the legacy of a tainted past

17.06.12

It is important for the bereaved to be assisted to accept their loss and to move on. Now that Rangers are dead, a thing of the past, I believe that their crimes should die with them. Obviously, Lord Carloway and his two colleagues will have to reconsider the sanctions in the light of Lord Glennie's ruling. However, the liquidation of Rangers does render this all rather irrelevant. It is akin to imposing a life sentence on a suicide bomber just after he has pressed the button.

Charles Green did not buy Rangers FC. That club is dead. What he purchased was the body parts. It is, of course, important to maintain the fantasy that the club still lives. He wishes to attract the customer base from Rangers (1872–2012) to his new club. Fortunately, Charlie and the boys are targeting an evidence-resistant subculture who want to believe that the 'Gers are still alive. When their club WAS still with us they did not accept that it had a serious illness. That is why they didn't mobilise to save their club in time.[1]

Now the Magic Cardigan Consortium has swooped in, like a paramedic one hour after the gravediggers have thrown in the last shovelful of dirt. This will only fuel the denial that many of them are in about the death of Rangers. In the crazy world of marketing we are often invited to believe many preposterous notions. It is seductively suggested that if we buy a product then we will acquire certain personal qualities and abilities. In the advertising world there is an in-house technical term for such a concept: pish.

Advertising people are creative. They always see another angle to market the urine they are promoting. Perhaps Mr Green will be advised on the rebranding to: "I can't believe it's not Rangers!" Some cynics may feel that it is the targeted customer base that should be branded. However, I am not a cynic.

The dual contracts probe by the SPL has been formally put on hold. I have been aware for some time that people in senior positions weren't keen to proceed with that investigation. I am convinced that Rangers (1872–2012) fielded ineligible players during the EBT years. Subsequently, victories are null and void, and titles will have to be stripped from the deceased club. That said, there should be no penalty imposed on the new club. That goes against all natural justice.

Charlie and the boys no doubt would have been counting on the support of the Glasgow media. However, the decision of the Walter to swoop means that there will be no honeymoon for the Yorkshire man. Since February there has been a craving among the denizens of the Glasgow sports desks to find good news stories for the Ibrox klan. When word of the Magic Cardigan Consortium reached the hacks there was air-punching euphoria among some of them. In the offices of one major title there was an embrace of relief between two dignified hacks.

The bottom line is that these papers have to sell lots of copies to survive and Rangers people are the main market. The media in Glasgow are caught between the rock of reality and the hard place of peddling the cosy fantasy that Rangers are still alive. Not all Ibrox chaps are so

---

1   http://www.scotzine.com/2011/09/why-its-too-late-for-gers-for-change/

disassociated from reality. They know the club's history hasn't been lost, but it is concluded.

However, depressed people don't tend to buy newspapers and voraciously consume the column inches for every detail of bad news. The BBC has been generally better on this story than most of the print sector. Jim Spence has been on the money, referring to Rangers as "effectively dead" and "140 years of history disappeared today" – those statements are evidence-based.

Subsequently, whatever the appellant tribunal finds apropos the disrepute charges, it should be recorded and we should all move on. It would be as effective as giving a driving ban to guy who dropped dead last week. It is a matter of record, but meaningless in the here and now. Moreover, if I buy the dead guy's car then I shouldn't have to serve the driving ban. The crime dies with him.

Rangers committed many crimes against sport, but they are dead. A new club has acquired the assets of the deceased club. Rangers are dead and those are the facts.

It's time to move on.

Our man in Nyon

19.06.12

It would appear that there is some confusion about Rangers on Planet *Fitba*. So I called my UEFA contact. He knows about this stuff. Scotland is a far off country of which he knows little. However, he lives on Planet UEFA and he knows their rules better than most people. He considered it risible that a liquidated club could be considered anything other than dead. "The football club is ended when the liquidation happens," he told me.

For the guys in Nyon it is not up for debate; a new company set up to operate in the stadium of the old outfit is viewed as an entirely new football club. The three-year exclusion from European football is not a "ban", but merely a rule that a club must exist for three years before UEFA will allow them into any of their competitions.

Anyone in the Scottish media who pretends that there isn't a new football club being set up to play out of Ibrox stadium is either too stupid or to venal to do their job. The idea that the new club would be allowed in the room to decide on their future in the SPL had my contact utterly baffled. He was surprised that any league in Europe would allow this in their rules. Tip of the hat is due to Bella Caledonia for their pursuit of this one.[1]

That the folks at the SPL don't seem to be acquainted with their own rules suggests we are dealing with rank incompetence rather than some malevolent conspiracy. More Mr Bean than the Borgias. UEFA guy was very interested to learn about the dual contract case. When I explained that RFC (1872–2012) fielded ineligible players in around 700 matches and that they were invalidly registered to disguise a tax evasion ploy, I knew I had his full attention. "Yes, yes, the records must be amended if this is true." When I told him who the SFA president was and of his history in the offending club he simply did not believe me. He had heard the name, of course, but didn't know of Campbell Ogilvie's club career as a brilliant administrator of the dead club.[2]

I believe that we are still only at the start of unravelling the extent of the crimes committed over the last twenty years by RFC (1872–2012) against Scottish football. There may be a clamour to inflict punishment on the new club for the crimes of the old. However, this is simply unjust and, according to my UEFA guy, illegal in his bureaucratic worldview. This is a new club which will not be allowed to participate in European competition for three years. This isn't a punishment on RFC (1872–2012), but the rules that pertain to any new club.

The people who ... err ... "govern" Scottish football should realise that they're not dealing with Rangers and move on. Rangers are dead and people should get used to that reality.

The Scottish spring

25.06.12

Achieving a common purpose among enough people at a time of national crisis has been a centuries old problem in the land of my birth. In Scotland's heroic age, auld Alba always had a fighting chance of repelling an invader if enough guys turned up for the big show. Gathering the clans was a vital process. A suitably Machiavellian foreigner might seek to indulge in a wee bit o' divide et imperia. Buying off a clan

---

1 http://bellacaledonia.org.uk/2012/06/18/the-man-from-tea-12/

2 http://www.philmacgiollabhain.ie/the-utmost-good-faith/

chief or two was always a good move. When that didn't happen and the dressing room was as one, fair Caledonia could cause a few medieval cup upsets.

As I write this, I have just learned that the Perth men have joined in what is starting to seem like a Scottish Spring on Planet *Fitba*. Six weeks ago it seemed a done deal in the corridors of power that FC NewCo would be allowed straight back into the SPL. The men in the big leather chairs at Hampden even peddled the risible notion that the NewCo wasn't a new club.

Yesterday I spoke with a couple of Inverness Caledonian Thistle fellas. They wanted to remain anonymous, but they assured me that their guys were in rebellious mood and wouldn't tolerate their clan chief taking the king's shilling on this one.

The immortal Jock Stein knew that "football without fans is nothing". The people who run the national game in Scotland forgot that central reality. I hope that the rebellion spreads to the fans of SFL1 clubs. Those clubs are more reliant on their paying customers as there is no TV deal. Moreover, the smaller numbers of fans mean that people in the boardrooms at Falkirk and Hamilton actually know their supporters.

The only morally defensible choice is Division Three for the new club that wants to play at Ibrox. This is not an extraordinary punishment; it is just the rules.

The rebellion started because a parcel of rogues wanted to subvert basic fairness. This messing around means that Dundee and Dunfermline still don't know if they are "Club 12". It almost certainly won't be the new club playing out of Ibrox.

The people in power could have avoided all of this had they simply applied rules without fear or favour. Another perennial problem for Scottish kings was the "over mighty subject". Rangers (1872–2012) wielded influence in the national game that went beyond their success on the field. Even in death, the people ostensibly in charge of Scottish football seek to give their baying fan base, in denial over their loss, preferential treatment. The solution to this problem is simple; the new club starts in Division Three.

Now, as is often the case with the rebellions, the top guy has left the country. What kind of national game will Mr Regan come home to? Hopefully, one in which the ordinary people have a greater sense of their own power.

Independence Day

04.07.12

Today was one of those rare days when the good guys won. The growing rebellion among football supporters across Scotland scuppered the plans of the powerful.[1] Just because people occupy influential positions, it doesn't mean that they're better than the rest of us. It is important when faced with people in power who act against the common good that you have an effective and civilised method of getting rid of them.

The people who buy the season tickets, the club merchandise and spend inside the stadium on match days were not, initially, being listened to. Six weeks ago, NewCo to SPL was a done deal. With each passing day the fans of the dead club that used to play at Ibrox have confirmed, by their own actions and inactions, my harshest assessment of them.

The inability to have a public gathering without it descending rather rapidly into a bigoted karaoke needs no further editorialising from me.[2] However, their failure to organise any meaningful movement in a peaceful democratic city in the age of social media is remarkable.

The SPL vote today was a massive personal setback for Neil Doncaster. NewCo to SPL was very much his project, his plan. He is damaged goods, just like the league he heads up.

The mainstream media have played a shameful role in this entire saga. They should have informed the public, but instead they spewed out propaganda about the dire consequences of not allowing NewCo into the SPL. Expect them to do the same with the Division One fallback position.

The rules state that new clubs start in Division Three. That is what should happen. Today is no Brian Dempsey moment. The rebels have not yet won and they may still lose to the massed ranks of marketing types who don't understand what motivates the people who sustain the game. They are supporters, not customers. They love a football club, not a brand.

The great Scottish football war now will now see its climactic battle in the SFL. It is the worst of times and the best of times for the national

1   http://www.philmacgiollabhain.ie/the-scottish-spring/#more-2881
2   http://www.philmacgiollabhain.ie/bomber-command/#more-2891

game in Scotland. There is no doubt that it is a time for heroes, not placemen. Turnbull Hutton has emerged as an unlikely, but authentic voice of decency and sanity on the steps of the national stadium. If justice finally prevails, those who cherish liberty will be dancing in the streets of Raith.

Hearing clearly

05.07.12

Listening is an undervalued skill for journalists in the digital age. When Stewart Regan made his "social unrest" observation, most of the hacks in the presser didn't pick up on the significance of it. They ignored what he said and then barged on with questions about the SFL, the SFA application by Sevco and other such insignificant matters next to public order. Those two words should have stopped everyone in their tracks; instead, Regan was bombarded with breathless questions from airhead hacks. Thankfully, they were not all of such a low calibre in the presser.

I have spoken to one experienced journalist who was there, and he remains quite clear on what the SFA chief executive was speculating about. Regan was concerned about the Ibrox mob's capacity for trouble. That is my guy's settled view of what the Englishman was on about. The SFA chief executive has tried to row back from the original "social unrest" comments.[1] Mr Regan obviously thinks it is unlikely that, in the event of there being no football at Ibrox in the coming season, the "Famine Song" choir will take up a genteel hobby and be good citizens. I agree with him on that. Mention the words "social unrest" in connection with supporters of the deceased club and it conjures up images of Barcelona, Pamplona and, of course, Manchester. Perhaps he is correct that Edmiston Drive is a sort of underclass crèche that provides a genuine social service to the rest of society.

However, I take the opposite view that Rangers (1872–2012) was a gathering point and a source of affirmation for the worst elements in Scottish society. Augmented by the finest specimens of Rathcoole and the Shankill Road, Ibrox has been a culture dish for some very toxic societal pathogens for over a century. Of course, Regan's comment does unwittingly heap greater pressure on the SFL clubs in their upcoming

1 http://www.bbc.co.uk/sport/0/football/18719894

deliberations. Turnbull Hutton and the other chaps may have another issue to consider when they decide on the Sevco application to their league: public order.

No pressure then . . .

Just apply the rules, Mr Regan

06.07.12

It is now clear for anyone who wishes to see that those in leadership positions in Scottish football find the rules a bit of an obstacle to their plans. I have noticed in the debate over the way the SFA is currently acting that no one has yet mentioned that NewCo in Division One is a breach of FIFA statues – article 9 of the regulations governing application of the FIFA statutes, to be precise. Quite clearly, league participation must be based on sporting merit. The SFA and SPL must abide by these statutes in terms of their own articles and rules. NewCo has not earned the sporting merit to be in Division One and so I believe the SFA are acting in clear breach of FIFA Statutes. If Mr Regan doubts me he can check page 62.[1]

Please read Section 9.1 on sporting merit and then think about what Mr Regan proposes for Sevco into SFL Division One. Section 9.3 on the changing of names and company structures should also concentrate those fine minds at Hampden. Section 9.4 should inform Mr Regan where the buck stops. Finally, he may wish to consult the SFA's articles of association.[2] I think he may find 3.B on page 24 has something within it that should focus him.

From my reading of these rules, both international and domestic, the sweetheart deal that he apparently wants to wangle for NewCo simply isn't on. Just apply the rules, Mr Regan, because that is what you are paid for.

---

1 http://www.fifa.com/mm/document/affederation/generic/01/48/60/05/
   fifastatuten2011_e.pdf

2 http://www.scottishfa.co.uk/resources/documents/SFAPublications/
   ScottishFApublications2011-12/Scottish%20FA%20Handbook.pdf

Judgement day

13.07.12

Well, this is it. Unlike a Duff and Phelps deadline, today really is a line in the sand. The people who gather at Hampden this morning have a fundamental decision to make about Scotland's national game. Today, Scottish football can emerge from a long Ibrox-imposed nightmare and start again, or it can die. Those are the choices.

It is a simple enough decision. The people who will congregate around the big table on the sixth floor have to vote for either marketing or morality. That will tell the world if they represent clubs or just brands. Are the people who buy the tickets supporters or are they just customers?

This is a day when the good guys, like Turnbull Hutton, MUST win. If they lose, the marketing monkeys will forge ahead with their vision of soccertainment. The game in Scotland can die today. That will leave a gap in my life. Thankfully I have the GAA to fill that void. I hope you too have alternatives because after today you might not have Scottish football in any meaningful sense.

Today really is the day.

Links

http://www.philmacgiollabhain.ie/
    sfa-to-move-against-paul-mcbride-qc/   13.04.11
http://www.philmacgiollabhain.ie/
    questions-about-rangers-in-europe/   25.10.11
http://www.philmacgiollabhain.ie/
    questions-that-should-be-answered/   01.12.11
http://www.philmacgiollabhain.ie/unanswered-questions/   02.12.11
http://www.philmacgiollabhain.ie/
    petition-sent-to-the-sfa-about-rangers-uefa-licence/   05.12.11
http://www.philmacgiollabhain.ie/
    the-second-contract-fact-or-rumour/   24.01.12
http://www.philmacgiollabhain.ie/
    the-need-to-be-crystal-clear-about-the-uefa-licence-story/   19.01.12
http://www.philmacgiollabhain.ie/the-utmost-good-faith/   26.02.12
http://www.philmacgiollabhain.ie/the-sfa-on-a-sticky-wicket/   06.03.12

http://www.philmacgiollabhain.ie/game-on/   14.03.12

http://www.philmacgiollabhain.ie/the-right-to-due-process/   15.03.12

http://www.philmacgiollabhain.ie/is-feidir-linn/   24.04.12

http://www.philmacgiollabhain.ie/due-process/   25.04.12

http://www.philmacgiollabhain.ie/help-required/   26.04.12

http://www.philmacgiollabhain.ie/a-watershed-moment/   06.05.12

http://www.philmacgiollabhain.ie/planning-blight/   08.05.12

http://www.philmacgiollabhain.ie/justice-served/   17.05.12

http://www.philmacgiollabhain.ie/campbell-ogilvies-garden/   22.05.12

http://www.philmacgiollabhain.ie/decision-making/   22.05.12

http://www.philmacgiollabhain.ie/franchise-football-in-scotland/   22.05.12

http://www.philmacgiollabhain.ie/
    smart-moves-for-powerful-people/   23.05.12

http://www.philmacgiollabhain.ie/the-great-escape/   24.05.12

http://www.philmacgiollabhain.ie/on-rule-66/   30.05.12

http://www.vavel.com/en/uk-football/scottish-premier-league/glasgow-
    rangers/166421-rangers-the-movie.html   30.05.12

http://www.philmacgiollabhain.ie/a-game-changing-gaffe/   01.06.12

http://www.philmacgiollabhain.ie/
    dealing-with-the-legacy-of-a-tainted-past/   17.06.12

http://www.philmacgiollabhain.ie/our-man-in-nyon/   19.06.12

http://www.philmacgiollabhain.ie/the-scottish-spring/   25.06.12

http://www.philmacgiollabhain.ie/independence-day/   04.07.12

http://www.philmacgiollabhain.ie/hearing-clearly/   05.07.12

http://www.philmacgiollabhain.ie/just-apply-the-rules-mr-regan/   06.07.12

http://www.philmacgiollabhain.ie/judgment-day/   13.07.12

Postscript

Looking into the future is an admittedly imprecise science at the best of times. Moreover, I make no claims to be a clairvoyant. However, if you have stayed with this book to these last few pages then I hope that I have demonstrated a track record over the years on matters Rangers of being more than occasionally on the money.

Ah yes, money. In the coming period I expect Binder Dijker Otte & Co. (BDO), HMRC's approved liquidators for Rangers Football Club, to be following a lot of that down Ibrox way. They will want to know why Rangers Football Club no longer has any assets but has a paltry £5.5m in an account currently controlled by the club's administrators, Duff and Phelps. I suspect they will be intrigued, perhaps even perturbed, to find out that £1.5m of that sum was used to secure possession of the "heritable properties" of the Albion car park, Ibrox stadium and Murray Park training ground. Looking into a "sale under value" is one of their things, you understand.

Under the 1986 Insolvency Act, don't be surprised if the BDO boys are in the Court of Session with a very clear picture presented to the Outer House – probably in front of Lord Hodge. The same eminent member of the judiciary will also want to hear from Duff and Phelps whether or not there was a conflict of interest from their time advising Craig Whyte on buying Rangers. I rather suspect that those insolvency impresarios, formerly known as MCR, may have some serious questions to answer in the Outer House.

David Grier of MCR, before it was taken over by the global firm of Duff and Phelps, advised Craig Whyte on the takeover of Rangers in 2011. It is that transaction which is, of course, currently the subject of a full-blown criminal investigation by the Strathclyde fraud squad.

There is plenty of stuff coming down the pipeline on the legal front. Anyone who thinks that the days of embarrassing financial headlines emanating from Edmiston Drive are a thing of the past probably still thinks Craig Whyte is a billionaire. The police are also involved at SFA level, but for a far more sinister reason. At time of writing, Stewart Regan confirmed that he had been the subject of death threats and had received advice and protection from the police.

The nature of the allegations meant that the anti-terrorism unit had been involved.

I broke the story of threats to SFA personnel on 23 July 2012. However, I deliberately did not name Regan. The mainstream media caught up a week later when Regan revealed the information himself. Brilliant piece of investigative work, guys! *Chapeau!*

The downfall of Rangers has been a difficult time for the Scottish footie Fourth Estate. As Alex Thomson robustly observes in the foreword to this book, the mainstream media largely failed to report accurately on one of the biggest stories they will ever experience in their professional lives. The Rangers fiasco established the veracity and reliability of new media. Many fitba aficionados now consider blogs and podcasts as their source of reliable news and intelligent analysis rather than the traditional media organisations. Both old and new media meet on Twitter, and it has been a sight to behold the extent to which journalists from the BBC and major newspapers, forced by their employers to tweet, have been soundly trashed by a digital-savvy generation of punters. Like the Rangers story itself, they badly misjudged the new media revolution. Every time they derided bloggers they only wounded their own credibility. To the fitba public it just sounded like a vested interest cynically protecting its own turf from a new competitor. In the coming period there will be few Scottish sports journalists who will publicly deride bloggers and new media.

The new football season had not even started when the *Real Radio Football Phone In* was liquidated. Thirty minutes before broadcast, the people on the show were given the bad news. The radio station put out a statement about the show being axed: "When the show started more than a decade ago it was among only a handful of debate shows available to fans. Now, this type of content is widely available whenever people want it on many different platforms, such as internet forums, fan sites, specialist TV channels, other radio stations and social media." Quite.

Like the rest of the print sector in the UK the demand for newspapers in Glasgow is shrinking and several major titles exist on wafer-thin margins. The traditional media lost a massive amount of respect during the Rangers saga and it remains to be seen if they will make the changes that will see them regain the trust of the fitba public. The people in charge of the big titles will need to call time on the practice of obediently accepting PR-generated fairy stories about Rangers and passing them off as "exclusives".

The overworked staff on sports desks were reduced to being mere "churnalists". Quite simply, the guys on the sports desks became little more than typists for the spin doctors employed by Rangers and Craig Whyte. This was a type of journalism that had made many of the hacks very fat under David Murray. Some of them remain one-eyed and poisonous towards the contribution of new media to the accurate telling of the death of Rangers. However, their time is passing and they know it. If the fitba Fourth Estate starts practising journalism again then there will have been a good outcome from this shameful fiasco. If their failure in reporting the Rangers story accurately is not a wakeup call, they don't deserve to be called journalists.

This entire saga has shown that the future of fitba journalism is digital. Moreover, much of that output will be generated by bloggers and citizen journalists. The platforms have changed and the level of interaction with the public is beyond the comprehension of many older members of the hack pack. Some journalists will adapt, but others will be like old goalies in the 1990s when the pass-back rule changed. Suddenly, some previously confident keepers looked befuddled, hesitant and out of place, and it was clear to all onlookers that their day had passed. I expect the influence of new media to grow on Planet *Fitba*. This is, of course, no different to other areas of human discourse, like politics and current affairs.

As for the Ibrox klan, sadly there seems little evidence of any evolution in their worldview. If anything, the condition may be about to worsen. They have now added victimhood to their Herrenvolk certainties for they are utterly convinced that their beloved club has been unfairly treated. The reality, as has been demonstrated here, is that the people in leadership positions in Scottish football did their utmost to facilitate the NewCo Rangers into the SPL. The Ibrox crowd continues to incubate hatred towards the Catholic Church and Irish Catholics in particular.

Sevco Scotland is currently signing players. One of them, Dean Shiels, is from Northern Ireland. The chances that he would be from the Republic of Ireland and destined for the first team at Ibrox are next to zero. The emotional contract between the customers and those who operate the Ibrox franchise apropos anti-Irish racism appears to remain extant. Sadly, this suggests that the old hatreds have come over with TUPE. Now Sevco Scotland Ltd appears to have a chief executive who is willing to push tribal buttons. Charles Green said that some of the business decisions taken against Sevco Scotland Ltd were fuelled by "bigotry". This is precisely what the Edmiston Drive lynch mob wanted to hear.

The future does not look bright for those who believe that a large section of the Ibrox klan needs civilising. At time of going to press it was revealed that two men had been arrested in connection with alleged sectarian chanting at the "Rangers" v. Peterhead match on 11 August. The men were arrested following a joint operation involving the Northern Constabulary and Strathclyde Police. Their officers were assisted by colleagues from the Grampian force and the Football Co-ordination Unit for Scotland (FoCUS).

My sources recently informed me that FoCUS officers would attend *every* away match involving fans from the Ibrox club this season. The operational plan is to film the Fenian blood-waders in their natural habitat, identify them after the event and then give them an early knock on the door.

This may be a new club, but they are selling the same product to the usual suspects. That is why young Dean Shiels from Northern Ireland is acceptable, but a Republic of Ireland international would cause consternation in the cheap seats at Ibrox. The young Ulsterman's new team-mate is ex-Hearts hard man, Ian Black. The midfield enforcer is reportedly being paid £7,000 per week. Ex-St Johnstone striker Francisco Sandaza has also been given a good personal deal to play for the Ibrox club.

The question for those in charge at Sevco Scotland Ltd is how they continue to trade with Division Three revenues and an SPL wage bill. An insolvency event for the new club would, of course, be beyond parody. Mr Green and his associates are currently putting together a share issue. It must succeed or Sevco will have to be bankrolled by a rich investor or face going into administration.

The success of the share issue will be down, in large part, to the "feel good factor" around the fan base, because they will be the main buyers of the shares. It is clear to anyone but the innumerate that the current wage bill at Ibrox is not sustainable and that without additional revenue streams or harsh austerity the long-term viability of Sevco must be in doubt. However, it would be risible to assume that the current owners of Ibrox stadium are there for the long haul. Moreover, I expect that clear divisions in the Green consortium will become more visible in the coming period.

The entire Rangers collapse has smashed up everything in its path and that includes reputations. Stewart Regan has been particularly bruised. The buck stopped at his desk and he frequently dropped the ball. The death threats he is receiving from the Rangers klan will probably only reinforce in his own head that this northern posting wasn't worth the rations. Do not be surprised if the man who boasted a 20/20 vision for Scottish football realises that he saw very little of this shit storm coming, even when it was clearly visible on the horizon to the rest of us. His co-conspirator on the sixth floor may well follow him out of Hampden, because Neil Doncaster of the SPL has shown himself wedded to the same failed business model.

The first competitive game for the new club contained all the components that led to the death of Rangers. At the eleventh hour a "conditional membership of the SFA" was granted, despite the fact that no such category exists within the Articles of Association. So when Sevco Scotland's Rangers took to the field on 29 July there were *two* Rangers. The original club established in 1872 is still in administration and awaiting liquidation, but it is still legally in existence. Sevco Scotland's Rangers played Brechin while Rangers Football club remained a full member of the SFA.

The visiting fans partied like it was all OK. They were happy because they could sing about "Fenian bastards". They also chanted about hating Stewart Regan, and the Sevco chief executive applauded the singing. It was the start of a charm offensive that is still in full swing. Bereft of leadership the bears crave an alpha male with the minerals to stand up for their "traditions". Mr Green has proved to be adept at playing to the gallery. His words are very much his own and he is not parroting any PR prepared script. Whereas Craig Whyte would read out a statement prepared with the help of communications experts bought in to provide that service, Charlie is rather unrehearsed. Consequently, I cannot see this ending well for him or the new club.

Charlie has already entered into some very public Punch and Judy spats with the people who govern the game in Scotland. The bears love it, but this grandstanding will create further bad feeling between the new club and the people on the sixth floor at Hampden.

However, it isn't all happy days for the Ibrox klan in Division Three, as liquidators BDO have still to step on to the stage. The Rangers klan can be partly forgiven their hubris because the people who run Scottish football have tried so many manoeuvres to maintain the Ibrox brand in the top flight. Sevco's front man, Charles Green, boasted before the game about being "debt free" and he did so without a hint of embarrassment or shame. At the back of this book there is a list of the 276 creditors left unpaid by Rangers Football Club.

Rangers, under Sir David Murray and latterly Craig Whyte, spent money they didn't have to gain a sporting advantage over their rivals. The British taxpayer, the Scottish ambulance service and the newsagents near the stadium were left to pick up the tab.

The Rangers klan has several touchstone words that define them – all tribes have such a restricted code – and a key word for the Ibrox lads is "dignity". Indeed.

The amorality of the Sevco situation is difficult to defend. The people who run the Scottish game were revealed to be wedded to a marketing strategy that needed the Ibrox brand at the centre of their business model. This meant that any crimes against sport or common decency committed by Rangers could not get in the way of business.

Like the Ibrox fans, the people in leadership positions at Hampden are largely in denial about what has happened and what the long-term significance is for the national game. The legacy of the downfall of Rangers has still to be properly addressed. One of these is the dual contracts issue.

The SPL has established an independent commission under the chairmanship of Lord Nimmo Smith. Alongside him will be Mr Charles Flint QC and Mr Nicholas Stewart QC. If this postscript is an attempt to look forward then I predict that these three eminent legal brains will conclude that Rangers FC operated a dual contracts system in contravention of the laws of the game. If the allegations over dual contracts are proven then over 700 matches are involved. Quite simply, we are about to be told the finer details of the biggest scandal in British sporting history.

Of course, it wasn't just domestic games where ineligible players may have been fielded. The "EBT players" also took part in European matches. In that event do not be surprised if some of the Ibrox club's vanquished opponents from the UEFA cup run in 2008 make official representations on the matter.

If the demise of Rangers is not a cautionary tale for those who run Scottish football clubs then they don't deserve to survive. The model for the national game in Scotland must be Scandinavian, not English. Rangers chased a dream of European glory to equal the past achievements of their city rivals. This was to be attained by importing high-quality foreign players on stellar salaries. This put the club into a debt spiral from which it never recovered. The future must be home-grown and largely Scottish. Planet *Fitba* was like an economy that stopped making things because it was easier to import them. When those imports were paid for by borrowing then it was a road to ruin. The fitba future must be self-sustaining or there will be no future at all. The company which now trades as "The Rangers Football Club" will need to raise cash and do so quickly. Expect a share issue soon, and if the original Sevco investors can, say, double their money they, might well do walking away at that point.

Like Bill Miller before him, Charles Green and his associates thought they would be taking their NewCo into the SPL. That was Plan A. However, the SPL spring among the fans scuppered that done deal. Getting NewCo into the SFL1 was Plan B for Regan and Doncaster, but they did not factor in Turnbull Hutton and his comrades. Now a financial Plan C is required. When Charles Green's Sevco Scotland Ltd bought the assets of Rangers from Duff and Phelps the question was whether or not the Ibrox klan would trust the new regime with their cash.

Since the new season started even those in the blue half of Glasgow who are opposed to Sevco have been forced to concede that Charlie has played a blinder. John "Bomber" Brown urged the fans to starve Sevco of cash and initially it looked like they were obeying that call. However, Mr Green appears to have won over manager Ally McCoist; after an ambiguous silence on the matter he called on the fans to buy season tickets. Deferential to the last the bears obeyed.

When Rangers faced the imminent threat of liquidation they could not organise among themselves to save their club, looking on rather helplessly as its life ebbed away. However, they do get ten out of ten for obedience. Sevco season ticket sales are now over 33,000. The prices have been cut by around a third so it is not a comparable figure with the revenue that Craig Whyte brought into Ibrox in 2011, but the immediate cash flow crisis for the fledgling club has been dealt with.

The reportage by the mainstream media has been breathless and gushing. Suddenly, everything in the Sevco garden is rosy. However, the next twelve months will not be without their financial challenges for the new entity. A Sevco insolvency event next year would undoubtedly catch the usual suspects on the sports desks by surprise, but you have been forewarned, dear reader.

A share issue, perhaps as early as October 2012, is the next move from Charles Green and his associates. Best-case scenario for such a flotation would probably be £10m. In a move redolent of David Murray's stewardship of Rangers this windfall, should it materialise, would kick the day of reckoning down the road for a year, no more than that.

However, the stringent and forensic extent of the financial information required for this move may prevent such a move from taking place. Because of the shyness of the some of the Sevco consortium a share issue may have to be parked.

At time of writing there remains a clear disparity between revenue and expenditure, even with the healthy sales of heavily discounted season tickets. We should not be surprised that the investigative churnalists on the sports desks have failed to nail down Charlie on whether or not Sevco has a credit line. Inability to access borrowing was a fatal pathogen in the Whyte plan. The mainstream media in Glasgow seem committed to helping Sevco in any way that they can. Of course there is more than one type of media now on Planet *Fitba*. The "unhelpful" coverage on my site regarding, for example, the sheriff officers' social call to Ibrox in August 2011 did not assist Mr Whyte in his attempts to get the corporate equivalent of a payday loan.

Before Sevco bought the assets of Rangers, former Rangers director Dave King said that any NewCo would have to be bankrolled on a "non-commercial basis" for three years. That is exactly the time frame that American Bill Miller mentioned when he pulled out of the deal to buy the assets of the Ibrox club. In terms of the Sevco saga this is just the beginning. Although the first-tier tax tribunal has yet to deliver a verdict on the big tax case, the HMRC-selected liquidators BDO may soon write a new chapter to this farce.

As for the future governance of the game in Scotland, while the same people remain in charge it would be foolish to expect a different approach. There must be strange mineral deposits in the Mount Florida area of Glasgow – a type of fool's gold that renders moral compasses unworkable.

The media still seem wedded to the old paradigm and by peddling the tired old pro-Ibrox narrative they hope that their sales will somehow get back to the good old days. Currently they are parroting the party line that liquidation does not mean the end of Rangers Football Club. There is no precedent on Planet *Fitba* where the Ibrox outfit is treated without deference.

The arrangement whereby the registration ban did not come immediately into force, therefore allowing players to be signed, had football administrators and sports lawyers in other jurisdictions shaking their heads in disbelief.

Instead of the "slow lingering death" that Stewart Regan warned of if the Ibrox brand was not in the SPL or SFL1, Scottish football is about to undergo a detox from the financial doping that David Murray introduced in 1988. The national game needs to be cleansed of that toxicity and the downfall of Rangers was a very necessary first step in that process. What remains to be cleansed from the game and, indeed, Scottish society, is a sporting brand that has anti-Irish racism as its unique selling point.

As the strapline of this book states, Rangers self-destructed. It was their choice, but the people who run the game in Scotland tried to make it everyone else's problem. In a situation akin to the banking bailout, the taxpayer had to pick up the tab for the gambling habit of the casino capitalists in the City of London. Ironically, it was the Square Mile's own police force that provided the hinge factor when they raided Ibrox in July 2007 for evidence of skulduggery in the Jean-Alain Boumsong transfer to Rangers from Auxerre in 2004.

The Ibrox punters never did get that mega casino, but their club was surely gambled away as David Murray went double or quits to attempt to replicate Celtic's success in Lisbon in 1967. I said three years ago that it was a racing cert Rangers were finished unless a blue-tinged billionaire came up on the inside rail. The folks who cluttered up the pavement at Edmiston Drive during this saga reckoned that Rangers were too big to fail. They were wrong.

If there is to be true leadership in the national game then the clean-up operation must start immediately. However, that will probably only begin in earnest when some people on the sixth floor at Hampden start clearing their desks.

The death of Rangers has been reported as a catastrophe for Scottish football. However, many good things usually come out of disasters. Structural faults that had previously gone unnoticed are shown up to be glaringly obvious with the benefit of hindsight. Bad practices that had heretofore been concealed from public view are laid bare in the organisational wreckage.

There was something rotten in the state of Planet *Fitba*. The self-destruction of Rangers has been nothing less than Shakespearean. As for my own contribution to the telling of this saga? *I have done the state some service, and they know't. No more of that.*

Notes

http://www.telegraph.co.uk/sport/football/teams/rangers/9429885/Rangers-
go-the-wire-haggling-over-SFA-membership.html

http://www.bdo.uk.com/
Binder Dijker Otte (BDO)
The name BDO, first devised in 1973, is an acronym of Binder Dijker Otte
    & Co.
http://www.karslakes.com/articles/sec216_insolvency_act.pdf
http://www.dailyrecord.co.uk/news/scottish-news/
    sfa-chief-under-police-guard-1197912
http://www.allmediascotland.com/broadcasting/35627/
    real-radios-football-phone-in-axed/
http://www.purnells.co.uk/limited-company/creditors-voluntary-liquidations/
    phoenix-companies/section-216-insolvency-act-1986.html

Appendix I: list of creditors

Source: http://www.rangers.co.uk/staticFiles/fe/a8/0,,5~174334,00.pdf
A K Ray, Ross Hall Hospital, Glasgow £150
ADI UK, Preston £7620
AS St Etienne, France £252,212.39
ASL, East Sussex £2514
Acies Group, Edinburgh £2340
Adrian Coll, Balloch £1600
Alan Duncan, Glasgow £1400
Alexander West Property, Glasgow £2807
Alison Walker TV, Bearsden £600
Alliance Video, Surrey £204
Aon Limited, London £14,151
Arena Imaging, Derby £336
Argyll and Bute Council £406.80
Arsenal Football Club £136,560
Astra Hygiene Supplies, Dumbarton £61.27
Audi Stirling £396.05
Azure Support Services, Macclesfield £523,949.71
Azzurri Scotland, Burnley £34.63
BTW Shiells, Belfast £2917.39
Barr Environmental Limited, Cumnock £264
Base Soccer Agency, London £52,560
Bauer Radio Ltd (Radio Clyde) £702
Beyard Services, Beith £5559.60
Bhutta's Newsagents, Glasgow £567.45
Big Think Agency, Glasgow £14,265.60
Blooms UK Limited, Glasgow £70
Brabners, Manchester £12,999
Brentwood Estates, Manchester £42,963.06
Brian Proudfoot, Glasgow £2,802
British Gas £1,562.42
BT £1,292.13
Business Cost Consultants, Glasgow £6,240.60
Business Stream, Edinburgh £9,727.22

CNP Professional, Cheshire £719.96
CRE8, Gloucester £68,406.70
Cairn Financial, London £4,127.60
Cairns & Scott Caterhire, Glasgow £762
Cameron Presentations, Glasgow £8,795.99
Campbell Medical Supplies, Paisley £3,386.73
Camtec, Herts £552
Canniesburn Taxis, Bearsden £269.69
Capital Solutions, Edinburgh £11,423.40
Capito Ltd, Livingston £1,049.69
Carberry's Coaches, Portadown Co Armagh £1,200
Carnival Chaos Production, Edinburgh £672
Carol Govan, Glasgow £600
Cask Productions, Glasgow £1,980
Cask Sports, Glasgow £2,919.60
Catercare Scotland, Stewarton £420
Celtic FC £40,337
Charlton Chauffeur Drive, Glasgow £792
Chelsea FC £238,345.43
Childcare Vouchers, London £1,143.74
Chilli It, Chester £416.52
Chris Clarke, Kilmarnock £150
Christine Siebelt, Milngavie £1,100
Citrus Office Solutions, Lancashire £4,304.24
City Electrical Factors, Glasgow £215.40
Clyde Productions, Glasgow £180
Coca Cola £10,133.91
Colin Suggett, Sunderland £741.80
Collstream Limited, Derby £5,779.37
Collyer Bristow, London £40,691.22
Colours Agency Glasgow £1,980
Computer Links, Livingston £2,146.32
Computershare Investor Service, Bristol, £23,855.03
Craig Services & Access East Sussex £900
Culture & Sport Glasgow £10,338.96
Daily Record & Sunday Mail £312
DealBureau Commercial Finance, Southend £10,000
Debenture Holders (various) £7,736,000
Decco Limited, Glasgow £174.72
Dell Computer Corporation, Berkshire £272.85

Direct Medical Imaging, Lancashire £230
Disclosure Scotland £372
Dominique S Byrne, Nuffield Hospital, Glasgow £160
Dr David A S Marshall, Bridge of Weir £160
Dundas & Wilson, Edinburgh £24,027.84
Dundee United FC £65,981.49
Dunfermline Athletic FC £83,370.13
E.ON £8,827.14
Eagle Consulting, Inverness £40
Eagle Couriers, Bathgate £96.60
Eden Springs, Blantyre £644.64
Edinburgh Audi £5,197.08
Electrical Waste Recycling, County
Employees Various £TBC
Durham £18
Enterprise Rent-a-Car, Stirling £9,000
Events Audio Visual, Clydebank £300
Exchequer Corporate Finance, Surrey £4,000
Executive Hire, Harlow £1,060
FES FM, Stirling £80,874.93
FL Memo, London £116.86
FX Signs, Glasgow £15,546.56
G Media Management, Cheltenham £995
G4S, Surrey £295,036.24
GTG Training, Glasgow £396
Gareth Neil Design, Glasgow £3,200
Gerry McGeoch, Glasgow £150
Glasgow Audi £1,041.62
Glasgow City Council £5,000
Glasgow City Council (Council Tax) £2,008.21
Glasgow Leading Attractions (The Willow Tea Rooms) £1,525
Glasgow Taxis £TBC
Glencairn Crystal Studio, East Kilbride £354
Gordon McKay, Blackridge £150
HOBS Reprographics, Glasgow £270.15
HSS Hire Service £67.10
Hamilton Brothers, Bishopton £115.56
Hay McKerron Associates, Milngavie £3,600
Heart of Midlothian FC £800,000
Hepscott Water Systems, Morpeth £1,190.28

HM Revenue & Customs £14,372,042
Hrvoje Bojanic Beethoveova, Zagreb, Croatia £2,898.42
Hutchesons Educational Trust, Glasgow £550
ILC Media, Preston £2,040
IMG Media, Chiswick £180
Impact Signs, Cumbernauld £9,482.79
Integrated Cleaning Management, Hampshire £3,329.19
Inverness Caledonian Thistle FC £39,805
Iris Chorus Application Software, Devon £5,973.60
Iris Ticketing, Devon £37,210.42
Iron Mountain, Livingston £1,271.16
JCM Business Consulting, Paisley £2,745
JJB Sports £19,390.59
James Gordon (Engineers), Galston £1,437.68
Jewson, Glasgow £930.60
Joe Lennon Picture Framing, Bearsden £840
John Deere, Gloucester £41,191.59
K7X, Ayr, £240
Kalamazoo Secure Solutions, Birmingham £4,017
Keith Hawley, Glasgow £2,600
Kevin Cameron Radio Service, Paisley £600
Kube Networks, Glasgow £7,672.08
L & S Litho, Glasgow £17,035.04
Lothian Power Clean, Larkhall £194.34
LSK Supplies, Glasgow £178.58
Lawrie Furnishings, Paisley £607.20
Limelight Networks , Arizona £2,333.49
Link Seating Limited, Worcestershire £606.98
Loomis UK, Nottingham £2,248.08
Louis Grace Electrical, Glasgow £1,087.84
Lyco Direct Limited , Milton Keynes £2,381.27
MSM Solicitors, Paisley £420
MacGregor Industrial Supplies, Inverness £106.76
Mackinnon Partners, Gourock £200
Manchester City FC £328,248.71
Manea Florin Bucharest £37,500
Mar Hall, Bishopton £5,511.90
Marsh Ltd UK, Norwich £779.10
Martin Dawes, Warrington £654.74
Media House, Glasgow £19,200

MediaCom, Edinburgh £11,544.42
Menzies Hotels, Derbyshire £257.40
Michael Douglas, Glasgow £100
Milngavie Mini Market £413.29
Modular Property Holdings, Glasgow £20,930.22
Motif Promotional Clothing, Glasgow £27.29
Murray Group Holdings, Edinburgh £278,964.30
Nairn Brown (Glasgow) £1,492.50
National Car Rental, Leicester £162.52
Navy Blue Design Group, Edinburgh £6,960
Newline Products, Glasgow £7,001
Newsquest (Herald & Times) £1,500
Nexo S.A., France £1,799.37
Nicola Young, Glasgow £3,500
Noble Grossart, Edinburgh £18,612
Nordic Scouting, Oslo £20,000
North Glasgow College £11,041.80
OHSS, Edinburgh £234
Officefurnitureonline.co.uk, Dumfries £338.40
Ooyala, California £733.92
Opal Telecom £169.72
Orebro SK £150,000
Oxford Hotels & Inns (Carnoustie) £3,709.96
PR Newswire Europe £300
PTS - Plumbing Trade Supplies, Leicester £30.42
Paramed, Howwood £1,050
Parklands Country Club, Glasgow £500
Parks of Hamilton £7,256
Paton Plant, York £1,450.16
Perform Group, Middlesex £346,097.43
Pineapple Aroundshot, Co Durham £2,316.96
Pineapple Photographic, Co Durham £5,875
Ping Network Solutions, Glasgow £4,020.25
Plum Films, Edinburgh £3,000
Posh Deli, Glasgow £260
Postage by Phone, Essex £510.80
Premier Cash Registers, Glasgow £12,600
Prime Commercial Properties
Management, London £10,805.53
Professional Pre-Season Tours (Libero), Glasgow £60,000

Quick Shift Tyre Service, Glasgow £48
R.F. Brown, Hamilton £1,681.44
RBS WorldPay, Cambridge £180.66
RS Components Limited, Northants £204.95
Rangers Lotteries Ltd, Glasgow £105.80
Reed Business Information, Surrey £2,764.80
Renfrewshire Council HQ £108
Restore Scotland, Paisley £579.74
Rigby Taylor Limited, Bolton £10,762.16
Rodgers Security Systems, Glasgow £342.50
Ross Hall Hospital, Glasgow £770.50
Ross Promotional, Glasgow £1,022.88
Royal Mail £3,262.54
SDL Group, Glasgow £1,350
SFA 11,089.04
SG World, Cheshire £577.56
SIR Teknologi, West Sussex £TBC
SK Rapid, Austria £1,011,763.44
STRI, West Yorkshire £17.28
Saffery Champness, Glasgow £31,028.01
Scot-West Business Forms, Glasgow £749.60
Scotprint, Haddington £7,514
Scotrae Productions, Greenock £17,058.94
Scottish Ambulance Service £8,438.40
Scottish Hydro Electric £62,527.30
Scottish Power £302.44
Search Promotional Merchandise, Buckinghamshire £6,240
Season Ticket Holders (various) £TBC
Shanks Waste Management, Southampton £122.58
Sharon Agnew, Glasgow £460
Shawfield Timber, Glasgow, £786.24
Shell UK £7,637.94
Shields Land Rover, Glasgow £246.75
Shred-it Glasgow £444
Sign Plus, Dunfermline £2,473.22
Signature Industries, London £1,507.90
Simplewaste Solutions, Clydebank £17,626.26
Sinclair Pharmacy, Glasgow £1,909.79
Slater Menswear , Glasgow £688.31
Solutions.tv, Glasgow £2,652

Sound Acoustic Productions, Glasgow £12,000
Souters Irrigation Services, Cumbernauld £456
Spike Multimedia, Giffnock £5,312.50
SPL £22,500
Sporting iD, Tyne and Wear £144.70
Sportopps.com, Belfast £150
Sports Alliance, Bury £2,006.65
Sports Revolution, London £5,034.52
Stellar Football, London £72,000
Stirling Fire Protection £1,149.30
Stockline Plastics, Glasgow £258
Strathclyde Police £51,882
Striking Imagery, Cumbernauld £113.51
Stuart MacMorran, Clydebank £422.50
Summit Asset Management, Surrey £70,555.88
Susan Thomson Your Sonsie Face, Glasgow £40
TNT £1,255.39
Tabs FM, London, £1,980
Tellcomm Limited, West Midlands £6,435.89
The Arco Group, Hull £443.43
The Brite Bulb, Bishopbriggs £3,209.64
The Burnbrae, Bearsden £1,403.88
The Business & Property Bureau, Bearsden £7,376
The Business Incentives Group, Glasgow £1,893.60
The City of Edinburgh Council £90
The Fees Company, Edinburgh £118.16
The Financial Times £3,480
The Scottish Football League £3,859.92
The Premier Property Group, Edinburgh £103,210.96
Thistle International Freight, Paisley £128.42
Thistle Storage Equipment, Cumbernauld £140.40
Thomas Cook Sport, Manchester £129,216.56
Ticket Team, Netherlands £873.36
Ticketline Network, Manchester £11,668.67
Ticketus, London £26,700,000
Trade UK (Screwfix) £77.01
Trident Trust Company, Jersey £40,689.90
UK Fast, Manchester £689.78
US Citta di Palermo, Italy £205,513.04
Umbro £1,756.05

University of the West of Scotland £135
Vodafone £204
Voicescape, Manchester £786.84
William Henderson, Glasgow £275
Yuill & Kyle Solicitors, Glasgow £1,486.80

Appendix II

SFL Meeting (Hampden Park, Tuesday, 3 July 2012, 11.00 a.m.)
Jim Ballantyne opening:
Airdrie declare a **conflict** of **interest** as they might benefit from promotion as a result of any decision.

Dundee's position exactly the same.

Stranraer don't feel conflicted in any way.

No one has spoken to Dunfermline Athletic about the promotion issue.

David Longmuir has stated that Dunfermline and Ross County are part of the **promotion/relegation** settlement.

Presentation:
This is not a recommendation document – it is just facts.

Figures quoted which may have a bearing on the decision from SFL **clubs**.

Neil Doncaster will present on SPL figures in detail.

Stewart Regan will present the SFA view.

David Longmuir – Your Game, Your Club, Your Future:

Buck been passed to SFL.

SFL asked if we can accommodate solution.

SFL have integrity, heart and won't be bullied.

We are all in this together.

Today is about giving clarity, based on facts rather than speculation.

Eurozone analogy with one economy affecting all others. Time for IMF (SFA) to step in.

5 scenarios:
SPL – not an option.

Third Division – £16m lost due to Sky, Clydesdale Bank want compensation, Irn-Bru getting threatened with **brand** boycott by fans. Scottish **government** will not step in and will allow SFL to make their own decision. Settlement agreement £2m would disappear.

First Division – Sky won't walk away. 30% reduction from walking away from overseas rights. Weatherseal, Clydesadale Bank will. Look for compensation. It is financially possible to recover.

SPL2 – Not supported by SFA. Not desired route from SPL Clubs (although contradicts SPL **exec**.). SFL could legally challenge this.

Rangers terminated or suspended. Emotive language. Would lead to complete financial meltdown. Where would Sky go? Lose fans probably. Settlement agreement would disappear. Where does that put Scottish football in the food chain?

Summary shows First Division option last (hence a heavy hint without recommendation).

One-off fee of £1m as a "one-off".

Play-offs for Division One in same format as Divisions Two and Three.

New distribution model to attempt to protect revenues.

SFL Clubs would be getting the same revenues as 2008 for Monetary Award.

Copyright royalty falling off the end of a cliff . . .

Question from floor (Turnbull, Raith Rovers): William Hill sponsorship of Scottish Cup – major conflict of interest for this important revenue stream, due to Ralph Topping's position if he denies revenue to all **clubs**. This is another example of something that is driving SFL Clubs to say "**enough** is enough!" SPL have no credibility, ethics or honesty, we should not be swayed by them.

Governance model:

Governance drives strategy and, more importantly, the integrity and brings everyone together.

3:2 split for **board** composition and voting structures. Neil Doncaster will add shortly.

Benefits delivered:

Board will make a call on the £1m split.

Could be 50:50%, could be 55:33:12%. For the **board** to decide.

Neil Doncaster presentation (same presentation as gave to SPL last week):

Costed options for dealing with Rangers FC "problem".

Rangers are a football club that have existed for 140 yrs.

NewCo own a stadium, training ground and some contracts.

Sevco 5088 have applied for a transfer of share from OldCo to NewCo.

Rangers FC have two separate companies.

OldCo still have a membership of SFA and SPL.

Bristol City (1982) and Middlesborough (1980?) are examples of insolvency.

ND's own team Norwich as well?

Since SPL created in 1988, four insolvencies without NewCo.

Mirrors Airdrieonians, Gretna and Livingston, not English **clubs**.

SPL rules recognise distinction between **club** and legal entity.

Three options costed:

SPL vote YES to NewCo

SPL vote NO and go into SFL Division **Three**

SPL vote NO and go into SFL Division **One**

Option 1 – SPL vote YES to NewCo:

Eight supporting votes approved.

SPL commercial agreement remains intact. £17.4m broken down.

Celtic **£3m**, Rangers £2.6m, Others various . . . bottom £0.6m

Option 2 – SPL vote NO and go into SFL Division Three:

Severe commercial damage

Sky:

Sky £50m over **five** years (**thirty** games per season).

Sky will not confirm that they will definitely terminate the deal if Rangers are out of **the SPL** for at least three years.

ESPN:

£30.3m (**thirty** games per season).

ESPN will definitely terminate if Rangers are not in the SPL or SFL Division **One**.

Sportfive: (Overseas rights):

£2.7m (12/13) and £2.75m (13/14)

Explicit contract option if Rangers are not in SPL. Sportfive will terminate immediately.

Assumption (actually clause in the contract) that **four** Old Firm games will be provided.

Other Broadcasting:

Combined revenue £2m, of which 50% will disappear.

£19.264m total **broadcasting** income will drop to **£4.54m** which £14.724m reduction in **income**.

Sponsorship:

A number of SPL partners and sponsorship (Panini, Coca-Cola, etc) £2.5m to £1.5m drop in sponsorship.

Total Revenue for SPL Distributions:

Rangers £17.4m (SPL) vs £1.7m (SFL Division **Three** or out of game)

Result will be SPL **clubs** taking, on average, a £1m hit and this will lead to potential insolvencies across the Scottish game.

Questions from the floor: (I will say **floor** if I couldn't see who was speaking, as was typing and listening intently)

"What about the **season tickets** and walk-ups that will walk away as they will liken Scottish football to World Wrestling Federation?"

No argument from Neil Doncaster to points made. Scottish football has a problem and we need to deal with this.

"Settlement agreement – in what way is this payment compromised by these scenarios?"

Neil Doncaster's view is that SPL will have no money to pay the distribution.

"SFL **clubs** are affected the most. Why do we have to bail out the SPL? Why can they not bail out themselves?"

Neil Doncaster no answer – "I'll come onto this – all will become clear!" line again.

£2m settlement would not be able to be paid?

Questioned. Actually it would be – it would leave only £1.7m and Neil's view is "the game" cannot afford to pay this. Again, clearly wrong – "the game" here means SPL **clubs**, not SFL **clubs** as we are already being penalised with the **financial distribution** model skewed heavily towards the SPL **clubs** and the Old Firm, in particular (or the Top **two** in SPL, which has historically been the Old Firm in the majority of cases).

If SFL Division One:

£17.4m down to £12.6m (including £350k from UEFA).

Club 12 will get £0.6m as a relegated **club** placed 12th in the SPL.

Proposal from the floor (Mike M, Alloa Athletic) to change the **governance** structure first. Governance is critical to the future of Scottish football.

Neil Doncaster acknowledged and accepts, but wishes to move to voting structure issue.

16 July – SPL voting structure change:

Members resolution to change the voting structure.

SPL 11:1 or 10:2 voting structure currently would change to 9:3 for most, unless it's contractual and that stays at 8:4.

Questions from floor:

"This is all about money! You have never mentioned the customer. They have spoken and you will p*** them off and lose the customer base".

Neil Doncaster's view is that there will be some customers that want to let Rangers disappear. The SPL **chairmen** he has spoken to think that the most palatable option is SFL Division One.

"Why are SPL Clubs gambling their future (with sporting integrity?) by passing this vote over to the SFL **clubs** to make the decision. Why have you not been able to persuade the SPL **clubs**?"

Neil Doncaster's view is that some SPL **clubs** have made their point on the vote without knowing all the facts first. This may be potentially unwise!

"Can Rangers **FC/NewCo** take a year out?"

Neil Doncaster's view is that this does not work for TV broadcasting. This is the same as Division Three as subscriptions will fall off the cliff!

"Surely the market will not fall apart if Rangers go to Division Three? Manchester United would still attract TV rights, if relegated?"

Neil Doncaster's view – **buyer** of the rights for Scottish football wants Old Firm games.

Annan Athletic FC view: This will not affect us. We have only been into our overdraft **three** times since 1979. We have a **financial/business** model and we stick to it. We cut our cloth accordingly, as do many SFL **clubs**. This may actually get rid of some of the expensive foreign players and bring through the young, Scottish players. This can be positive and we can use this as an opportunity.

Hamilton **Academical** FC view: We cannot afford Rangers to go to SFL Division Three, as a **club** in Division One with our costs.

Queen of the South FC: Cannot **make** a decision about one unified body at the moment. Want a commitment to move forward/**heads of terms** about governance and voting rights.

David Longmuir: This would be the first page on any new document.

Clyde FC: We have c. 8,000 seats, so short-term hit for **NewCo** in Division Three would be good for Clyde, but is it worth it? We have the smallest budget. Cash £244k net income   but we can deal with this. We live within our means now.

We cannot accept this as a major financial problem that we cannot deal with – we would cut our cloth accordingly for loss of SPL **distribution** filtering down.

Heads of terms wouldn't fill us with any trust. There is a complete and utter lack of **trust** in SPL. It is based on greed. It is a bankrupt business model.

Let's sort out Scottish football over a couple of years. Your model is bankrupt and bust. Let's face it, we are 42 turkeys voting for **Christmas** and we are having our heads shoved into the oven. The SFL **clubs** are being slowed cooked and the SPL **clubs** are being quickly microwave-roasted. Either way, the game's up!

Stenhousemuir: "The whole **PR has** been an utter disgrace. SFL have been asked to go against the wishes of the vast majority of our supporters who have said that they will not be back. This is based on threats and aggression, rather than a sensible, mature debate. Aberdeen have said Rangers should be in Division Three. Why can you (SPL) not control this **PR in** a joint way."

Neil Doncaster's view is that there is no **PR campaign**?!?

Eric: "More clarity on Rangers taking a year out. Can you not go to broadcasters and broker a deal based on restructuring Scottish football? Can you not sell this to the **broadcasters**?"

Neil Doncaster's view: "No. Where is the Rangers subscription money for them?"

Floor: "Big assumption here that it's automatic promotion. What happens if Rangers go to Division One and don't get promoted?"

Neil Doncaster's view: "Then we have a problem this time next year!"

[Quite staggering. The gun has now been **cocked**.]

Stewart Regan:

Three issues to deal **with/charges** to answer over the Rangers situation . . .

1. Bringing the game into disrepute
2. EBT
3. **NewCo**

These are all big issues and have not been closed.

The **apellant tribunal has three** options.

Lord **Carloway**

Termination

Expulsion

Suspension is a realistic outcome. Rangers could be out of the game for some time. How long – don't know?

(Someone from the floor later pointed out that a **suspended** sentence could be a fourth option?)

Some **clubs** have borrowed beyond their means and will be significantly damaged by this.

Two options to move forward . . .

Appellant **tribunal**

Collaborative solution

Long-term withering on the vine . . .

Division One option put forward and SFA say this is the only option that works. SFA **board** not wishing to wave Rangers through to SPL. SFA **board** will not support this. Transfer of membership application can be stopped by SFA.

Rangers have to go somewhere? They won't be allowed to play in another country.

If we cannot agree on the Division One option, then the SFA **appellant tribunal** will kick in.

Trying to see before the **appellant tribunal** if we have a collaborative solution. It's all about communication and bringing people with you. It's about judgement. We have a really difficult few years ahead of us, if we cannot get this correct.

SPL2 is not the preferred option, however, this may happen if we cannot agree and **appellant tribunal** apply sanctions.

Transfer embargo and out of Europe for four years. SFA believe this is a reasonable set of sanctions.

Clyde FC: "What is the SFA's view on SPL joining SFL? We have a model, this is not based on greed. Why do SPL not trust us enough to do this?"

Stewart Regan's view: "Every **club** has the ability to have their say. But the governance structure should be linked to the balance of power (media contracts, etc) and this is the distribution model at the moment."

Alloa Athletic FC: "Let's sort the governance model quickly. This cannot happen without letting us **have** a voice. We need to defend those that are affected. Perhaps we need to take this away and let the SFA decide what happens and that is the same for all **clubs** – leadership needs to be driven from SFA and away from SPL and SFL. Campbell Ogilvie should be allowed to step aside on the PR and the SFA (Stewart Regan, Rod Petrie) step forward.

Stewart Regan's view: Work has been done for months. The only way to consider proposal is to counter with other changes as well. Until we have a plan, we cannot say anything. We need to widen the net and develop a plan and Stewart will step up to the media. We will never please everyone as we have such a range of emotions.

Alloa stated that they were uncomfortable taking a vote that may result in the **downfall/insolvency** of **ten or twenty clubs**. The SFL are in a really difficult situation here . . .

Floor: "This is a once-in-a-lifetime opportunity. We agree with Henry McLeish's proposals, which were aired already. Pyramid structure governance, etc. we need leadership!"

Stewart Regan's view: We cannot go past "Go" until we agree what happens to Rangers and we have a ticking time-bomb.

"This should have been done a year ago!"

Stewart Regan's view: Agree completely. Blood has been allowed to become bad over last **fifteen** years and there is mistrust. This event will happen again. (DD: It definitely will. The SPL model is bust and this is not just about Rangers, there are other SPL **clubs** close to going to the wall. ND stated that at least **six** SPL **clubs** will be severely affected by this and close to the wall. The **clubs** in the SPL are relying on Sky's August payments (£695k?) and this may be withheld if Rangers are not in the **top two** tiers of Scottish football come the start of the season?

"But you are creating a class structure with A and B shares. It's unbalanced at the moment."

Stewart Regan's view: Big issues that are left are mainly commercial and this is weighted towards the top of the game.

"Are we not setting a very dangerous precedent here, with Aberdeen [for example], etc. going into liquidation? What happens to their debt? Do we have the same **rules** for them, to go into Division One?"

David Longmuir's view: That is a risk . . .

Clyde FC: "When you give different people different types of shares, you create a class society. We can fix the governance, but not cobbled together. The loser is 42 **clubs** at the moment, the winner is the future and the generations of youth, if you get the governance right."

Floor: "This group is not minded to be the ones to make the decision. Who sent the **governance** document? Who thought SPL2 was a good decision?"

Stewart Regan's view: Have not seen the governance document that sets out SPL2 proposal. SFA board will not sanction SPL2 and would open the appellant tribunal option. It is Neil's only option to keep the financial model alive if SFL reject the Division One option.

Dunfermline Athletic FC: "If SPL clubs change their minds tomorrow on NewCo going back to SPL, will SFA block this? Is tomorrow a waste of time?"

Stewart Regan's view: SFA will not support this. We will reserve the right to block the transfer of membership. This is my view as a board member, one of seven board members and the view at the moment, based on previous discussions at SFA board on the sins that have been cast by OldCo. SFA board will take a very dim view of any membership transfer of OldCo to NewCo, to allow them to be parachuted straight back into the SPL.

This is all news to most of the SFL representatives and member clubs. This is a damning example where the three bodies do not discuss with each other closely enough as the SFL document did not bring this out implicitly. The three bodies work in the same building and how this is new news is staggering and highlights the need for governance change! This is also the second time that Stewart Regan has mentioned the blocking, so we are all in no doubt that NewCo cannot go into the SPL. This is not an option now, no matter how the SPL vote goes.

David Longmuir: Scottish football does not do confidentiality well. This is the day we can give you all the facts and now you have the facts we need to learn lessons from this.

Floor: "SPL chairman phoned this morning and said if we didn't vote for Division One, then the SPL will likely vote for an SPL2."

Clyde FC: "The language all suggests that Division One is the only option here, financially. I do not believe that it is actually. We, the majority of SFL clubs, can survive this, as we have cut our cloth accordingly and have a business model which is balanced and not based on greed. No one has mentioned the customers here. We need to listen to our customers, not think about a quick fix with cash. Our customers are priority. They have spoken. They will walk and will not come back to Scottish football. There will be no goodwill and that will create a far bigger financial Armageddon. The articles of the governing bodies suggest that we should be doing what is correct for Scottish football as a whole, at all levels, and this is not at all levels, it is based on the higher echelons."

Stewart Regan's view: If we do not make a decision today, SPL clubs will not make a decision tomorrow. (What?!)

Clyde FC: "You have the leadership opportunity to take this decision and take it out of our hands. You could allow NewCo back into the SPL and we sort this in two years."

Stewart Regan's view: SFA cannot allow the club members to allow a NewCo to parachute into SPL.

Floor: "Can the First Minister speak to Sky?"

Didn't catch the answer.

Floor: "Time questions. No vote today. SPL may not vote tomorrow if they do not get a steer . . . SFA can't step in, etc. Does anyone have a trigger point where we need a decision and leadership takes over?"

Neil Doncaster's view: It is for the clubs to decide.

Stewart Regan's view: If not decided by the start of the season, then we start the season with eleven clubs or we promote another club into SPL and backfill the Third Division with another membership application for a suitable club.

Break:

Unfortunately, someone tweeted Stewart Regan's comments during the meeting, so laptops and iPads were banned and I had to stop taking minutes . . .